Chotti Munda and His Arrow

Chotti Munda and His Arrow

Mahasweta Devi

Translated and Introduced by

Gayatri Chakravorty Spivak

Blackwell
Publishing

350 Main Street, Malden, MA 02148-5018, USA
108 Cowley Road, Oxford OX4 1JE, UK
550 Swanston Street, Carlton South, Melbourne, Victoria 3053, Australia
Kurfürstendamm 57, 10707 Berlin, Germany

First published by Seagull Books Private Ltd

This edition published 2003 by Blackwell Publishing Ltd, by arrangement with Seagull Books Private Ltd

Library of Congress Cataloging-in-Publication Data has been applied for.

ISBN 1-405-10704-9 (hardback); ISBN 1-405-10705-7 (paperback)

A catalogue record for this title is available from the British Library.

Set in 11/13 pt Baskerville
by Kolam Information Services Pvt Ltd, Pondicherry, India

For further information on
Blackwell Publishing, visit our website:
http://www.blackwellpublishing.com

Contents

vii

TRANSLATOR'S FOREWORD

ix

'TELLING HISTORY'
AN INTERVIEW WITH MAHASWETA DEVI

1

CHOTTI MUNDA AND HIS ARROW

289

TRANSLATOR'S AFTERWORD

293

NOTES

298

THE SELECTED WORKS OF MAHASWETA DEVI

Translator's Foreword

I T HAS BEEN MY PRACTICE to underline the words in English in the original. It makes the text awkward to view.* I do this because I prepare a scholarly translation, in the hope that the teacher/scholar will get a sense of the English lexicalized into Bengali on various levels as a mark of the very history that is one of the animators of the text. This is the first novel where Mahasweta articulates tribal history with colonial and post-colonial history. Much of her earlier work was concerned with colonial history and precolonial history. After *Chotti*, the text of tribality frees itself from the burden of a merely 'Indian' history.

This is the first novel by Mahasweta Devi that I have translated. In the hope that the teacher/scholar will move to Mahasweta's racy Bengali with its occasional lyric simplicity, I have included page references to the original.* I have used the first edition (1980) of *Chotti Munda ebang Tar Tir*, published in Kolkata by Karuna Prakashani.

One of the most striking characteristics of the novel is the sustained aura of subaltern speech, without the loss of dignity of the speakers. It is as if normativity has been withdrawn from the speech of the rural gentry. For the longest time I was afraid to attempt to translate this characteristic. Yet, as Barbara Johnson says felicitously, a translator must be a 'faithful bigamist.'[1] In the interest of keeping the faith, I had to try; straight, slightly archaic prose killed the feel of the book. To my great delight, among the first things Mahasweta Devi said to me when I reached Kolkata was (in my translation, of course), 'Gayatri, what I am really enjoying in your translation is how you've shown that dialect can be dignified.' Shown! It was she who had 'shown' this in the text and created a test of faith for me.

I can only hope that other readers will echo the reaction of the first famous reader of *Chotti Munda and His Arrow.*

Gayatri Chakravorty Spivak
Kolkata-New Delhi
5-6 January, 2002

NOTES

1 Barbara Johnson, 'Taking Fidelity Philosophically' in Joseph F. Graham (ed.), *Difference in Translation* (Ithaca: Cornell University Press, 1985), p. 143.

*Publisher's note

Gayatri Chakravorty Spivak's translation of the Bengali text included underlining of words which appeared in English in the original, as well as page references to the original. This edition dispenses with both of these editorial practices.

'Telling History'
Gayatri Chakravorty Spivak
interviews Mahasweta Devi

GCS: Chotti Munda, the hero of your novel, is a figure of continuity, from the Ulgulan,[1] to the Emergency,[2] and post-Emergency.

MD: When, in the 60s, I would go to Munda villages, their marketplaces or anywhere, they would talk still of Birsa's uprising and of Dhani Munda who was a legendary figure. And you say Emergency and post-Emergency. I used to visit that region from '63 to '75 continuously. I have seen with my own eyes what the Emergency meant, what was done. The criminalization of politics, letting the lumpen loose in the lower caste and tribal belts.[3] Inhuman torture and oppression. I have also seen resistance. That is the time when Naxal boys were harboured there, given shelter, allowed to escape.[4] What *Chotti Munda* or my other stories and books depict is a continuing struggle.

Tribal history is not seen as a continuity in Indian historiography. (I use the word tribal, not indigenous people or aborigine, because it is appropriate to the Indian context.) Yet it is still continuing, the tribals are still being evicted from their land. Indeed, Birsa Munda comes late. His movement was from 1895 to 1900. Before that there were many tribal rebellions.[5] The first Santal rebellion was Baba Tirka Majhi's rebellion (1780–85). I receive letters about this because I wrote a short novel, not so very well written either, on Baba Tirka Majhi. He was ultimately hanged and a statue erected in the heart of Bhagalpur. That place is now known as Tirka Majhi Chowk. To appease tribal voters the government have named a University after Sidhu-Kanhu, the Santal rebellion heroes.[6] There is a Baba Tirka Majhi university in

Bhagalpur. There they want to erect a statue. Some people at Bhagalpur University claim that Tirka Majhi is fiction, that nothing like that ever happened. I go back and find and check and write to them. Tirka Majhi's name does not come into the official histories.

Yet after each rebellion—always related to land and labour—they were evicted from their home places. In the context of the tribal world of Eastern India, which is what I know, they migrated towards Bengal, they were taken to Assam as tea garden labourers, kept in Bengal to clear the mangrove forests in the Sunderbans, the indigo planters brought them, this is continuing history, there is no break in it.

GCS: In the novel, you emphasize the role of story—*galpakatha*—and rumour—*kimbadanti*—in Chotti's life. And the novel has an open end, a thousand hands raised but the conclusion forever suspended. Please tell us about the relationship between history and story. You don't for example talk about the actual followers of the Birsa cult—the Birsaites—at all—

MD: No.

GCS: And you have put some details in Chotti's life which are like Birsa's life. Keeping pace with the historical continuity this is a sort of fictive continuity. I want you to talk about the relationship between what is called history and story, the writer writing a story as she attempts to set the record straight.

MD: These people do not find anyone writing about them, and they do not have script. They compose the stream of events into song. By being made into song, into words, they become something . . . a continuity. Their history is like a big flowing river going somewhere, not without a destination. Not without. These phases come like small streams joining into it, making their history. I wrote in *Pterodactyl* [7] that the tribal world is like a continent handed over to us, and we never tried to explore it, know its mysteries, we only destroyed it. It's very difficult to reknit that entire experience without knowing what their potentiality was, how much they had to give. We did not respect them. About *Chotti Munda*. I find that Birsa's uprising did not die with Birsa. And so through the figure of Dhani, I wanted to say that there had to be a magic arrow, not magic in the narrow sense, but an arrow that Dhani Munda wants to hand over. This arrow is a symbol for the person who will carry on that continuity. Chotti is an emblem of that.

GCS: In a sense, as a reader, I felt that to understand what that magic is was part of my task.

MD: Yes. And this is unwritten history. I had to learn it by being with the people. For all those years, in those years, I was technically married to someone, but that life was very barren, so that was the time when I covered many miles on foot. I know those places, the riverbeds, the trees . . .

GCS: The role of the imagination is so important: the imagination holds the river, the stone, the tree. Everything you have said so far makes it clear that what you do is, in your own words, to read between the lines of tribal experience—

MD: Which is not written—

GCS: Yes, the unwritten lines, to read between the unwritten lines of the tribal story, the tribal experience, the songs. In this novel, by insisting like a refrain that everything in Chotti's life becomes *galpakatha*, you have actually not seen this as a deficiency. You have seen this as the creative principle itself, and of history as well.

MD: What I can do must also be woven into a song and sung, this song continues, then another phase, another song, these songs are sung here and there—that it continues to live, this is also resistance. Thus they are making the thing alive. Chotti here is a symbol or representation of tribal aspiration. This is why the beginning of the book opens into a mythic ancestor—continuity placed within an open frame at both ends.

Indeed, it is not only at the two ends that the book is open but also at the centre. In my travels I saw this old man with whom I was not so well acquainted. I knew other tribals well, and all of them revered him, oh he's a legendary chap, and all these [archers] you see here and there, he is the person who has taught them all. So that legendary Chotti Munda provides me with a legend at the book's centre. Where did I see him? One day I was travelling by bus. Some tribals stopped the bus because they wanted to go somewhere, there was a mela—a fair—not a big thing, but there will be an arrow competition. I was entranced. They climbed on to the top of the bus. Archery was very much in their blood. And in Hesalong market I saw this fantastic archery competition, for which an old Munda was brought as judge. He sat on the platform. It was a time honoured tradition that at the end, being the best archer of the area, he would shoot last and hit the target. All these things get stored in the brain somewhere—

It struck me then, I have to write about the tribals, I have to, because these things will vanish, there will be more industries . . .

GCS: . . . yes—

MD: I have to document it, these things will vanish. And thus came *Chotti Munda*. In it, so many experiences, I had stored them so lovingly—*Chotti* is my best beloved book. I had such a great *asthirata* in me, such a restlessness; an *udbeg*, this anxiety: I have to write, somehow I have to document this period which I have experienced because it is going away, it is vanishing.

GCS: It's vanishing, yes, yes . . .

MD: Today, if I go back, I will not find them like that. It has all been sullied, been polluted, and they are very vulnerable. I have read about the American Indians, when smallpox and other diseases came, they had no resistance against it, and these people had no resistance against the cultural invasion that took place. It is cultural, it is economic, it is connected with the land, with everything, they want to rob the tribal of everything.

GCS: In this book you say that India is village but we do not hear from that India. Today, we hear a lot about globalization and the urban. I would like you to talk about the continuing importance of the rural, and also of the role of the lumpen—Romeo and Pahlwan are two such characters in your novel.

MD: From '72 to '75—and '75 brought in the Emergency—Mrs Gandhi's younger son, Sanjay Gandhi, and his Youth Congress unleashed a great deal of harassment upon the people. The region in the background of which I have written the novel was one of these areas. During Emergency, nothing happened that did not happen before, although the lumpenization in the lower echelons of politics was perhaps made more systematic. But during Emergency everything came out. In the newspapers at that time. Since the time of Independence we have had a free press, but at the time of Emergency for the first time rural reporting got some coverage, for the first time investigative reporting came about. Because Emergency was also the time when part of the middle class, part of the student population, were touched, like the Naxalites. Their homes were invaded, middle-class smugness was broken to pieces. And yet the break-up of the Emergency was not because of such measures. It was precisely because tightening of centralization was interfering with the operation of the power-lines in country towns and villages, backed up by the lumpen element, that the Emergency was not allowed to continue. I have tried to show that in *Chotti.*

GCS: Yes. I'd like to go back to the importance of the rural. If I could just point at what I think is one of the astonishingly powerful things about the novel, is that you actually show, not just Mundas acting, but Mundas and outcaste Hindus coming together. There is the self-consciousness in Chotti Munda that Munda customs will become things that are only done on festival days, that in today's India, we have to be together. This togetherness of the rural, please say something more about that.

MD: I am talking about a place of great caste difference between the lower castes, but with the tribals they were one in everything. The Munda is considered the first comer in Indian tribal society. Other kinds of tribals, building a hut, or doing something new, would have to invite a Munda boy who would come and consecrate it. He had to be brought, offered sweets, given a gift. And I was exhilarated to see all those so-called lower castes, the Dusads, Ganjus, Chamars, doing the same thing, inviting the Munda boy. Festivals thus became joint festivals. They joined the railway porters when any puja was there, and the porters in turn went happily to join their Sohrai, Karam, Holi [celebrations].

GCS: I see. Therefore, when you were talking about them coming together in their struggle, you were also as a novelist recording something you were seeing at work.

MD: It is my firm belief in the last phase of my creative years of my life that this solidarity is resistance. This is the only way to resist globalization. Globalization does not mean that someone from America, some white man, is coming and doing something. When the British left, they left our brains colonized, and it remains like that. If we have to know about tribals, we have to go back in tradition, in oral tradition, re-read something that is not written, or written in human beings, generation after generation. But we also celebrate its changefulness in the name of solidarity today. Changing their tradition, indeed. You have seen the Sabars,[8] cultivating their field, just this triumph, they have dug a well and water is coming up, they have never done agriculture but they are doing it; this changefulness is resistance against globalization. Globalization is not only coming from America and the first world, my own country has always wanted to rob the people of everything. The tragedy of India at Independence was not introducing thorough land reform. A basically feudal land system was allowed to stay. A feudal land system can only nurture and sustain a feudal value system. A feudal value system is anti-women, anti-poor people, against toiling people. It is the landowners who formed the ministry, and became the rulers of the country, why should they do anything else?

GCS: It is my understanding that the main demand, even at the time of the Ulgulan, was that the Khuntkatti[9] way of agriculture should be restored, and that they were able to get some legislation from the British. Of course, no lasting impact was made because, as you say, those in power managed to stop this. But in fact the Mundas were talking about the kind of thing that would have helped land reform.

MD: Yes, yes, yes. They wanted the rulers to allow their land system to stay. The land distribution system could have been implemented while keeping their own system alive. In those regions, when they clear forests, suddenly they come across a place with a big stone. When they bury their dead, they place a stone. You realize that this was the site of a Khuntkatti village. This was found in the Santal rebellion oral tradition kathas or sagas also, that Khuntkatti villagers chose villages founded on calculation. Somewhere they would go, and what shall I say . . .

GCS: Put the stake down . . .

MD: Put the stake down, and then they would start a village, because their own village had become overcrowded.

GCS: Your novella *Pterodactyl* was published about a decade after *Chotti Munda?* That novella seems to me to be more tragic. There seems to be a kind of a pessimistic grandeur to it. Will you comment on *Chotti* as an early tribal novel—*Aranyer Adhikar*[10] was of course before that—it seems to me more upbeat, there is more hope in it. Am I right in saying this?

MD: But in *Pterodactyl* also there is hope, because they are saying at the end that they will plant thorns and eat the tuber. They're learning to cope with the modern, they aren't accepting defeat, they will not be crushed. They know charity will come and go, that the government will do nothing. But they are not accepting defeat. *Pterodactyl* is the crux of my tribal experience. I do not see them as defeated and crushed.

GCS: No, I didn't mean defeated and crushed. I suppose I meant withheld.

MD: Pessimist, it's not pessimistic.

GCS: Well, maybe that's the wrong word. Tragedy is after all the grandest kind of literature there can be. I was wrong to say pessimistic. There is this kind of disillusionment with all this aid and these government efforts. They have decided that they will survive from the thorn, that is a little bit different from the way Chotti manages with the Daroga in spite of his disillusionments.

MD: *Chotti* was written when I came to this house, when I was for the first time liberated from the middle-class inhibitions—in a surge, written from my connections with the first forest movement, the Gua firing in which nineteen tribals were killed, but the government gave out that only eleven persons were killed. Then Laro Jonko, that dauntless, fantastic woman warrior of the tribals, she came here. I could not enter Singhbhum but, with the help of Laro, I got reports, who all were killed and who was buried where. So I wrote that article for *Economic and Political Weekly*, that these persons have been killed, but their names have not been included. Gua firing.[11] That was the time I saw the forest movement. They worship sal trees, and the government was introducing teak (saguna). The cry went up: *saguana hatao*, sal *bachao*. This became a war of the tribals. They destroyed teak nurseries, planted sal. I was very close to them in those days. You can read about it in *Dust on the Road*. Out of this feeling of exhilaration came *Chotti Munda*. I was dying to write that story, it was Puja time and no paper would print it because it was so long.[12] So ultimately from Bangladesh, Ekhlasuddin Ahmed came and took it, and the Eid number of *Bichitra*, Bangladesh, published it first.

GCS: I see. And that was 1979?

MD: That was 1980.

GCS: When you say that *Pterodactyl* is the culmination of your tribal experience, I agree with you completely. I have felt that there is in *Pterodactyl* your knowledge of the Sabars. When you wrote *Chotti Munda* you did not know the Sabars yet.

MD: No, no . . .

GCS: That kind of uncanny silence, that resonant silence of the Sabars, which is its own kind of resistance, that's in *Pterodactyl*, that's why *Pterodactyl* is a more mysterious text than Chotti. Chotti belongs to—

MD: Yes, *Chotti* is very open . . . it's like sky, and jungle and river . . .

GCS: I think one of these days you should write about the woman warriors. In the police reports there's plenty of mention of intrepid women who were actually fighting. They were also punished by the authorities, and I wondered why in Dhani Munda's memory, there is no recollection of these brave women—

MD: He wants to go back to Sali, he said I want to go back to Sali. About Sali, in Birsa's story it's written extensively—

GCS: Oh, I know—

MD: And Birsa wants to go to Sali. He wants to see Sali's son Pariwa, Pariwa who was formally adopted by—

GCS: Yes, by Birsa.

MD: When Birsa was arrested, Sali was with him and another woman. He was with two women, and those two women forgot his directions and they tried to cook something. Steam went up, and the police came and caught him. And again we come back to rice. Rice remains the motivating factor. Hunger.

GCS: There you go. Absolutely. Chotti's wife, you represent her as a wonderfully brave, resourceful imaginative woman. But she is an exception, she is a leader. I want—

MD: Motia is a leader too. Women do not do it all the time by going to the battlefield and raising their machetes. But Motia, in her own way, that Dhobin, who kicked at Tirathnath and went to open a laundry in Patna—that is women's resistance as well.

GCS: Yes, you're quite right, I agree with you, but I still would say, as an obstinate reader, I want you, one of these days—

MD: I will write, about Laro—

GCS: To write about the women warriors.

MD: Laro is someone I know, I will write about her. And about women participating, those were again tribals brought from the Chhotanagpur plateau, settled in Sunderbans, who took part in Tebhaga.[13]

GCS: I'm not being a literary critic here or a translator, it is just a reader's request.

MD: I know, I know.

GCS: I began with Draupudi after all, she was a fighter. She fought in the end in a woman's way—Senanayak was afraid in front of a woman's body.[14]

MD: By just making them nonexistent, they do not exist for her, all this male stuff, they are trying to do this, by mass raping, by gangraping also you just cannot destroy a woman's spirit, she does not recognize their existence, they are nonexistent for her.

GCS: But I think it is good that you point at these women who are in the interstices of *Chotti Munda*, who resist in their own way. Let me now ask you about the international reader. Your work has been very beautifully translated into many Indian languages. I hope you will approve of the fact that I don't translate for the Indian reader who doesn't read any Indian languages. I translate for the readership in the rest of the world. I would like you to say something, if you would, for the international reader. I am thinking also of the figure of Amlesh Khurana in your novel. I was wondering if you would say anything specifically to the well-meaning South Asian diasporic, what's called NRI [Non-Resident Indian] here, I'm also particularly interested because I'm one of them. Amlesh Khurana lives abroad.

MD: Gayatri, you surprised me. I never expected that you would translate my story, and I'd become known to the non-Indian reader. Amlesh Khurana—I have not come to that part of the book as yet—went as an NGO to help them, with foreign funds, isn't it?

GCS: Let me interrupt you since you wrote it a long time ago and haven't come to it yet. It's the Government of India that loves Amlesh, NGO culture is not around yet. He's very well meaning, but he has this artificial picture, he doesn't know the reality of the place, so he tries to help through this totally unrealistic idea, he wants Munda villages, he wants leper villages, he wants untouchable villages, he thinks that everything is in nice little compartments, and that's what I was talking about when I said South Asian diasporics who have an idea about the place they came from but don't really know what it's like, and they will read your novels and stories—so if you want to tell them something . . .

MD: You see, reading my books here also, not to think of readers beyond India, but sitting here in Calcutta, I'm always receiving earnest offers from people who want to go to the Kheria Sabars[15] and work for them. I always tell them, they won't accept you. What have you done for them to accept you? You don't know tribals. Your grievance and mine, Gayatri, has always been with people who cannot respect them, do not know them, cannot realize that they are superior human beings, although often obstinate. These people come with well meaning ideas, this sort of approach, and tribals have a lot of resistance. The tribal will say yes to everything, but he will remain basically closed. The international NGOs will pour money in one place, provide the expertise of skilled people, to raise the place that has submitted a project. This is indirectly serving the interest of the so-called colonizers, because that place automatically becomes cut off from the rest of the area, creates anger, distrust, and then the developers start making money from it. In very few cases does the effort reach, to use the actual Government of India jargon, the target beneficiary. That kind of help is not needed. Now the tragedy is that the Government of India itself has become a beggar. And everywhere the state governments are giving in to the NGOs. So many NGOs, for so many purposes, so much money. They want their packaged programmes, literacy completed within this and this, then inoculation, then—

GCS: That's globalization, to take away the redistributive powers of the state and to give everything to these NGOs who only want their money spent on time. Philanthropy is not democratic. These NGOs are philanthropic at best, they are not democratic.

MD: Yes.

GCS: I have come to feel and maybe this is not correct, that in fact it's not really a great deal of money spent that is needed—

MD: No.

GCS: I feel like saying to people, if you want to help, don't go.

MD: Let them be.

GCS: This is my feeling, leave them alone. If you want to help—

MD: Just let them be. I've seen many places, many organizations, where I disagree with the purpose with which the money is given, and I am angry and disgusted.

GCS: Now, Mahasweta-di, I want you to forget all our discussions and to put yourself back in the frame of mind, take your time and think about it, more than twenty years ago, in the frame of mind where you wanted to write, you said that you wrote in a frenzy, you wrote in seven days, what was it that you wanted to do and what was it that you felt you had done? Take yourself back to then, not to today's Mahasweta Devi, but the person in those years and tell me about the novel in your own way, and about the character.

MD: Yes. I had been going to Palamau, and touring all over the district of Palamau, it was forest. At that time, the forest and trees meant so much to me, still do, and I saw how they sustained themselves. I'll never forget those fantastic days when I'd go to the

Chotti nallah—the rivulet. Chotti is actually the source of the Damodar. When it enters Bengal it becomes Damodar. But where Chotti starts, the source, it was fantastic. In the morning I'd find, on the sands of the river, tracks of bears; in the night they come, cross over, eat berries and go. And I saw the bridge where Chotti saved Tirathnath. On two sides there are two low hills, and there is a slope, the train goes up. When elephants crossed the rail lines, the train stopped there, it was fantastic to see, an entire train stopping, letting the elephants pass in their slow grandeur. . . At that time I found the animals unconscious, because the train did not matter to them, did not exist for all these trees, birds, snakes . . .

GCS: I should let you have the last word but I have to tell you something. You know what fills me with the greatest anguish, it's Birsa—twenty-five, a twenty-five-year old boy of such courage, dying in jail, that last stuff, you know, vomiting blood, making that sound, and dying suddenly. That fills me with anguish. You know, we hear of death in custody, and that is an intolerable thing. But when I think of Birsa in his twenties, with that kind of courage and imagination and leadership, dying that way in jail, that fills me with anguish.

MD: Slow arsenic poisoning. I made a conference with the doctors. And he dragged his chains, in a small room, from this end to that end. You have read my story 'Lifer'—it's like that. Terrible. Birsa himself was a gentle person. He did not learn to kill alone. Of course they learn to use arrows and other weapons, but they don't go to kill alone. They also help nature to survive. They use weapons, but they are not bloodthirsty. They are basically gentle, polite, highly civilized, and this innate blood civilization runs back thousands of years. A tribal lives in harmony with the nature around him, with human beings, even intruders. With everyone. So when he kills, it is a necessary killing.

GCS: And in fact, in Singh's book, in the Appendix, there is a conversation between the lawyer and the judge. The way in which they decided that these people were violent, it's a farce.[16]

MD: An absolute farce.

GCS: There was no justice.

MD: About Chotti also, throughout the book you'll see, Chotti is never raising his arrow to kill anyone, he is basically a civilized polite person. If we think of what Gandhi means, patience, tolerance, forgiveness, tribals have it. The way they suffer us is because they have a very ancient civilization. They can do it, we cannot. We get angry, lose our tempers, become beasts, they do not. When they do it, one must understand their extreme desperation. In Birsa it was like that, and in Dhani don't you find it fantastic that he had to go back to Sailrakab?

GCS: I think the conception of Dhani's character is extremely beautiful.

MD: Fantastic, na? Because I read that Dhani suffered for so many years, I had to make Dhani like that.

GCS: But you never met him?

MD: No. Dhani it was impossible to meet—

GCS: Of course, of course—

MD: Because it was so long ago . . .

GCS: When in this novel, Chotti is likened to Gandhi, I thought of the ancient Lochhu Sabar[17] who was in the national liberation movement—as if Lochhu was speaking, but you hadn't met Lochhu yet!

MD: No, no, I hadn't. But when I went to the Sabars, I found answers to all my questions, everything I had written about tribals, I found in them. That's why I'm so vulnerable about them, so touchy, one can take advantage of them so easily. That's why I cannot do anything when I think of their faces. Lochhu-da and you and me in Akarbaid. Do you remember with what dignity he said, 'Stop, I'm narrating history.'

GCS: I'm now telling history—ami itihas bolchhi. Yes, I do remember. Let us end here, Lochhu-da on history is a good place to end. Thank you again.

NOTES

1 The second half of the eighteenth century saw the disintegration of the tribal agrarian order in India under a steady influx of non-tribal people—land hungry peasants and unscrupulous traders—accelerated by the local administration acting in collusion with the British administration. The tribals reacted to these developments in the form of a series of uprisings in an attempt to throw out the intruders from their homeland. The process of armed resistance and revitalization movements aimed at reconstructing tribal society continued sporadically, finally blending and culminating in the last uprising of the Mundas, the Ulgulan or 'The Great Tumult', led by Birsa Munda (1874-1901), the legendary tribal leader, from December 1899–January 1900 in the

Ranchi and northern Singhbhum districts of Bihar. The uprising was suppressed, ending in the surrender of the insurgents, followed by the capture and death in captivity of Birsa Munda. See K. S. Singh, *Birsa Munda and His Movement 1874-1901: A Study of a Millenarian Movement in Chotanagpur* (Calcutta: Oxford University Press, 1983). (It is accepted practice to use the word 'tribal' in the Indian context—as distinct from Muslims, Hindus, and other religious communities.)

2 During the period 1971-77, when Mrs Indira Gandhi (1917–84) was Prime Minister of India, the country faced food shortage and rising prices (1973–74) leading to political grievances, popular demonstrations and movements, discontent among a group of MPs in her own Congress Party, a countrywide agitation led by Jayaprakash Narayan against corruption and misrule, and finally a ruling of the Allahabad High Court on 12 June 1975 declaring Mrs Gandhi's 1971 election invalid. Jayaprakash Narayan, originally a member of the Socialist Party, had shifted his ideological position to a point where he advocated non-party democracy; his moral credibility led to him being chosen to spearhead the united opposition to Mrs Gandhi. The leading opposition parties joined forces and organized a mass mobilization campaign demanding her resignation. In a final bid to decisively end all opposition to her continuance in office and to keep the discontent among her political opponents at bay, Emergency was declared by the President of India on 26 June 1975, under Article 352 of the Constitution. All her principal opponents—in the opposition and in her own Party—were arrested. Civil liberties were curtailed and strict censorship imposed. See Paul R. Brass, *The Politics of India since Independence* (Cambridge: Cambridge University Press, 1990).

3 The term 'lumpenproletariat', originally used by Karl Marx, is used to denote, in Marxist terminology, 'the amorphous urban social group below the proletariat, "the scum, the leavings, the refuse of all classes", among which Marx included swindlers, confidence tricksters, brothel-keepers, rag-and-bone merchants, beggars and other "flotsam of society"; lower classes of society who are unorganized and uncommitted to any political or ideological position'—Samik Bandyopadhyay (compiled and ed.) *The New Samsad English Bengali Dictionary* (Calcutta: Sahitya Samsad, 2000). This is the connotation of the word lumpen—lexicalized as a noun, and allowances made for differences in social idiom—in the Bengali and Indian context as well.

4 '. . . the Naxalite movement in West Bengal, broke out in the tribal region of Naxalbari in northern Bengal in May 1967, when a policeman, Sonam Wangdi, was killed by armed tribals resisting a police combing of the village, killing nine, including six women and two children. The regional movement grew and spread fast, drawing in a wide assortment of elements, including a considerable section of urban students; but with inadequate organizational control and sharp differences in the leadership over both ideological and strategic issues, mounting persecution, and, above all else, the Left establishment's use of state machinery both to disinform the people and the ranks alike and to drive power to the extreme of brutality, the movement collapsed in 1971.' [Samik Bandyopadhyay, Introduction to Mahasweta Devi's *Mother of 1084* (Calcutta: Seagull Books, 1997), p. xi]

5   The expansion of British domination in India and the growth of an Indo-British administrative system, compounded with ruthless extortion, fraud and oppression by up-country merchants and moneylenders, led to economic, social and political discontent, particularly in agrarian and tribal society throughout India. Agitations and militant movements started in different regions—the most notable among these being the Bareilly Rising of 1816; the Kol Rising of 1831–32 and other uprisings in Chhotanagpur and Palamau; Muslim uprisings like the Ferazee disturbances at Barasat in 1831 under the guidance of Syed Ahmad and his disciple Meer Niser Ali or Titu Mir, and later the leadership of Deedu Mir; the Moplah outbreaks in August 1849, 1851, 1852 and September 1855, and the Santal Insurrection of 1855–57 led by Sidhu and Kanhu (see note 6). See Kalikinkar Datta, *The Santal Insurrection of 1855–57* (Calcutta: University of Calcutta, 1988), p.1.

6   The Santal brothers Sidhu and Kanhu were regarded as the 'chosen ones'—apostles appointed by their God (Thakur) in a revelation. Leaders of the Santal Insurrection, 1855–57 (ibid., pp. 14–15).

7   Mahasweta Devi's *Pterodactyl, Puran Sahay, O Pirtha* was first published in the Bengali literary journal *Pratikshan* in its Special Autumn Issue in 1987. Subsequently published by Prama Prakashani in 1989. Available in English translation by Spivak in *Imaginary Maps* (Calcutta: Thema, 1993; New York: Routledge, 1993).

8   The Sanskritized 'Savara' means hunter. The Sabar or hunter tribe is today reduced to extreme social disenfranchisement, but retains some of the precapitalist communitarian virtues.

9   Khuntkatti: Tenure of the members of the lineage (*khunt*) who reclaimed lands (*katti*). The original land tenure system of the Munda (see notes on p. 295 for details).

10   *Aranyer Adhikar* was first published in serialized form in 1975 in *Betar Jagat* [a fortnightly programme magazine (now defunct) published by All India Radio, Calcutta]. It was first published as a book by Karuna Prakashani in 1977 [Baishakh 1384 B.S.].

11   'On 8 September 1980, the Bihar Military Police (BMP) confronted by tribals assembled under the flag of the Jharkhand Mukti Morcha in the small, picturesque town of Gua [in Singhbhum distict], chased some tribals who had to run to the hospital carrying a comrade injured in police firing. Eleven were shot dead within the hospital. The BMP had, according to a tribal, fired 60 to 70 rounds and people of the surrounding area remain convinced that many more than the officially admitted number of 11 died that day'—Mahasweta Devi, 'Witch Sabbath At Singhbhum', *Economic and Political Weekly*, 3 October 1981, collected in Maitreya Ghatak (ed.), *Dust on the Road: The Activist Writings of Mahasweta Devi* (Calcutta: Seagull Books, 1997), p. 48.

12   Publishers of periodicals all over West Bengal bring out Special Autumn Numbers ['*sharadiya sankhya*'] just before Durga Puja, the major annual religious festival celebrated around October each year, which is perhaps the most important socio-cultural event of the annual Bengali calendar.

Poets, novelists, essayists, playwrights are commissioned well in advance; major graphic artists and designers are involved in planning the layout and design; leading contemporary artists contribute illustrations and covers. This is also a forum for discovering new literary talents. A particular play or short story or novel would normally be reworked by the author and subsequently printed by a publisher in a revised/enlarged version. Some of the greatest works in Bengali literature have emerged as part of this process. This is also the time for annual vacation, with holidays for Durga, Lakshmi and Kali Puja—all of which follow, one after the other—usually adding up to a substantial number of days, and families often buy a couple of *sharadiya sankhyas* as reading material, a custom that has become part of the urban Bengali ethos.

13 Tebhaga: [Lit. three shares] A movement of tenant cultivators or share-croppers (1946–47), led by the Communist Party, against the jotedars or rich peasants in the four districts of North Bengal, demanding a radical revision of the crop-sharing system so as to reduce the landlord's share of the produce from half to one-third.

14 Mahasweta Devi's story, 'Draupadi' in Spivak's translation, *Breast Stories* (Calcutta: Seagull Books, 1998).

15 The Kheria Sabars are a minority hunter tribe, concentrated mainly in Purulia district, West Bengal, but also to be found in the forest areas of Medinipur and Bankura districts of West Bengal. Officially notified as a criminal tribe [by the British Government] (with Lodhas and Sabars) in 1871; denotified in 1952 by the Government of India, and accorded the status of a 'Scheduled Tribe' according to the 1947-49 Constitution of India. Cf. Mahasweta Devi, 'The Kherias of West Bengal', *Economic and Political Weekly*, 7 September 1985; collected in Maitreya Ghatak (ed.), *Dust on the Road*. See also *Bortika*, Kheria Sabar Special Number, July–December 1987.

16 This exchange, reported in *The Bengalee*, 23 May 1900, between the Munda's Counsel and the Magistrate, illustrates a typical day in the trial of Munda prisoners—Singh, *Birsa Munda*, p. 259–66.

17 During the movement for Indian Independence in 1942, Lochhu Sabar mobilized thousands of tribals, armed with bows and arrows, and under the leadership of the Gandhiite leader Rebati Chattopadhyay attacked the Burrabazar Police Precinct [thana] in Purulia and was arrested with several others. He spent ten years in jail. He is 88 years old and lives in Jehanabad village in Purulia District in southwestern West Bengal.

HIS NAME IS CHOTTI MUNDA. Chotti is of course also the name of a river. There is a story behind a river giving him a name. Stories grow around him all the time. It seems that mica or coal came out of the ground wherever his forefather Purti Munda went. As a result stories grew about him as well. Purti brought his wife and kids from Chaibasha to Palamau. Cleared the forest and settled a home. This time weapons of stone emerged from under the soil of his fields. Immediately there was talk. Suddenly one day many kinds of people—White-Bengali-Bihari—appeared and evicted him from his home. Stone Age arms give the right to the Government's Department of Archaeology.

His spirit was quite broken. Why does coal or mica appear if he breaks ground? Why do Whites-Bengalis-Biharis appear right away? What is the reason? Why can he not live in peace anywhere? However remote the place he travels to, something will come out from under ground, immediately a big settlement will grow there. His Mundari world will shrink. He doesn't want anything, after all. A small village. All the locals adivasi, worshippers of god Haram. Followers of a priest, the pahan.

That he's failing at this, is Haram god angry with him then? Pahan says in a melancholy voice, Purti Munda! T'woulda been better if ye'd been Hindu, been Christian. Now if we keep ye, our lives will also be spent wanderin' this way.

His wife said the same thing. Where'er ye go, why da things come out from under ground?

Come, let's go elsewhere.

They made a home by Chotti River. The riverbank is like a high hill, and the hut is on this slope. He fishes in the bosom of the river at evening. One day at glimmering twilight he saw amazed that there was gold dust in the sand that had come up in his net.

He sat down on the sand. He remembers how White men and Biharis jumped at the sight of coal and mica, how instantly they disfigured adivasi areas with slums of tile-roofed dwellings. Who knows what such people will do if they see gold? These hills, these forests, this river will once again be spoiled. With great loss of spirit he brought up sand once more in his open palms. Gold again. Now he decides. The Hindu enthusiastic sect Sadan, Christian missionary and tea garden recruiters, all three want to get him. Purti Munda went in search of the recruiter. Let his wife and kids live. At departure he tells his wife, there's a kid in your belly. Call him Chotti if it's a boy.

Purti Munda was most ill-fated. In search of the recruiter he enters a prosperous Hindu village and sleeps under the very tree from whose roots the stolen plate of the landowner begins to emerge. As a result he is caught and jailed immediately. Recruited as soon as freed. Then Mauritius. What happened after that is unknown. But river names keep inscribing themselves as the names of his descendants. That is the reason why the two great-grandsons of Purti Munda are named after rivers—Chotti Munda and Koel Munda. Their home is still on the banks of the Chotti. Even today. But Purti Munda's wishes were not fulfilled. He had escaped for fear that outsiders in search of gold would make the place all mixed up. Now the Southeastern Railway runs three miles from the spot. There is a station called Chotti. The reason that there is a station for this settlement is that the settlement is populated by Biharis, Bengalis, Punjabis. The adivasis stay at a distance, in villages. Once a year the place named Chotti fills with adivasis. At the Chotti fair on Bijoya, the high holiday celebrating the Hindu great goddess's triumph. Adivasis from thirty villages nearby come to this fair on that day. They make huge tigers, elephants, horses of paper stuck on bamboo frames. They carry the animals and dance. Women dance too. They drink moua, the adivasis' berry liquor. Non-adivasi men are forbidden to go near these dancers at the fair. If they do they might harass the adivasi women sexually and the State dislikes fires in dry grass. Police come from the Tohri thana to avoid such incidents. The dance goes on from eleven in the morning to three o' clock. Then the real fun of Chotti fair starts. The fair is held in a spacious field. There is an adivasi archery competition there in that meadow. The target is gradually moved back. Hitting the final bull's eye is exceedingly difficult. Two iron rings are tied onto two successive bamboo poles. There are three such rings. The bull's eye must be hit through all these rings.

A most exacting feat of archery. From the adivasi side the prize is a pig. For a long time now the police Daroga gives five rupees. Tirathnath Lala-the-trader gives five rupees, Harbans Chadha the owner of the brick kiln gives five rupees, Anwar the fruitseller gives five rupees. Every year there is fierce competition around this test. Every year the Daroga thinks, there's sure to be rioting. Yet every year the contestants stay up the night eating pork and rice—the meat of this pig and a couple more that they slaughter—and drinking liquor. The Daroga is annually astonished that there is never a quarrel between the winners and the losers.

Chotti Munda says, Why s'd there be quarrel? One village wins at a time. It's now no more than a game. Why s'd there be a quarrel over't?

Until about eighteen years ago Chotti Munda won the contest each year. But the final time he won, his kinsman Donka Munda had said to the judges, 'Tis no' right.

What is not right?

To let Chotti Munda enter t' field.

Why?

Everyone knows his arrer has a spell on't. Th' arrer will hit bull's eye e'en if he shoots with eyes shut.

Chotti! Is this true?

Yes, Chotti had said.

Then, surprising everyone, he had pulled out some other person's arrow from the target. Had said to Donka, Gie me yer bow.

Putting the arrow to Donka's bow, pulling the string, he spoke to the arrow, Ye'll get a bad name me son, ye hav'n't been able ta hit t' bull's eye, go me son, hit t' bull's eye now.

He shot talking and hit the bull's eye. Donka touched his knee and showed respect. Shall I show wit' bow of each who failed, Chotti had asked. True, there is a spell. But see I didn' use t' spellbound arrer. I hit t' bull's eye with me grandson's arrer. But it's also true that I'll not swerve from t' bull's eye as long as that spellbound arrer is with me.

Then it's not right that you join the game, someone had said. You're sixty now, why not be a judge? There is always one from your community.

A' right.

From then on Chotti Munda is a judge at the games. What sure aim, the Daroga said. If only you held a rifle.

A man-man shoots an arrer, Chotti had said. A man-zero shoots a bullet.

The Daroga swallowed the remark because it was Chotti's. Why he eats Chotti's words is another story. Everything is for story-telling in Chotti Munda's life for many reasons.

II

THERE WAS A GREAT FLOOD in the Chotti river the year of Chotti's birth. Stones floated in the sweep of the flood-water. The flood lost force as soon as Chotti was born. It was then that the Brahman station master had said, This is not an inconsequential child.

This is the original story. The station master didn't even know of Chotti's birth. He wouldn't have said it even if he had known. No one would have understood even if he had said it. For the station master's tongue was too short. His speech got garbled. He made do with gestures. It's futile to say these things. The story had been around for a long time. The flood had gone down by its own law. That too no one remembers.

Chotti was obstinate from childhood. Koel's hand was truer in archery. But Chotti's resolve was to be a master archer, to pierce the bull's eye at Chotti fair. He went to his sister's in-law's house when he was an adolescent. There he saw his sister's grandfather-in-law, Dhani Munda. Dhani must have been close to ninety when Chotti saw him. Dhani counted his age by the measure of the two maturing and ageing cycles of the sal and teak trees in the forest—from his childhood to this day.

Dhani Munda is old but not decrepit. He winked at Chotti and said, I have a spellbound arrer. If ten birds fly in t' sky, an' ye tell th' arrer get me t' third one, it'll do it.

Is this true?

Ask yer sister Parmi.

Milking the she-goat with his sister he says, Sis, did he speak truth?

Parmi says, No one knows. But he knows howta shoot arrers. But if he shoots an arrer, t' police'll catch 'im.

Why?

Don' know.

Chotti gets very excited. He was fourteen then. The Chotti-area was burning with drought. Parmi's father-in-law was a good guy. He said to Chotti's mother, There aint no grass in yer fields, sand runs around on the riverbed, pushed by t' sunburnt wind. Send yer eldest son. He'll tend cattle. There's no drought that side.

I too'll go, Koel had said.

Can't keep two, sister's father-in-law had said.

So Chotti Munda goes to Parmi's father-in-law's house. A big village. By the bus road, near the police station, the Mission and the Sadan Ashram. It's not possible to grasp today that these adivasis, the Mundas, were the ones who first lived in the village. Other Bihari sects and castes now dominate the village. Poor upper-caste, rich upper-caste, etc. The Mundas live at a distance. Their settlement is also large. The Mundas labour here, in this village, in the fields and barns of the Hindus. Parmi's mother-in-law sells goat's milk. There the drought is not as consuming. Chotti remained there about a year. Worked very hard. At harvest time, when everyone—Parmi's father-in-law, husband, brother-in-law, mother-in-law—went to do bonded labour, he milked the cows and goats alone, delivered milk, herded cattle, all by himself. Parmi's parents-in-law really fancied him. What a pity they had no unmarried daughter. Then they could have made the lad their son-in-law. But they both told Chotti only one thing. Don' go ta Dhani Munda.

Why?

Don' ask. And ne'er ask him to hold a bow an' arrer. Dhani Munda's t' brother of me great-grandfather. I still say, when t' bow's in his hands, Munda society and families are in danger.

Hearing all this an alien attraction toward Dhani grows in Chotti's mind. What has Dhani done? Why does everyone give him this fearful respect?

He would look askance at Dhani. Dhani did nothing all day. All Mundas have machetes. Dhani's machete is incredibly sharp and some random marks are inscribed upon the wooden handle.

Dhani worked wood all day and made lovely toys for the Munda children. He spoke to no one. He cooked his own rice. Did not eat mixed meal, ghato. The village blacksmiths made machetes, floor-knives, scythes, spades, trowels. Dhani sat in front of the smithy and put together wooden handles for them. When did he learn such carpentry?

Parmi would say, No one knows.

Dhani was a man of much respect. If he was not seen in the shade of the raintree in front of the smithy a constable would come looking from the precinct. The police that took a cut at the market, went to the house of landlords and moneylenders on feast days and fast days, that almighty police comes to Dhani and asks in such a soft voice, What ho Dhani? Why haven't we seen you for a few days?

Feelin' sad?

Dhani! You know everythin' after all. Don't go anywhere please, I'll lose my job. You've grown old, show some sense.

Yer job, ye show sense.

I beg ya!

T' day I feel like it, I'll cast a spell, become invisible and take off!

Don't, Dhani!

Why're ye jerkin' t' Mundas aroun' at market and takin' cuts?

Who said?

I say. Daroga must be told. If ye cross t' Mundas—takin' cuts again! Understan'? Then Daroga too will hafta answer. Yes, I'll not tease t' Munda people. But e'en t' Gormen don' want new torture and t' Munda roughed up.

No new torture, just the old one. Chotti didn't understand which one was new and which one old. He understood when Parmi's father-in-law's group went to give bonded labour to the moneylender at harvest time.

Where d'ye go? Dhani roared.

Bond labour!

Yes grandpa.

Ta gie bond labour? Dontcha know? That bond labour is one among all th' ills he fought against?

He is no more Grandpa. Forget his name.

Oh Birsa! Not e'en fifteen years. And Mundas still shake for fear of t' rod.

Dhani left the house. Sister said to Chotti in the afternoon, He won' come if t' people of t' family call him. Ye call him.

Where's he gone?

To t' forest.

Why not give me his food? Else I'll look, call him, then he comes ta eat?

He doesn' eat our food.

Lemme look then.

Chotti went to look for Dhani. That business of looking ties him to another new and important story. Everything in Chotti Munda's life is a series of stories. Like many other stories of Munda life this narrative is also epic. How the earth was made, how that earth was burnt in the fire of Shengelda, how a man and a woman survived, how a new earth was created—these are the perennial stories in Munda life. Chotti didn't know that the new epic of Munda life had been created twenty years ago. Dhani tells him. As a result of the relationship that grows between him and Dhani, Chotti also becomes a part of the epic, and his ultimate destiny becomes as enormous and suggestive as that of epic heroes.

All this happened in 1915. When Chotti was fifteen. He looked and looked and found Dhani in the depths of the forest. Dhani sat on a stone beside a spring. He lifted his eyes when he saw Chotti.

Chotti held his feet.

Why grab me feet?

Teach me ta shoot an arrer.

Me?

Yes. Ye are t' god Haramdeo of archers.

Why d'ye want ta learn? All Mundas shoot, no? What new skill will I teach ye?

I want to win at Chotti fair.

Oh, for that?

Is that a nothin' goal?

Suddenly Dhani laughed at the sight of Chotti's glowing face. How shall I teach ye, he said. If I hold an arrer the polis'll again lock me up.

Why?

It's a long story. I want to tell t' tale, but there's no one to listen. And t' Munda folk here are broken-backed, livin' on t' kindness of t' Diku-Hindus. They won' let me stay in Chaibasha. There's still people to hear me there. They won' let me stop there.

Who won'?

Gormen.

Why?

That is a tale. Ye are a Munda. A man came to this world for all o' ye. Father Earth. Lord Birsa.

But I know of him.

Ye know? Who told ye?

Me mother's pa. Me grandad.

What's his name?

Hara Munda. It seems that there was a lotta fightin'. Our god died. And then a lot of polis trouble. Then grandpa came here from Ranchi. That's it, I know no more.

I, Dhani Munda, was his mate.

Ye! But ye're old.

So what?

Ye saw him?

Day after day. Even prison mates. And so I'm homeless, and so I'm not to pick up an arrer.

Why?

As if in the unbearable pain of not being able to speak, Dhani spoke, They know I'm t' Haramgod of archery. They think if I lift an arrer I'll call t' great revolt—Ulgulan—again.

I won' tell.

Ulgulan! What happened? Where's th' ownership of Khuntkatti villages? A life with no moneylender's ledger, no bonded labour? Where're Mundas happy? Still they fear. If I lift an arrer t' polis'll vent its force on them. I won' live here.

Where will ye go?

What's that to ye? Scram, scram, get outta here.

Chotti came away that day. But as long as this bonded labour went on, Dhani departed at the crack of dawn. As if he couldn't bear to look upon the bonded sweated work of the Mundas for an infinite debt repayment. Chotti would finish his own chores and follow him around. In the mean time one day a huge uproar. Parmi's mother-in-law said, From tomorra I'm not goin', me boys're not goin'.

Why? Dhani was curious.

Elders are much revered among adivasis. Ye are t' senior man, said Parmi's mother-in-law, ye give judgement and tell me, why s'd I go?

Ye were goin' though.

Why was I goin'? For yer brother, for these boys' dad's great-grandpa. Ye were a fighter, ye didn' tell t' Gormen about yer own brother, yer dad, yer boy. How was yer brother?

I don' know. T' ones I thought brothers're all gone. I haven' sown me seeds all in one bitta ground like ye. I don' recall today where I went for t' Santals' big revolt, their Hul, where I sharpened me arrer in t' Sardar's fight. This me Lord taught me, blood kin is not ever'thin'.

Parmi's mother-in-law says in a dry serious voice, I know I say nothin' to yer face, but I keep pride inside f'r ye, and I say nothin' for there's nowhere to go if t' polis make trouble.

So say now.

For some famine on some faraway day yer brother took ten seers rice at country measure—which comes to less—gave free labour for that bond, his son me granpa-in-law gave it, me father-in-law gave, we are givin'—okay. 'Tween wet an' dry, me land is just that tiny bit, wan' ta harvest me paddy, I wan' two days off and they won' gie? Don' gie, I won' go. Let 'em do what they want. And let me tell yer too, if t' Lord's Ulgulan had happened, t' Mundas would ha' lived. Did they? Tell me?

Dhani shook his head, Ye folks' moneylender's not a good sort. Moneylenders are not good sorts. If everyone labours on bond, and ye alone don', comes to nothin'. And this is all Hindu settled, where's th' adivasi? Ye wanna die fightin' alone?

But t' deer'll eat me paddy?

They won'.

Why? T' deer've reformed?

Dhani says, This too is t' new age rule. T' great-grandson's wife answers back.

The next day Dhani says to Parmi, Take rice from yer house and cook. Chotti and I'll harvest t' paddy. Chotti'll come at midday to take our food. Look I trapped hare. Roast t' meat.

A lot of forest in those days. Hare-bear-deer-hedgehog-partridge-pigeon—no dearth of meat.

Less than an acre of land. Government-deposit land. It was Dhani and Chotti who harvested the land. After the first day's work Dhani said, We'll sleep on a bamboo-frame in t' field at night. If not there's as many peacocks as deer.

Suddenly Chotti graduates to Dhani's companionship, comradeship. On a frost-dripping night in the harvest-month of

Aghran, at the unearthly moment when the starry heavens had come surreptitiously close to the earth, when in the royal forest of Jajpur the elephants were breaking down the bamboo groves, Dhani says to Chotti, Wanna learn to shoot arrers? There's t' stag eating paddy darkling. Canya hit it?

But I can' see!

Gimme yer bow.

Dhani stood on the machan. Shot the arrow leaning forward slightly. Tomorra we must drag it off, he said. We'll eat meat. Come, let's guard it from close. Otherwise t' leopard'll grab it.

Chotti thought it was all magic. But the deer was real. A huge buck. The two sat there. I'll sure leave, said Dhani. But I'll teach ye and go.

Me bow is small.

I've a bow.

Ye do!

Of course. Stashed it in t' jungle. Take me machete in yer hand. Feel t' handle with yer fingers.

What design is scratched there?

In the starlight Dhani smiles like the invincible soul of the forest. Me lord wrote his name by his own hand there, he said. This is his name. Ye don' know how to read, nor I. No need. If ye feel it with yer fingers t' spell'll enter yer fingers as well.

It will?

Absolutely.

Then?

Then ye'll win at t' Chotti fair! In yer time there is no Lord, no Ulgulan, no fire in anyone's soul to change t' Munda's life, no piercin' of moneylender, polis, an' soldier with' arrers in t' heat of that fire, but there's t' Chotti fair. Gormen babysits t' Munda tribe that way.

Everyone knew who shot the deer, but said nothing. After the harvest Dhani had said, How long can ye feed on this light white rice? Sow pepper, more money in't.

Parmi's father-in-law had said, T' land belongs to t' Lalas— traders. Given us to farm cos there is no good crop. Soon's they know pepper, they'll take away. We too know pepper grows there. Knowin' we can do nothin'. It's enough that t' rice grows.

All th' arable land belongs to t' Mundas and th' Oraons.

That was in yer day. We've never seen landownin' Mundas and Oraons. All t' land is Diku land—Hindu land—since long ago.

What all did we see?

Now even more police pressure. We'll eat game and ha' fun, but now they scare even if they see t' Munda dance and sing. Right away t' polis come to see what's up. And t' polis'll charge board, lodgin', travel.

T' fight goes on.

Ye know, yer great-grandsons live in Jijubhatu?

What's t' use knowin'?

Dhani felt driven somehow. He took Chotti to the jungle. He called the jungle Our Mother, Dhani said. Let me learn ye t' jungle. With jungle learnin' ye won' die starvin'. What isn't there in t' jungle?

It is a precious experience to live with Dhani. It is then that Chotti learns to know the sweet-rooted creepers, to learn the springs full of fish, to learn to trap deer. When to pick dropped feathers for the market from the special place where peacocks dance.

Won' ye teach me archery?

There are red and black fruits of the kunchtree in the forest. From the kunch you can make kuchila poison. There was some terrific haste somewhere inside Dhani. Otherwise why teach Chotti all this? Chotti is only a poor Munda lad. He came to his sister's house in a famine year to live on a bite to eat. Whose only life's dream was to shoot an arrow to win at the Chotti fair.

And Dhani taught him to parrot the story of a long gone revolt. When Birsa was a student at Chaibasha, it was Dhani who had told him, You're born to be Father Earth.

Dhani was always crazy, at the time of the Santal Hul Dhani was a lad of twenty. The Kherwar revolt, the Mulkoi revolt of the Sardars, and then Birsa's revolt. Armed struggle is also an addiction. He went to all the revolts in the hope that Mundas would establish villages in forest and arable land and farm rightfully and in peace, and that other adivasi groups would do the same. But looking at the peaceful farming Mundas he understood that he had not wanted this peace. It is not known if peace was to be had in an area free of moneylending, Gormen and Diku, for adivasis don't live that way anywhere in India. He felt very much alone. Yet the police will immediately be alert if they see a bow in the hands of the eighty-one year old Dhani Munda. The Mundas must not create trouble again. Most complicated affairs, these.

T' most important thing in archery is concentration. Be stable on one sightin', shoot yer arrer. Look, there's a ripe bitter apple hangin'. Make it fall. Look, a herd of deer. Let's see ye kill t' stag? Listen to a huntin' tip. When ye kill, finish with one arrer. Don' make t' prey suffer for nothin'. Why does yer hand shake to pull t' bowstring?

There's something drives Dhani inside. Some days he beat up Chotti mercilessly. I teach so carefully, he'd say, And ye forget everythin'? Drop t' fruit from t' tree—why did th' arrer hit t' branch?

The day Chotti killed the green dove hariyal from behind green leaves at dusk in the glimmering twilight that's kind to the new bride's face, Dhani said, Ye'll get there. Sitting on the platform that day Dhani said, Are y'asleep, Chotti?

No, lookin' at stars.

See that star in t' North. It's no' movin'. We knew our way, forest and hill, by that star.

I've seen.

Heard t' Sadans sing Mahabharat at t' railway tishan?

Yeah.

Arrer fight.

Yeah.

Where did t' Hindu gods learn to shoot those arrers?

Where?

From us folks.

Us folks.

Yeah. Keep in mind—ye don' have long to learn how to shoot an arrer to win at Chotti fair. Howsomever, food or no food, shoot an arrer every day. Skill runs off without practice.

I'll shoot.

I'll teach ye t' real skill after these lessons.

Ye'll teach?

Yeah, there's no end to instruction. Now learn to drive yer eye in t'dark. See how many straight trees on t' field edge.

Three.

Nope, five. Check in t' mornin'. Must learn to drive th' eye in t'dark, to walk t' forest in t'dark.

Why?

Don' know. Lemme keep teachin' yer. How much longer will I
last? And what other Munda laddie will come to learn arrer-
shootin' from me?

Will ye die?

No Hul, no Mulkoi struggle, no Ulgulan. Me lord said I'll be
born again in t' belly of a Munda mother, Dhani! No trace of that
either. T' Mundas now work bonded labour with down-low heads,
they die at t' hands of t' moneylender. All's become t' train line,
t' polis watch, t' muscle force of King-Emperor and Daroga—no
end in this—me mind's not in such a world Chotti.

Don' die.

I'll die after I teach ye t' real skill.

To tell the truth, the matter of staying with Dhani was itself so
exciting and joyful, that the matter of archery at the Chotti fair
was becoming increasingly secondary. Dhani had to labour greatly in order to complete the task of teaching how to shoot an
arrow. In the morning he worked the bit of settled land belonging to Parmi's family. From midday on, educating Chotti in the
forest. As soon as it was afternoon he had to sit in front of the
smithy. Otherwise the police would come to his place to search.

At that time there were not too many trains on that line. There
was still a lot of jungle all around. The Marwaris had not yet started
employing contractors to break stone and export morraine. The
forest department hadn't started cutting down the ancient sal forest. So there was lots of game. A lot of old time landowners. A lot
of private forest. Thanks to Chotti's arrow lessons a lot of deer
and hedgehog was consumed. Parmi's father-in-law was happy as
well. Now Dhani ate with them.

Ate rice, however. Will not eat mealie, No, he'd say. Me lord
fought so that Mundas could eat rice like Dikus. This was among
t' many reasons he fought.

A little valley in the middle of the forest. Covered with grass.
Dhani would draw an eye with lime on the tree. Chotti shot
arrows. Dhani would increase the distance. Learn fast Chotti, he
would say.

The day Chotti hit an eye painted on a tree through two rows,
Dhani said, Good! Now if ye practise every day ye'll win at t'
Chotti fair sure as sure.

Now teach t' true skill.

I will.

As soon as he said, I'll teach, Dhani seemed to change for a moment. His age increased amazingly and he became an old man of a million years. If you are that old, age drops off your skin. As in the Hindu god's temple in Bishangarh. Although seven hundred years old, the age of the humans, monkeys, elephants, birds carved on the temple does not increase. Dhani became like that. Told someone in a low voice, I can' be alone any more. Me time has come.

Then he became the everyday Dhani again. Let's stop a coupla days, he said to Chotti. Lemme catch t' lay of t' land.

We must hurry.

Why?

Holi Colourfeast is just ahead. There'll be hunt games in t' forest.

Let a coupla of days pass. Git away now. Leave me alone for now.

What do ye listen for all by yerself?

Dhani sighs and says, D'ye hear someone cry?

Why, no?

He could.

Who?

Dhani didn't answer that question. Drew out his first remark and said, T' forest cried. Told him, Birsa, Diku-Master-White man—together they've made me unclean, naked, undressed, clean me up. Chotti gimme yer word, ye'll not tell no one all that I've told ye?

Won' tell. Swear on me bow.

As soon as he gave word Chotti understood that his age too climbed up. The intolerable burden of proceeding with Dhani's secret guarded was his alone to bear.

Two days later Dhani said, Let's go today. Took Chotti way-deep in the forest. Look ahead, he said.

In two days Dhani has built a straw effigy. The straw man stood in front of the tree.

Chotti! Look with care.

I'm lookin', yes.

This is t' real instruction, Chotti.

Why s'd I kill humans?

One must, from time to time.

Something raises an urgency in Dhani's voice. No time, no time for him. He was born in 1834. He was a young man at the time of

Sidhu-Kanu's Hul. From Hul to Kherwar, from Kherwar to the Mulkoi struggle, from Mulkoi struggle to Ulgulan, walking from revolt to revolt, grinding the poison-berry of the wild creeper, he has reached eighty-one in 1915. Now he's in great trouble. Expelled from Chaibasha. 'Dhani Munda is not to enter Chaibasha Police Station area on peril of death.' And Dhani Munda wants to live only there. There are still those villages there that joined in Birsa's struggle. Dhani wants to hear Bolpe Bolpe, the Ulgulan song. He wants to see Birsa's adoptive son Pariba, his initiate disciple Sali. He wants to die in Birsa's last battlefield, Sailrakab in the Dombari Hills.

Here Dhani Munda is most lonely, most solitary. But Chotti has wanted to learn archery from him. Let's give him the real instruction. Something drawing him somewhere, there's no time. Dhani realizes that the times when he lived a real life are now past. Munda are agricultural by blood. Dhani was never that. The fight was to wrench a peaceful life for one's kin, but the goal of the battle was not fulfilled. Let's teach Chotti. Chotti, let me thread ye to the tales and sayings of Munda life by teachin' ye to pierce the straw man. But what does Chotti say?

Why must one kill people from time to time?

We killed.

Why?

We won' eat mealie, won' obey t' terrorizin' moneylender, Diku, polis, will occupy arable and settled rural land, will take back t' right to t' forest.

Did ye?

No. We got nothin'. Someone showed us t' way. We fought. Someone might show ye folks t' way. All t' reasons remain, Chotti. If such a day comes ye too will kill. And yes, raise Dhani Munda's name and kill. I'll be at peace then.

Kill humans!

If need be.

What is't, what is't in yer hand?

Me bow. Look. Ye'll hit t' chest, here, this way. Go fetch that arrer. Most pricey arrer. Look let me show ye. Ho! there behind t' straw man a bird in t' tree. A green dove. There I kill t' bird. There's a whole buncha birds in t' sky? Kill ten? Gimme yer buncha arrers. Look ye! Ten birds, ten mouths to feed at home. Now look I hit t' man's chest agin. Hold it, raise t' bow.

Not once, but day after day. Finally Dhani said, Now practise will do whate'ers pos'ble. Somethin' to be learnt fer life caint happen so quick.

Will ye go somewhere?

Why? Why ask this?

Dhani became cautious. How will Chotti know, he's trying to return to Sali, to Pariwa. Where there is much peace.

But we'll play hunt at t' Colourfeast Holi? Surprise everyone?

Holi? Let's see.

Moneylender'll give liquor, colour.

What else'll he do?

There'll be dancin' front of moneylender's house.

Everyone will go?

Everyone.

Dhani's eyes become dusky. Smiling a bit he says, Then I must first see Holi fun.

Yes.

Holi arrived. Dhani had said, Go, go play hunt. I gie ye me arrer thinkin' of this day.

Yer arrer? Mine?

Yes. Most feisty arrer! This is an arrer to keep close Chotti, don' shoot unless there's great need. No one can ever beat ya if ye keep this by. But keep up practice.

Sure.

Holi madness in Murudi that day. The Hindus' festival. The adivasis' Hunt Holiday. Drinking, song, and dance after the hunt. The moneylender gave liquor to the adivasis, and colour powder to the outcaste Hindu villagers. Chotti killed a tusky boar. Tremendous applause for it. It gets to be dusk before everyone's game can be taken back to the village. Dhani wasn't home.

After that departure, Dhani did not return. The police came, there was a search, but Chotti knew he wouldn't come back again.

Being buddies with Lord Birsa's co-worker Dhani Munda is another story in Chotti Munda's life. Chotti heard its conclusion later. After his return from Murudi.

The account is like a rumour, the rumour that travels all the time, somewhere or other, in some way. History advances because rumour happens. Such is the rumour that by it Dhani Munda becomes perennial. His starving, fierce being becomes a detail in a copious epic.

The rumour is like this.

Dhani Munda, accused and convicted in the Munda riot case headed by Birsa Munda, did his prison term in Ranchi je-hell. After his release, he was sent to Murudi village under Tahar police station in Palamau, with the order of staying out of Chaibasha. There was a police precinct in Murudi. Dhani was a dangerous criminal. The precinct was alerted about him. It was desirable that he stay under cover. For he believes in Birsa's delirium in je-hell, 'I'll come back again.' It is dangerous to credit the delirium of the dead. It is also incorrect that Dhani should be armed. Especially bow and arrow. If kept for a while this way Dhani would die by natural law.

Murudi Precinct and Tahar Police Station were in great trouble because Dhani disappeared. His whereabouts could not be ascertained and Ranchi and Chaibasha were alerted. Mundas love to die at home. Dhani was an unruly man. Chaibasha is not his home, and those he left behind were indeed his kin. But Chaibasha was once his field of work. Where can Dhani go? The names of many villages emerge after rummaging through fifteen-year old files and paper. Rummaging into all this, a certain Mundari-knowing Munda-enthusiastic Father of the Chaibasha Mission enlightens the officer in charge all of a sudden. He says that on the anniversary of Birsa's death Birsa's old comrades go to Sailrakab and share his memory. In secret. Therefore where Dhani can go is no longer an expanded area. It's clear that Jejur Police Station is nearest to his destination. In the month of June, as Birsa's death day approaches, many Dhani Mundas are captured. Many of them are called 'Dhani'. Unfortunately, none of the captured ones is the sought-after Dhani. Over-enthusiastic police beat the markets and, capturing scores of Dhani Mundas, they exhaust the Station Officer. Gradually it seems that the entire affair might be a sheer invention.

Everyone dozes off again and one afternoon a great uproar is noticeable in Jejur market.

The constable announces, Oh, Dhani Munda is coming! Daroga Muneshwar Singh runs at speed with his head-constable and witnesses an incomparable scene.

Machete in one hand and holding his bow aloft in the other a thin but wiry old Munda comes forth. On both sides are assembled adivasis. He is calling out loud, I am Dhani Munda! I was kicked out, I've come agin. Where is t' station, eh? I never seen a station. No one forbids me lads, I have come.

Halt, stop! Muneshwar Singh shouts.

Dhani shakes the folds of his toothless face and laughs in child-like glee, saying, Nowhere a polis tha' kin hold me back. I've come, me lads, I'm that Dhani Munda.

Dhani Munda! Dhani!

Ye're Donka!

Dhani!

Ye're that Hara Munda!

Dhani!

Hey Kanu! Where's that Sali? Where's that Pariwa?

The old greet the old joyfully and Muneshwar Singh sees a frightful possibility of another Munda uprising in this. Dhani swings machete and bow in air in an irrepressible exaltation and says, dancing, I've returned home lads! He stoops and sits, Lemme eat dirt, lemme eat home dirt! Home soil has t' sweet smell of rice lads! Lemme eat earth! In truth he rubs his face in the dirt, Donka starts to weep, Dhani laughs and weeps, Muneshwar Singh shoots him in the head.

Thus, dangerous Dhani Munda dies as a result of ignoring his expulsion order and the Mundas, without a written language, mingle Dhani-tale with the tale of Birsa and make Dhani eternal.

The story comes to Murudi by the police chain and in time Chotti knows it. Thus another story is added to Chotti's life. Everything in Chotti Munda's life is one story after another.

III

YES ALL'S A STORY IN CHOTTI Munda's life. Munda language has no script. So they turn significant events into story, and hold them as saying, as song. That's their history as well. Dhani Munda's news reaches Murudi police precinct in the proper way through police accounts.

This is how the news reaches Chotti village: When lord Birsa was in the je-hellhouse, Dhani Munda alone knew that the lord will return. This body will die, but his kernel and his spirit will not perish. He is the Earth Father, the engenderer of the world.

Dhani knew that. The lord's body dies. Dhani slaves in the je-hellhouse.

> Dhani, ye came out of t' je-hellhouse.
> Big polis boss said with red eyes
> Ranchi and Chaibasha are forbidden for ye
> Ye won' lift bow and arrer
> Ye won' come to Ranchi and Chaibasha
> When ye outed from t' je-hellhouse
> Big polis boss said these words, these words//
> Dhani, ye came out of t' je-hellhouse
> An arrer of fire showed ye t' way
> Ye came to Murudi
> When ye left t' je-hellhouse//
> T' ones with whom ye stayed in
> Murudi were given grace
> Murudi's water-sky-earth became blessed
> Dhani, ye stayed in Murudi//
> Dhani, Father Earth called ye
> On t' day of his body's death in Sailrakab
> He comes to look for his disciples
> He calls loud shakin' t' hills,
> Hey who's kept me in mind, who's forgotten
> Who's here crazy for Ulgulan, for Revolution!
> Father Earth called ye//
> Ye said, Hey I've come
> Ye climbed up on t' black cloud
> Ye came to Jejur on t' black cloud
> So many humans at Jejur market!
> They said eat barley paste, eat rough molasses
> When ye came to Jejur//
> Ye said home soil is me molasses,
> That soil ye took in yer hand,
> Soil became rough molasses
> Eatin' that soil ridin' on t' black cloud
> Ye went, whoa! To Dombari
> Ye vanished into Sailrakab stone//
> T' Daroga wept, slapped forehead, and went off
> Ye vanished into Sailrakab
> Called out loud, on t' day of t' death

Of Earth Father's body
I'll call y'all in one voice with him//
Ah! On Sailrakab stone now flowers bloom
Ye are those flowers

In this way, becoming song and story, Dhani comes back to Chotti Munda. As long as he hadn't, Chotti sat as stone looking out to the river. When he got Dhani back in song and story, he became human again.

On the day of the Chotti fair, Chotti Munda went as well. Old Sugana Munda was the judge on behalf of the adivasis. He is also pahan in his own village.

The judges' seat is on rush mats spread on the platforms where the marketeers keep their wares. Sugana, the Daroga, Baijnath the Lala-trader, these are the judges, the prize givers. The competition began. Seeing Chotti Sugana asked, Ye're Bisra Munda's boy?

Yes pahan.

Ye're but a brat.

Let me try once.

No adult Mundas in Chotti village?

They're there too.

Why one arrer?

If I can I'll pierce t' target with one arrer.

Ye'll join t' first round?

Final round.

Go, join it. Ruin t' village name.

Chotti didn't ruin the village name. He was wearing a yellow dhoti. He'd stained it with the yellow dye of the kusum flower. In his hair a wooden comb. Putting Dhani's arrow to the bow he memorated Dhani in his mind. Dhani's words, he must forget all. Ye're there, and there's a bull's eye.

Only him, and that eye.

Chotti shot the arrow.

The arrow pierced the iris.

Joy. Surprise. Elation. The dance of the Mundas of Chotti village with Chotti. Nightfall. Pork is cooking. Rice on the boil. An ocean of tears breaking in Chotti's chest. His dad Bisra put the vessel of liquor in his hand. From now on ye're a man, said he. A male! Now I get ya hitched.

A match was proposed by that pahan, Sugana Munda. He had a granddaughter. He really fancied Chotti. He looked great because of the food and tender loving care in his sister's household. His bravery matched his cool head.

I've no' a thing at home.

Who has what at home!

Two months' grub don' grow on t' land.

That's their fate.

Ye can get a good groom.

That's a good groom. I wanna give close to home. Give a sow and a she-goat to t' grand-kid. His fortune will turn with it.

Bisra sighed. Lemme tell his ma, said he.

Why does he want yer son?

Ye know.

Not a mean lad. Named for t' river.

That's just a clan rule.

Top o' that . . . in Murudi . . . folks say, mebbe he learnt some spell fro' Dhani Munda.

Let that be. Dhani Munda! Why talk o' him? Talk of m' boy. Ye wanna bring danger? Do a call-polis?

No, no.

And why's yer mind shook up wi' it? Dhani was a Birsaite, and Lord Birsa had no faith in chiefs?

Still . . .!

In Chotti's society the mother's respect is equal to the father's. Chotti's mother heard everything and said to her husband, It's no' a bad idea. T' Polis-Daroga, t' Lala-trader, t' contractor, t' jungle-babu Forest-Officer, all have good relations with Pahan. We have not a thing to talk about, t' tale of Purti Munda's gold-prospecting our only property. Chotti's spellbound arrer-tale is about ta become another new property.

What's that!

Everyone says t'was a spell on th' arrer. Spell! In fact his hand is sure. Here he shoots deer, there bird, we eat meat, they're all jealous, huh. Where's th' arrer-spell?

So, t' wedding plans?

Awright.

Hafta feast t' folk.

Will borrow.

Borrow! No one's done it in t' clan?

Everyone borrows.

If ye borrow tis never repaid.

Their chief Bharat Munda said, If it's prime land t' moneylender lends. That land of yers is poor, moneylender won' lend. What's his gain in grabbin' that land?

Then tell a way out?

Let t' marriage be. Feast later.

If ye say so.

Where's t' boy?

Does t' bit 'o work that's to do, else he's shootin' darts in t' forest.

This time ye got a lot.

That we got. Ten rupees.

Whatcha do with' it?

Chotti's ma bought a cow, and . . .

Chotti's ma said, Kanu Munda's going to his father-in-law. He'll live there. His wife is now Daski's dad's only child. T' brother died. His land mighta worked out.

Don' mess with that. T' land's in hock to t' moneylender.

Then I won'.

Listen, now it's t' month of Kartik. Sixteen miles to go. But t' kings of Narsingarh do a Kali Fair t' next month, in Aghran. There's an arrer contest there. I'm very sad no one from Chotti village ever wins in tha' game. Ye get cash, pig, even clothes.

A young lad, won' send that far.

Dintcha send to Murudi?

Woulda died of no food else.

But Chotti was dancing. All in his life is stories. He is sixteen. Koel is fourteen. Dad went with him, also Pahan.

What target must be pierced?

Don' know.

Narsingarh Fair is also very big. Many contests. The target was a clay pitcher on a platform, on it a gourd. Patterned in whitewash. The pitcher will be full of water, the arrow won't touch the pitcher, the pitcher won't lean, the gourd must fall. At first the other archers laughed when they saw Chotti. Then, knowing who he is, they start whispering. Yes, this is indeed that Chotti Munda, who spent time with Dhani Munda. Dhani shot arrows in the dark and killed boars by sound, shot geese on the wing in dusky twilight. His arrow is spellbound. No one can defeat him. Chotti was listening to everything. In his mind he memorated Dhani.

The gourd was felled by the arrow, the pitcher stood. Bisra and the Chief looked at each other amazed. Then the Chief started to dance. Won, Chotti village has won. The Chief's son took second prize ten years ago, no one's done it since then.

A pig, a cloth, five rupee notes.

Slaughtering the pig and a celebration with the local adivasis. The boy who came second says to Chotti, Let's go to t' Jujubhatu Fair two months from now, in t' month of Magh. There they give a pig and ten seers of rice.

Ten seers of rice!

Yes mate. I'll feel a hope if ye're there.

I'll ask Dad. I'll ask Pahan.

Pahan said, drinking, Of course.

Chotti returned home thoughtful. Returning he says to dad, Aba! Ye'll let me go to all t' fairs all year all around here?

And ye'll play yer arrer? Spend yer life that way?

Not to spend life tilling Moneylender's field like ye, Aba. All shoot arrers. But this is a practice thing.

What d'ye mean?

If I get money playin' me arrer ye'll give yer feast with it.

Enough t'jest buy rice?

Buy rice, make liquor, I'll bring meat.

Bisra kept quiet.

Mother said, Not to borrow?

No. Borrow means bond labour, and all in t' family line will give bonded labour. I saw in Murudi, I see't here too.

Everything is a story in Chotti's life. No Munda boy has behaved like him. Lala Baijnath said to Bisra, What's to worry about cash? Borrow, pay with labour.

Nope, won' borrow.

Won'?

No.

Don' then, yer wild brain.

Don' fault me, Lord.

Fault? Why fault? Boy's playin' th' arrer, bringin' in lots of money. But what do I hear of a spellbound arrer?

That's just stories, King.

Lala Baijnath said to the Police Daroga, I don't understand Bisra Munda's plans.

Why? He's a good guy.

Why doesn't he borrow?

Let him not. Look Lalababu, don't ye poke him. There's no trouble with tribal people in my area. I don't want any trouble. My job is for seven more years, I want to do my job in peace. It's a problem if ye make trouble with tribal folks.

No no, why should there be trouble?

How does Bisra's boy win in every arrer play?

His arrow is spellbound.

Can that be?

Sure thing. Hear my tale.

Tell me.

Do ye know the King of Narsingarh?

How will I know such a moneyed man? Know the name.

He had an older stepbrother. He should have been king. Heir to the seat. He went to hunt, and stayed in a forest house, thatch roofed bungalow. Their own land. The current king's mother got hold of the estate manager. Her son must be king. But the British Commissioner won't hear of it. Manager-Sir gave his word.

So where's a spell here?

In his area there was Bharat Mahato. A heavy shaman. Hearing the manager he said, I'll get t' job done, but I must have four acres of land—ten bighas—without ground rent. Manager-Sir said yeah to this wish. That very night Bharat spoke a spell and floated a burning clay light in the wind. Floating and floating the lit bowl burnt the bungalow. Eldest Prince perished.

Younger Prince was King?

Was, but there's more.

What?

Manager got a bad idea. He called Bharat and said, Here's ten rupees. Ye can't get the land. Bharat said, If ye say so, yer Honour. Ye keep this money. But this isn't a good thing to do. Then, the Manager-Sir sits in open office, suddenly fire breaks out in his entire body in front of everyone. He died burning.

There can be such things, ya.

So why can't Bisra's son have a spellbound arrow?

Merchant-Sir, Lalaji, if a man has a spellbound arrow, will his days go on an empty belly, wearing a ball-bag?

Whatever you say.

Whoever holds the arrow will hit the target?

Godamercy! That arrow is his, controlled. If another tries to hold the arrow it will become a venomous snake and bite him.

Let's forget him. A Munda, a savage, they always shoot arrows. Arrows are their companion.

Yes.

Chotti hadn't a clue that stories were being made up about him outside the Munda community as well. He practised his arrow every day then. And hunted. The day before market day. The police from the post buy the birds and game that he shoots. The station master too. If he kills a stag he cleans the skin with salt and ash and sells it at the big market. And he goes from fair to fair, for archery contests. Koel said, Chotti? Ye've got a spellbound arrer, after all. Then why d'ye practise th' arrer like mad ever' day?

That practisin' is t' spell.

Chotti brings twenty-five rupees in a year just playing the arrow. In 1915–16 twenty-five rupees is a lot of money. His mother bought another cow, rice for the feast, liquor, even a silver nose-ring for Chotti's bride. That is cause for great happiness. And village-respect for both Chotti's parents goes up. The bride brings a pig, a she-goat. The mother has two cows. At this time the rail line goes up to Tohri and the shelters are put up for the rail-way people. They are outsiders. Chotti's mother supplies them milk.

This is the time of the greatest peace and joy in the life of Chotti and his family. For a most trivial reason the good times are broken up.

Lala Baijnath was not pleased with the well-being in Bisra Munda's household. The particular reason was that Baijnath's field and yard work was generally done by local Oraons and Mundas. And some untouchable castes. Baijnath prefers to have adivasi labour. Adivasis work for incredibly low wages. Don't like bickering. They work as they give word.

It's very easy to bind the adivasis in debt. If they once put their thumbprint on paper, they give bonded labour for generations. Of course this is just as applicable to untouchables.

It's much more comfortable to work with untouchables and Mundas, with whom Baijnath has a creditor-debtor relationship. In whatever way, it is right that untouchable and adivasi should remain poor. Bisra is not all that poor anymore. Baijnath, enraged, called Bisra to his presence one day.

You don't want to borrow, don't borrow. But you'll come to work the land? It's hard to set eyes on you. I hear you're the Mundas' moneylender?

For Baijnath the word 'moneylender'—Mahajan, great man— is a word of respect. He'd forgotten that Mundas did not understand the usurer's trade. Bisra was insulted and said, Chotti, Koel, and I don' get time to herd our cows, goats, pigs so we didn' come. Called us moneylender, Lord? Munda borrows but doesn' lend. Doesn't suck his brother's blood by moneylendin'. You've abused me.

Because the two did not share a perspective these broken words made a snarl.

Baijnath said, It's abuse if you're called a moneylender?

A Munda does no' lend money.

I abused you?

If I say ye've become a Munda?

You're abusing me?

I abused ye?

Is there a bigger abuse?

What's Munda? Some loathsome thing?

Enraged, Bisra returns to the village. He went to Pahan's house and said, Lala Baijnath has called t' Mundas 'moneylender'.

Gradually all the Mundas were opposed. 'Moneylender', 'interest'—these words are thoroughly despicable to Mundas. This is most deplorable. Putting a thumbprint on paper at the behest of the moneylender it is in the net of interest that they are entangled. The Mundas didn't show up for sowing.

Everyone said that the merchant, the Lala, will go to the police.

Pahan said, Let 'im. We aint done anything wrong. And Daroga Mukunda Pandey. He knows us.

Baijnath went to the police. Praise be to Lord Viswanath! If Mukunda Pandey had been there he'd have said, Don't make trouble with the adivasis Lalaji. In my area there ain't no trouble. My job's for another seven years. I want to work in peace.

Mukunda Pandey isn't there. There's a lawsuit in Chhapra with his land. He's on leave. The acting Daroga's name is Mahavir Sahay. He has fifteen years left on the job. And he's hot-blooded, unwilling to shout 'Peace now' at the start of his tenure. The Chotti area is so remote, that he doesn't believe news will travel to Ranchi if something happens here.

He found out everything that took place. Then he said, Go home, I'll take a look.

Lala Baijnath lives in the same village. Each inhabitant is known to him. He lends money, takes interest, takes bonded labour. But since his world is also this village, he doesn't want to act so out of line that the consequences are dire. He certainly doesn't want to alienate adivasi labour. And he's scared as well. He said, Don't try to say much, please.

Mahavir Sahay says, Of course not. Why should I say much at all? If the job's done with little said?

Don't tell Bisra. Tell Pahan.

Baijnath says this because, according to the adivasi social system, the pahan or the priest is the chief of the village community. They sit with the pahan and settle any problem that comes up. It is in fact possible that the pahan and the village headman are two separate people. But that's not the case here. Baijnath knows the rules of adivasi society.

Mahavir Sahay thought, Baijnath's thinking that anything said directly to Bisra would lead to trouble. Doubtless that Bisra guy's a devil. He sent two constables to arrest Bisra.

The Munda-Oraons of Chotti village have never seen police enter the village to capture them. They didn't understand the situation at all. This is also true that upstream from the Chotti river there is a tiny waterfall, for the river's course descends two hundred feet there before flowing flat again, and an Englishman is about to strike camp there to shoot migratory geese. White man from Ranchi. The villagers thought that the police have come about the encampment. Even then the district officers would tour and pitch a tent to solve and judge local problems. Consequently, many complaints from adivasis and villagers received judgement in situ. The poor were spared a lot of tribulation. Because this practice was singularly inconvenient for landowner-contractor-moneylender it was gradually retracted with other excuses. It is not the wish of either the foreign or the indigenous administration that real relationships grow up between the officers and subject groups. It is more auspicious for the administration to keep the relationship completely unreal. Then in the officer's eyes, the humans can remain a mathematical calculation of supplied census statistics. And in the eyes of the people the administration can remain the king's elephants. Elephants that are no use to them, yet must be reared by them.

In the eyes of the villagers the two constables are, at first, a matter of curiosity. In their calm lives it is interesting to see the measured tread of puttees, red turban, boots. Children follow them.

When the two constables capture Bisra, busy pasturing cows, and put a rope around his middle, they become objects of amazement, then fear. News travels to Pahan. Immediately Pahan says, Come on, let's go see what's up. Suddenly he thinks he has grown very old. The police and the administration seem incomprehensible to him. He cannot imagine what use the Daroga can have for a timid quiet man like Bisra. The Mundas never understand what the administration considers a punishable crime.

A few people walk with Pahan. Sana Munda worked as a punkha-puller at the government bungalow, and therefore he is well-known among the local Mundas for his grasp of the mentality of Diku-Hindu and the police. He says, Lemme come too. On the way Pahan says, Good ye came. Who knows if Daroga understans Mundari language. Sana takes a metal pitcher. If t' polis get ye, yer thirst increases, he says. Yer tongue doesn't move, as if yer spit turns to sticky banyan-sap.

By the time they get there, Mahavir Sahay has already bloodied Bisra with kicks and cuffs, blows and slaps. In response to the pathetic questions of the pahan's group he says, I can't do without him. He doesn't himself go to work at Lala Baijnath's, and he's egged you on as well.

What'll happen to him?

Je-hellhouse.

Je-hellhouse?

Bisra knows Pahan's voice and groans, I won' go.

Lala will know if you will.

Sana asks, Ye'll put him in t' lockup?

What else?

Let'm go a bit, t'gie him water.

I have no water.

Pahan shakes his head, Let's go to Lala.

Lala Baijnath is both happy and worried at the pahan's words. Chotti is not yet such a lawless place that the adivasi-untouchable has to be curbed with lawsuits. The Lala's word is enough. For a lawsuit the Lala would have had to run to Khalari. It's not possible now. And if the adivasis are angry with this? The landowners and moneylenders of local villages will blame the Lala. The adivasis can get angry. They are a stubborn race. After everything, the Daroga will get the upper hand as well. This is hard to accept.

Baijnath says, I'll go see.

Come now.

Why now? He abused me, let him taste a little punishment? I tried to give advice, he abused me.

Pahan said, Lord! We never understood yer words and don' now. Ye said to 'm, gett'n to be moneylender. That's an insult in Mundari. Ye aren't guilty. He said, ye're Munda. 'Twas an insult, and fault too, on Bisra's part. For us there's no one but us to call our own. All hurt if one's hit. Today too we feel this hurt for all but we don' know if 'twill go on 'til our kids' time. So Bisra don' come to field, just chases cattle. We was all a'comin'. Well we ain't cos he was insulted. Ye said to Daroga that Bisra was rousing all Mundas.

I didn' say this.

So ye say true, or t' Daroga? See Lord, t' Mundas haven' done nothin' yet. If Bisra dies at t' station, he'll die by yer fault. Ye'll have sin. If everyone's mad then? He has a laddie, got a lot of fame at arrer-play, will he take it?

As soon as he heard this, Lala thought of the spelled arrow. Lordy lord! Mountain from a molehill—if life goes?

Come, let's go.

Pahan came to the station again with Baijnath and his followers. Chotti was there waiting. He wasn't home when the event transpired.

It is not known what words passed between Baijnath and the Daroga. But the Daroga let Bisra go. I didn't put him in je-hell-house, let him go, so there's a village-fine. Munda people must come and give me five rupees in Station. Within three days.

Chotti came forward. Said, Won' gie now. Gie ye when I win t' game at Fair. Now there aint five rupees in village.

Who're you!

Ye caught me pa.

Give cash! You?

I will. Munda don' lie.

They left. The two constables were greatly scared. They too live here and know regional news. The old Daroga was different. They did indeed catch and bring Bisra on this Daroga's orders, but they didn't beat him. Now they said to one another, that Chotti can sit in the village and kill them with the spellbound arrow. They have no doubt that Chotti's arrow has been blessed with a spell. If it weren't spellbound, Chotti wouldn't have won at every fair. If the Station and the Daroga want to die by torturing Chotti's father for no fault, let them. They don't want to die.

The two had a chat and went to Bisra's place in the dark of night. They called Chotti out of doors and both put their palms together. Said, Chotti! Ask yer pa, we took'm but did'n touch'm. But we took'm, we're at fault. Here's the five rupees fine! We're givin'. Our job's in the forest, so we're scared. Don't kill us, don't send yer arrow. We have homes, kids.

Chotti said, Did I say I'd kill ye?

All know y'know spells. If you send yer arrow it'll go across ten Stations and killa guy and get back to ya.

They put the cash down and ran. Chotti stood in starlight and tried to understand what had happened. Stories are growing up around him. He is becoming legend? He took the money and put it away. Next day he told the pahan, the Station-police gave me t' fine money. What s'd I do?

Pahan said, Ye're in Haramgod's grace.

Why?

Hey Lala is scared that ye'll fell him with t' spellstruck arrer. He too called me at night and ast that ye forgiv'm. He too gave fine money.

What're ye sayin'!

Ye know spells, me son. Otherwise no one's ever heard that t' Lala pays t' fine when a fine's put on a Munda village. What our dads never saw, ye showed us, a slip of a lad.

But hear me.

Tell.

Chotti wanted to say that he knew no spell. And this too he understood, that Pahan wouldn't believe him even if he said so.

So tell then, he said again.

Pahan said in a melancholy and serious voice, T' money's on yer behalf, lettin' ya know. Now we must return it to whoever's it is.

I too have come to say that.

Oh my Chotti! Ten rupees is a lotta money. Forty kilos of rice a rupee! But no one in Munda tribe has ever ta'en sick cash!

I said I'd give with arrer-play, and that's set. Otherwise I caint keep me honour. Me dad cries if a pig is cut. I will not take t' money of them that did catch that dad, from t' hands that caught, to pay t' fine for me dad.

Good. Let me gie't back. This is a good deed. With no fault we stay scared nine parts of ten. Cos of ye they stay one part scared of us. Even Lala's scared.

Chotti returned home. Told his dad, told everything. Listening and listening Bisra says suddenly, A bit more land to buy with th' arrer play.

Why?

Bisra said with driven and terrified eyes, Yer sister, that Daski, she's wed. Koel will wed. Ye'll mek yer family large. Then this land will be enough?

Buy if ye have to.

Even then barren land. If I buy fertile t' Lala'll grab.

No Aba, won'.

Also must do penance.

For what?

There, they took me to je-hell.

Where is t' je-hell, Aba? Just t' Station.

Ye know? Ye'll know. Yer arrer is spellbound!

No Aba, no.

A few days later Bisra said, Me mind is sore since that day Chotti. Hey, if ye tell a spell and blow th' arrer, can' that arrer ruin t' Daroga's arm?

Let's see.

Chotti went to his ma. No word but that, said Ma. Ya Chotti, his eyes roll, says whatever, is he crazy?

Pahan hears all and says, Cause for worry. C'mon, I'll tell all. Bisra's ma suckled me. I was a motherless boy.

It's harvest time.

But ye don' go.

No. Don' feel like it.

So Lala thinks ye'll surely off' im. I say, No, won'. Who knows what he understood? He's givin' us a snack, and a two pice.

Snack and two pice?

If ye don' go, send that Koel.

Chotti's ma's been burnt. 'Slong as yer baba don' know, she says. A tip of two pice! Salt-pepper-oil—a deal of goods.

Pahan also said, I'll say Chotti has no time. When they see Koel they'll know ye aint kep' yer anger on 'em.

Chotti sighed and said, I really don' get time. That cow's a devil. All t' time she goes in't forest. Tiger'll get her one day.

On the topic of tigers Pahan says, A tiger's makin' life hell in Neundra. Lotsa cows and calves killed. The area's pahan says if ye get that tiger he'll gie ya loads of rice. Told me t' tell ya.

No one there to do it?

Doesn't fall in a trap, doesn't eat if t' cow-carcass is pizened. Says, a tiger devil. Some bad spirit mebbe. Yer arrer will off it.

Lemme see.

Chotti sighed and got up to go. He is most worried about his dad. Such a mover and shaker now always melancholy with some species of fatigue. Hardly utters a word. Occasionally says a word or two to himself. Are they always sensible words? Suddenly the other day, he says, Allus et mealie, lately fer long by son-luck I'se eat'n rice, wear'n whole cloth, so they lock me up. Munda's at fault eat'n rice, wear'n whole (cloth). Me foredad knew, so he ran off seein' gold in water. He knew.

Today he stood in the yard and said, Where'd that tall tree come from? Weren't there before. Mus' cut down that tree.

The tree had always been there. Ma did her work with the boys lying in a hammock she tied to its branches. Is Father going mad?

This is one worry. Mother's supposed to be at the helm of the household. She too looks to Chotti for every little thing. Chotti is getting tired, becoming lonely, with the stony weight of everyone's faith, that Chotti knows spell, Chotti is special, he'll kill the tiger in Neundra village. What sort of expectation is this?

Chotti's mother says, I won' let ya go.

Pahan asked.

Let Pahan's boy go. That's not a tiger, it's a Dang-demon. If ye kill, it kills ya. Koel's sickly, yer dad's losin' his mind, and I lose ye too?

Have they come to beg me?

Ya can't go.

Chotti didn't have to kill the tiger. The British railway-engineer shot it dead. Chotti realized that he must win the arrow stakes with ceaseless practice. There's joy in winning, honour as a result of winning, prizes. There is the responsibility of keeping alive the legend that is growing up around him as he wins stake after stake.

But he hadn't wanted to be the hero of legend. He had only wanted the honour for winning at archery. Dhani Munda has turned his life around. But Chotti cannot analyse how it was done.

Trying to practise his arrow by setting up a target on a stone under a distant hill, another narrative got entangled with his life.

A Britisher had pitched his tent upstream from Chotti River. A Britisher from Ranchi. The villagers of Chotti had thought the White man must be an officer type. But in a few days it was known that the Whitey was raving mad. Paying for milk, butter, meat, whatever he's buying. Brought just two coolies, two horses. Pays even for the horse's grass, Pahan said. Paints wandering all day, writes something after dark in his tent, occasionally brings down a bird.

Even this had not made Chotti curious. At twenty-one, with a capable father alive, the weight of the household is on his shoulders. His soul is most melancholy. Now he tends his own bit of land, his brother herds cattle. Unruly cattle, so he too must go from time to time. Koel is already nineteen. It would be a mistake not to find a bride for him, not to do a wedding. His own wife is pregnant. A bride is needed to help his ma. He makes time to practise his arrow. He had put up the arrow that Dhani gave him. He just takes it with him on archery days. Dhani is now song. Riding on the black cloud he has mingled with Sailrakab. From time to time Chotti wonders, did Dhani ever exist? Or is he a dream, just an imagining? Then he looks at the arrow. Police! The police killed Dhani. The police caught his dad and beat him up for nothing. And it seems even the Daroga is now scared that Chotti might send an arrow and kill him. If he could have done it, Chotti would have told Dhani's arrow, Go kill the man who killed Dhani. How many stories there are around the Chotti who cannot make anything supernatural happen.

How many things does Chotti not know, didn't get to know because Dhani is no longer there. He didn't get to hear of the time when the Mundas were free, when Diku and Gormen and contractor and recruiter and missionary hadn't entered their lives.

Thinking and thinking he shoots his arrows, goes on shooting. To see if his hand was ready he killed a duck on the wing in the silvery light of the full moon. He walked into the river to pick up the dead duck and stopped. A White man. Holding the duck. The man said in clear Mundari language, Ye shot it?

Yes.

What is yer name?

Chotti Munda.

Named after the river?

After t' river.

Why? What day of the week were ye born?

Monday.

Then why aren't ye called Somra, Somai, Somna, as Monday is Sombar?

In our line one is named after t' river.

Where did ye learn archery?

Why? By myself?

Hey! Wonderful! Even with a gun I've never been able to shoot a flying duck in the moonlight.

Would ye like t' duck?

No no.

Take it, I'll kill again.

Better ye come tomorra, I'll shoot with ye.

White man, th' arrer is silent. If ye blast a gun there's noise and t' geese are scared. Ye won' be able to shoot an arrer?

What were you doing here?

Practice.

Why?

I'll play me arrer at t' fair.

Where's the fair?

Neundra Fair's coming up.

Come tomorra.

Why?

I'll draw yer picture.

My! Picher!

Yes.

Chotti returned home and said, Ma! T' Whitey is surely crazy. Says to me, Come tomorra, I'll draw yer picher.

Knows yer name-fame mebbe.

Nah! Just crazy.

The next day the White man catches him quick. Says I've come just to draw. Come, I'll go to yer village. First come to my tent.

The Britisher really comes to the village with Chotti. With a few pencil strokes he draws a picture of Pahan, of the open shrine of

Haramdeo. He said, I've come here really to tour. And to draw.
Therefore I draw ye.

Why are ye speakin' Mundari? Are ye a missionary?

No. But I've learnt Mundari.

Where?

In Ranchi.

Everyone was silent.

The White man said to himself, Strange! They speak to each
other, they gossip, and to me they just give answers to questions.

The pahan looks at Chotti. White means Gormen. Chotti has
brought Gormen along. Such a thing has never happened. So no
one knows what people do or say when such a thing happens.

Pahan's wife saves everyone. With easy woman-wisdom.
Mundari women smile often. Wife came forth smiling and gave
the White guy a string seat to sit on. And then said, Come come.

The village women came forward. One had popped maize in a
shining brass plate, bits of dry molasses. Another brought water.
Wife said, ye've come to a shrine. Drink some water. Next draw
our pichers.

Actually the women were amused to see the men's hesitation.
As the White man ate, the women made verses together and sang:

> Gormen has come to our place
> Gormen has made pichers
> Gormen hasn't brought a gun
> Hasn't killed us folks
> Gormen has eaten holy food.

Immediately the Whitey says, Sing again! Writes the song down.
The women sang again. Then all broke up in laughter. Sana's
mother is a wise old woman. She says, Not crazy, dears. Good
Gormen.

Then the White man goes with Chotti to see their house. He
has many wishes, to see a Munda's house, to see the paintings on
the wall.

The White man's name is Ronaldson. The brother of the
Secretary to the Governor of Bihar. Coming to Ranchi and reading Hoffmann's dictionary first aroused his interest in Mundas
and the Mundari language. He discovers that in spite of his failure to do anything useful in Britain, he has developed a skill in
learning Munda language. He feels he wants to write a book to

inform the reader about Munda villages and the Mundas. He is here for reasons of this nature.

He learns the sayings about Chotti and he goes with Chotti to Neundra fair. As usual Chotti hits bull's eye. The pig is killed and by Chotti's request the Mundas allow the mad Gormen to remain at their feast. The White man surprises them by not drinking, indeed he pleases all by swiftly drawing everyone's shape and form with pencil. The Neundra Pahan says, If ye're a good Gormen why do we suffer so?

The White guy says he doesn't know the answer to this, but what they should do, wherever and whenever the officers pitch tent, they should go directly and make their complaint.

Why 'ud they listen? Pahan asks.

Have ye tried?

No.

Try and see.

Thereafter Chotti and Whitey return to the White man's tent. There at midnight the White guy shows Chotti the pictures he's drawn. Suddenly Chotti sees a picture of Dhani Munda holding high his bow and machete.

Where did ye draw this picher?

In Jejur.

Ye went to Jejur?

The White guy says, This is a marvellous human being. The moment I saw him coming, I was in fact drawing, and I drew his picture. But the Daroga killed him. He is supposed to have been a great rebel. His name is Dhani Munda.

Will ye give me t' picher?

Take it. Wait, take it tomorrow. Let me make a copy.

Even drunk Chotti doesn't reveal that he knew Dhani. The next day the White man makes a present of his own likeness and Dhani's picture to Chotti and picks up his tent. Chotti hides Dhani's picture. Then he goes to market. By the station. To buy salt and oil. There he sees Lala Baijnath. Lala says reverently, Chotti! I spoke of your father to the Daroga, I was angry. I am most shamed for what happened then. And the Gormen White man is also your friend. Hey, don't say anything against me.

To whom?

Gormen people come, pitch tent.

No, I won'.

Pahan calls him and sits him down as he walks back. He says, Our honour's bigger cos of ye. Well I called ye to talk of yer dad.

What's to say?

Pahan sighs and says, Heard from me own father, me own grandad, but never saw with me own eyes. Some of us Mundas are sometimes in sorrow of mind. That sorrow never leaves us. T' sorrow kills t' man. Maybe Bisra took that way.

Chotti sighs and says, What to do?

Shall I try to do a puja?

See.

This year of 1921 is most memorable for Chotti. This year he becomes a father, and names his son after a river unseen by him. Harmu. He has not seen this river. He had heard from Dhani that god Birsa had been cremated on the banks of this river. Not by the Mundas. By Gormen. Mundas bury their dead. Gormen lit the god's corpse with lumps of dry cowdung, to insult god's body. Coming outa je-hell we each took a handful o' dirt from Harmu-bank, Dhani said. Ma said, Monday's child, Sombar's child, why not Somru? Where is that Harmu river?

If there's another boy name him as ye like, Chotti said.

Their son was born. That very year Chotti won many other arrow contests. That year Pahan arranged a puja for Bisra's welfare. After the puja, when everyone was busy eating, Bisra left the feast. Unnoticed by anyone. He walked half a mile, tied his dhoti to the branch of the mango tree in front of Lala Baijnath's house, and hanged himself.

A case of suicide. The Daroga came after the body was lowered. Why're ye here, Chotti asked. Why'd me Aba die? Me Aba never looked even when a pig was cut. Ye hit him for no fault and fro' that his mind was turned.

Mahabir Sahay's face darkens. He would not have borne such words from anyone else. But he kept quiet for fear of Chotti's rage and the suicide Bisra's vengeful spirit. Bisra's body was sent appropriately on its final journey. The entire episode must have struck Lala Baijnath's spirit much more strongly. For right after this he gives up his beloved landed property to his son Tirathnath Lala and goes to Banaras the Tirathrath—the highest of sacred places—and there, trying to dance on a wooden platform boat under the too-great influence of cannabis, he falls into Mother Ganga the Great and gives up the ghost.

Right after this Mahabir Sahay takes leave because of recurring fever. Pahan says, Chotti! Ye did good, very good. One of t' people guilty of Bisra's death died, and th' other's taken leave. Ye are very powerful.

Very powerful but can't fill five bellies.

Won' ye go to Lala's field?

Yeah, ye can't bully t' belly.

Pahan says, That'll be good. If ye're there then Tirath won' harm us.

Thus many more folktales align themselves with Chotti's life and because one can't shadow-box with folktales Chotti admits defeat and keeps up archery practice in the nooks and crannies of work in the field. In about three years he is a father again. Koel is wedded with Mungri, the sister of Sana Munda. Chotti's mother dies of snakebite on the way home from market. Drought descends on Chotti.

IV

DROUGHT, WIDESPREAD drought. During such a drought in some remote past year Chotti's mother had sent him to his sister's. Now Didi's family is large, and there's drought there too. It's also a time when there are few places to run to in this world.

The Mundas say, We'll go to Tirathnath.

Why? Chotti asked.

We'll borrow.

He'll lend?

If we gie a thumbprint he'll lend.

If ye put a thumbprint ye'll hafta gie bonded labour, become a bondslave.

We'll gie, then. To live now.

Listen to what t' pahan says.

Ye'll gie bonded labour for a thumbprint, f'r a bit of rice-wheat to eat, I'll not say 'yeah' to that. This bonded labour won' be quit in ten generations. Everyone falls into its trap. See all t' Ganjus, Dusads, Chamars, Dhopas—all the oppressed, tribals and outcastes—tied up in bonded labour. I won' say 'yeah' to no one. But thing is, can't say 'no' neither. Why not? Then ye'd say, If we put thumbprint on paper at least we'd eat.

Chotti says, What's t' way out?

There's no way out.

We work together, why not ask those Ganju-Dusads?

Then Chief said, Whoever wants can put his mark and take a loan. What can I say? I hear Chotti Munda can do everythin'.

What're ye askin' me to do? Chotti is furious.

Why get angry? Ye're poor and so are we. I say, t' White man will come to Tohri, he'll see there's famine, then he'll give aid, and if Gormen agrees to 'famine' t' White sirs and madams from t' mission will come too! Why n't ye go there and ask?

Won' t' police precinct ask?

This Daroga? This tax collector?

Let's go and say.

The Daroga said, What shall I explain to you? Savage scum that you are! Yes, there's a drought. But where's the famine? In a famine people will die, they'll run from the village, that's what a famine is! Is the government's money that cheap?

No one but Tirathnath has rice or wheat.

He wants to give.

But he tells us to put our mark?

Why should he give without a thumbprint?

Ye won' send a petition?

I will when the time comes.

Dharam Dusad came out of the Police Station and said, Chotti did ye understan' anythin'?

What's to understan'?

Tirathnath and the Daroga are as one. If the Daroga sends a petition now, we get some aid. Then Tirathnath can't bind this village in the surety of bonded labour. He now needs two hundred seasonal workers in the field. The work will be done without expense if the workers come by bonded labour. I know me great-grandfather took four pice worth of maize from his great-grandad with his thumbprint. I still give him bonded labour for that.

That's why he won' send a petition!

It's Asharh, the third month, the month of rain. There's no rain. Howsomever there's rain in Palash, Dahar, Komandi. P'raps here too there'll be. Who'll give a thumbprint then?

Come let's go.

Go.

Why 'go'? C'mon. We must all go.

Tirathnath hears of this as well. He seethes inside. The station is a place for promenades here, and what's more, in this banished place, one gets news of the outside world at the station. He sat at the station and told the station master, This Chotti Munda has started a lot of mischief. I don't know what happened between his father and my father, but he has not calmed down yet.

Why? Chotti is a very calm boy.

Such a drought. I am waiting to give people paddy and wheat. He won't take, he won't let anyone else take. And all the lowcaste Hindus have ganged up with him. Why? Because I'll write up receipts, I'll take bonded labour. To take bonded labour from adivasi and untouchable is my natural duty.

Tirathnath has a washer-caste mistress. The panderess of this love affair is another washerwoman, Motia. Motia came to the station looking for her nephew. Motia said to Tirathnath, Your dad called Chotti's dad 'moneylender', and all this sprang from that. And now you say about Chotti he's 'started mischief?'

When did I say that?

Look here! You just said it, and now you say 'no', Lord! Or is this too your natural duty? Whose ringleader is Chotti?

Gabbling to herself, Motia walks over to Chotti. She says everything at length and then says, Kill him with an arrow, love. End to all problems.

We'll all go to Tohri, Chotti says. We'll say it to t' White sir, t' sahib. Ye must also come.

But Gormen won' kill us?

No no. Haven't I been to Gormen? Don' I know?

Didn' Gormen come to ye?

Pahan also said, Yes, let's go. Chotti understands that although there is a pahan, it is upon him that the task of leading Chotti's Munda society is devolving. And because everyone credits his magical infallibility in archery, at time of trouble and danger even Dusad-Ganju-Chamar-Dhobi will obey him if need be. A worrisome thing.

No group like the one issuing from Chotti in June 1924 had gone before this through five miles of forest to Tohri for such a reason. The survey officer had struck camp. He also had the responsibility of ascertaining if there was famine in the area. The news should by rights have come from the Daroga at Chotti. It is the Daroga who is the government representative in rural areas. Chotti is a government forest area. Otherwise the region belongs to rajas and zamindar-landowners. Who are they, if not the Daroga? The officer is a Bengali. Since this is his place of work, he knows Mundari, Oraon and the local Hindi. Domiciled in Ranchi for three generations.

The Daroga says, What's this? Munda, Ganju, Dusad, all together?

We've a petition.

What petition?

Terrible drought, t' crows reel and die. No one has wheat, maize, rice, paddy at home. Starvin' to death.

What's your petition?

We told t' Daroga there, Let 'em know there's emergency here. He won' inform.

Who are you? said the officer.

Chotti Munda.

So it is! I didn't recognize ya—the Daroga said.

Why won't the Daroga inform? The officer knew the answer. The entire experience is well known to him. The landlords or landed farmers and the Darogas in an area watch each others' interests.

Chotti glanced at everyone. And then said, Lemme say then.

He said everything in detail. And added, Tirathnath says I bring people together. Yes, we're bound together. By hunger fire. I haven' roused anyone.

I don't think the government will open a centre here, said the officer.

Why?

Chhagan Dusad worked at the coalmines for a bit. Knows how to read and write Hindi. Sir, we'll die of starvation, he says.

Let's say aid comes, that too will take time.

This Daroga has no common interest with Tirathnath. If you all work Tirath Lala's fields, he says, Let him give aid?

He'll take our mark on bond labour receipts.

Seeing the thin indigent appearance of the men the officer says, Let's see.

He could not generate administrative interest. But he informed the Jain Mission and the Baptist Mission at Sartowli. Those two missions came to Chotti and opened free meal centres and carried on food distribution for nearly a month. Then it suddenly starts to rain. Chotti is also held responsible for the successful bringing of missionary aid. Pahan says everywhere with pride, Chotti knows Gormen. For that reason this help came.

In the ten days between the departure of the officer and the arrival of the two missions a most significant event transpires. There were no radishes or roots left in the forest. Sana's aunt ate tree bark and died of gastric pain and heavy vomiting. Then Chotti and other villagers put pressure on Tirathnath.

We won' put our mark on bonded labour contracts.

Give us our daily food as loan.

Take it out of our wages, t' right amount per head.

Are you going to kill me, Tirath had asked. Why push me? Gormen will give aid. Am I Gormen? The Sir-babu at the tishan is a Gormen man. Go to him. Am I the one bringing drought?

If we could kill ye lord. Feel like killin'. This bow stirs in me hand. Th' arrer says I want blood.

If you kill ye'll swing, Chotti.

But ye won' come back.

At this point Tirath's mother screams like a kite at her son. Your dad, she says, Sharecropping in this savage place, pushed Chotti's dad around and died himself. D'ye want to die too? My brothers open free food centres at such times. We are Jains. Will you go wanting if you give a bit? Give them their daily food. If he casts a spell and sends an arrow, will ya live? Arentcha scared?

Wife says, The rage of savage folks! Do they fear je-hell, fear noose? If they cut down someone in rage they go to the Police Station with the body on their shoulder and say, I killed for rage. And then they go to je-hell—and swing. When the washerwoman comes from her place, the arrow will strike.

Yeh, so easy to shoot an arrow.

Who'll save ya? Daroga?

You fool, says Mother, if you die you're gone. Whoever goes to je-hell and swings after, will yer breath come back?

His manager joins the chorus in support and says, At least give me leave of absence. They shot the manager when he tried to raise taxes at the zamindari of Latehar. I'm scared of the savage jungle folk.

Tirathnath considers this a defeat. Every landlord-moneylender-sharecropper is now taking thumbprints and making bonded labour permanent. He says with a sour face, Give them last year's maize. It's full of bugs. I couldn't sell it.

The manager says, I'll write ten seers for two and a half. Not to worry.

At this time Chhagan Dusad's booklearning comes of use. He says with great enthusiasm, Didn't give bonded work, gettin' our daily food, this is like a story-tale. Let me write down. T' manager will cheat like a bastard. That fucker is a tick on t' tiger's neck.

Tirathnath recounts the entire incident to the Daroga. Daroga tells the tale in Ramgarh, three months later, when he's on leave. This version goes to Ranchi, as follows: Chotti Munda got to-gether a huge group of Mundas armed with bows and arrows and lowcaste Hindus armed with spears, threatened the sharecropper Tirathnath, took away his keys and looted his granaries.

Since the police chain of command did not forward this news, the first receiver of this information did not give it any importance. He goes to the club in the evening. There in the course of conversation, the drought comes up for a moment and someone says with a smile, The Ranchi-Palamau-Chaibasha belt is good. Even the hungry masses do not loot grain. Not so in . . .

He cannot finish his sentence. A certain pre-retirement army doctor says, Peaceful? Do you know that twenty-two years ago, sit-ting in this clubroom we English trembled for fear of Birsa Munda? Of course we were able to defeat him later. But don't call them peaceful. Playing the tuila, dancing the group dance and then shooting arrows. A most complicated people.

The provincial governor's Secretary laughs drily and says in a controlling voice, We shouldn't forget that Alluri Raju, the leader of a tribal uprising, was put to death just the other day in South India. If there is any breach of peace in the tribal belt we should take it very seriously.

Who is this Raju?

The leader of the mountain tribals in the Vishakhapattnam agency.

What does it mean, 'put to death?'

Shot dead. Not sentenced to hanging.

Non-violent struggle, violent struggle . . .

The first receiver of Chotti's news feels greatly uneasy. The next day he gets special permission and meets with the provincial

governor's Secretary at his residence. At the meeting he wipes
sweat off his forehead and says everything that he has learned
about the incident. Then the Secretary's brother says, Such a
piece of news, and there is no report?

No sir.

How did you find out?

Via Ramgarh.

Is this yet another Munda insurrection? No, no you're saying
that other villagers were also with them. It sounds complicated.
Most complicated.

Can I do anything sir?

The one who asks is a young Englishman. As soon as he says
'Can I do anything' a procession of moving pictures flashes
upon his inward eye. There is a Munda uprising. He goes and
stops it. Promotion. Praise. The Secretary pours cold water on
his enthusiasm and says in a rough and bitter tone, Tell me
what you think you can do? The army to go in response to
police station gossip? No no. Everything about the Mundas is dangerous. Has to be managed carefully. I know this business of
moneylenders and landed farmers. Extremely vicious. If they
were not ceaseless exploiters we would have seen peaceful tribal villages. We will have to investigate with great caution and
care. If we see it's not much of anything, to stir things up might
really create trouble. Who will bear the consequences then?
That's enough for now. Let me look into it. What name did you
say?

Whose?

The Munda fellow's?

Chotti Munda from Chotti village. The village is on the Chotti
river. Excellent bird shooting by the river, and there are tigers and
elephants in the forest.

I see. Goodbye.

The officer departs. Now the spread newspaper moves from the
other chair. In a lazy voice the mad sahib known to Chotti says,
What name did you say?

Chotti Munda from Chotti village.

What has he done?

Didn't you hear?

I heard. Rubbish.

What do you know that you say so?

I know the village and the man. A wonderful young man. An expert archer. He wins at every neighbouring fair that has an archery contest.

This is not good news at all.

Why?

If he's such an expert archer the Mundas will make him a leader.

I'm interested in the Chotti affair. First find out what happened.

I will.

Then tell me.

Really Hugh, the things you get into!

Why?

Nasty incidents follow you around.

What did I do now?

You went to draw at Jejur market, there was the Dhani Munda incident. The fellow you befriend in Chotti is a rebel.

First find out. But I have seen that fat Lala. He is the devil's own. He should be taught a lesson. Do you know that half Chotti village is his bonded labour?

What can you and I do?

Bonded labour!

This is your bloody glorious India.

Do you want to see Chotti's picture?

Let me see. Hey! A good looking man.

A quiet, peaceable type.

Don't say that. That explains nothing. It's long before my time, but those who saw him say that Birsa had the sweetest smile.

You're afraid of ghosts. Birsa! I've gone around and observed. The Mundas are a peace-loving people of a happy disposition.

Let me do my own work.

Fortunately the Daroga from Tohri is located in Ramgarh. Summoned by the government he arrives trembling like a sacrificial lamb. Wiping his eyes he narrates the entire event. The Secretary realizes that Chotti had gone to declare famine.

Why? Why did you not report this?

Made a mistake my lord.

But Chotti was famine area. Whose report?

Then the land surveyor comes as well. He offers his account. The Secretary is mad with rage to hear this. That there was a famine and the Daroga hadn't reported it because Tirathnath wished to take thumbprints on bonded labour vouchers. The Daroga does not return to Tohri. He is ordered to show cause for his action. He is demoted and transferred. The Secretary says to the Police Commissioner, He belongs to your office. Explain to him that if he watches the landed farmers' interests and creates unrest among tribals and lowcastes, he'll have to spend the rest of his life in jail. A stupid scoundrel.

The new Daroga goes to Tohri and sends a report. All is calm. There is no turbulence. No complaints from Tirathnath either.

Now Hugh says to his older brother, Hey, it was me who told them to complain to the camping officer directly.

Now the Secretary sends his brother back to Britain. Any probing and digging will surely reveal that it was his brother who said this to the Mundas. Mundas acknowledge even murder with pride. An Englishman has said this. They will loudly declare that any Englishman is the government. How will he explain Hugh to the provincial governor? His brother has drawn pictures of Dhani Munda, Chotti Munda—all the dubious people! He says to his brother, Go back to Britain and publish your damned book. Don't include those two pictures in it.

Hugh smiles in response and as usual, on the publication of *The Flute and the Arrow*, both the pictures are to be seen in it. There is no time to make a row about this, for Hugh fulfils God's wish and brings relief to his brother by dying from an angry villager's spearthrust as he tries to draw pictures of adivasis in Uganda.

After the satisfactory answering of all questions, it is still in the Secretary's head that Chotti is a good place for a hunt. Chotti Munda is a famous archer in a community of archers. He wins archery contests in fair after fair. As a result there are many stories about him. Such a person can become a rebel if he's provoked in any way. He has influence over non-Mundas as well. Whatever the cause and effect, it's apposite if such a person is in jail. But the Mundas are a pigheaded lot. They are not even into petty larceny.

Why an archery contest at every fair? In answer he opens the Gazetteer and sees that such contests are an ancient tradition. It's an integral part of adivasi festivals. Supported by rajas and landowners. He lets the wish of the government be known unofficially, henceforth the news of famine will be accepted only if it comes through proper channels. This will keep the landed farmers and moneylenders happy. He also informs the proper channels of the following. Landed farmers and moneylenders must be kind to people at times of natural disaster. After all, they themselves are protected in a thousand ways these days. Is it unfair to expect some humane behaviour every two or three years in exchange? Is it too much to ask for a small change of heart? If one engages in charity due to change of heart it does not escape the government's eye. You can get a title on account of charity.

Trickling down the filter system this information reaches its destination one day. Then suddenly an extraordinary petition arrives at headquarters.

'Submitted respectfully to the Provincial Governor, parents of the poor, magnanimous Mother of the World Gormen. This wretch Tirathnath Lala is a longterm resident of Chotti village in _____ Revenue Sector and _____ Village Group. When in June 1924 there was a natural disaster, Tirathnath saved 117 villagers by giving them nourishment daily, whereupon the missionary memsahibs arrived. The villagers would have died without Tirathnath. Because there is no one to speak for this wretch, his service has remained unnoticed and neglected. Now if this wretch is blessed with an appropriate title that will be sufficient reward. This too is submitted, that this wretch has contributed a hundred and one rupees to the hon'ble Governor's famine relief fund. Etc. etc. . . .'

The government looks upon this plea with indulgence. A perfect case of change of heart. The title of Raisaheb is bestowed.

Thereafter, in the waxing phase of the moon the Secretary proceeds toward Chotti, to hunt and for no other reason. As he strikes camp in Tohri on the way, he goes to the fair on the request of the local landowner. To see adivasi archery. A spare but lithe Munda archer seems familiar to him. He also sees with what reverence everyone looks at him. He is startled to see the incredible skill with which the youth pierces the target. A tall wooden pole is planted in the ground. An eye is painted on the pole. A wooden plate is placed on top of the pole. There are holes on the rim of the plate. A network of coloured rope hangs from these holes. There are paper birds at the end of the ropes. The plate is turned around by a pulley below. The birds tied to the ropes are whirling at full speed. The eye painted on the pole is pierced through them.

Who is he?

The landowner wrings his hands and states, Chotti Munda from Chotti village my lord. He knows arrow spells. He has been coming first for many years now. Didn't you see, the others couldn't?

Chotti took the prize from the Secretary's hands.

Who are they? Screaming with joy, playing music?

People from his village.

All Mundas?

No, no, other lowcastes are there as well.

Thereafter the Secretary pitched camp for a day on the banks of Chotti river. Tirathnath had made every arrangement to look after the sahib's well-being. Chotti came fearful in answer to the Secretary's summons. Secretary said, Let me see if you can kill a flying duck on a moonlit night?

I can Master.

When moonlight drips from the harvest moon, the wings of the duck mingle with it. These are migratory ducks. They come to the sandbanks of the river at this time. At winter's end they depart, who knows where. Chotti lifts his bow and kills the duck with steady aim. The Secretary shoots a duck with his gun. The next day at the time of leaving he says to the pahan, Play your arrows, shoot birds, but don't let your men make trouble.

Pahan, Chotti, and the rest keep their heads bowed.

Your arrow's aim is truly fine.

Throwing this remark at Chotti, the Secretary takes his seat in his special compartment. A special train had come for him.

After this came Tirathnath's title. With indulgent affection Tirathnath spoke of Chotti, Mother! If Chotti hadn't come then, I wouldn't have given aid. My title came because I did.

I told you, he knows spells.

This is another tale of Chotti's life. Next came three young Mundas of Kurmi village. About six years later.

V

IN THESE SIX YEARS NOTHING important happened in Chotti's life. Nothing happens in Munda lives. In a fully Mundari village, amidst a lot of pain and poverty, some variety enters in the form of half-Hindu festivals such as Karam, Sohrai, or Holi—

the Colourfeast—or at the time of the worship of Haramdeo. In the Munda quarter of mixed villages even those festivals don't brighten up the soul. Excitement can be seen at the time of the Hunt festival. In the old days the hunt festival was only for the adivasis. Now other people also participate. The only joy is that the Hunt festival is regional.

Nothing else happens in Mundari life. In the life of a Munda like Chotti. With his brother he does his daily round—ploughing Tirathnath's land, ploughing his own bit of land. Like all Munda women his wife and Koel's wife are also tough and hardworking. Chotti's wife is somewhat domineering as well. There would have been problems if Koel's wife had not been altogether mild and peaceable. The older of the two tends cows and goats. Whatever they get by selling kids to the tishan or to the forest contractor they put in a tin box and bury by the clay oven. If money is buried close to the oven it will never be stolen. At harvest time she goes to market and buys rice, wheat, maize. The younger one cooks and does other housework.

Everything goes by that archaic rhythm, as usual. From the outside you'd never think there was any trouble. But if you live close to the station, news of the outside world sometimes comes down. The train doesn't always stop. But it's nice to watch even the passing train. The train means modernity, power, machine. It has no connection with the poor people standing on the platform. Still it's nice to watch. To watch and watch and return home in the dark.

In 1930 a new scene could be seen. Police in some of the compartments. The passengers wear white caps. They shout something incomprehensible.

Sana Munda gets the news and says, These Dikus are t' followers of King Gandhi.

King Gandhi, Chotti says. Who's that?

Do I know? All say a great king.

These're followers?

Yes mate. Raising reva-lutions ta chase off t' White man. So they're taken to je-hell everywhere.

So! So many Diku! No end to them?

Sana smiles at Chotti's ignorance. Ye caint count Diku, he says.

I go ever'where. I don' see so many Diku.

T' Diku's in town. Many houses, many roads, so many cars. They'll come to this jungle land so ye c'n see?

Chotti comes back with a sigh. Ye didn' go t' three fairs, says Sana. Why Chotti, me friend? What happened?

Where's t' time?

Right after this three young Mundas come to him. Dukhai, Bikhna and Sukha. They lower a pair of black hens near Chotti's feet and touch the ground respectfully.

What's this? Who're ye?

We're Mundas from Kurmi village.

Why've ye brought these?

We must talk.

'Bout what?

In secret.

They go to the riverbank. Ye did not go to all t' fairs this time, Sukha says. So we came to get news. One more thing.

What?

They look at each other. Teach us, Sukha says. We hold bow at birth. But we don' hit target like ye. Give us t' spell.

Ye want me spell?

Yeah.

Spell, spell, all see me spell. Look at me hand man, hard wit' pullin' t' bowstring. I practise all t' time. Will ye?

Yes.

Midday's th' only time.

F'r us too.

Too much heat then. Come before dawn.

We'll come then.

Why d'ye wanta learn?

Sukha smiles—innocent, transparent. Says, Ye're king in our eyes. But we can want to pierce t' target at t' fair?

That ye can. Why is Sukha so youthful? And Chotti is past thirty now! But he still remembers the joy under his heart at the triumphant glee of the audience after he hit the target for the first time. A roaring in the blood. It was as if his heart had burst with joy. As if a whole field of red flowers in the trackless fields from Chotti village to Tohri had blossomed in his chest. Yes, they too have the right to that joy. Although the king of the fair has to return to his dark room after hitting the target, still.

And, when y're gone, we c'n say we learnt from ya.

Ye're short tempered, lads. Ye fight with t' Nakata Raja's manager cos he takes a cut at market. I'll make ye run till t' breath's outta yer chests, then?

Give us a kick. We'll eat dirt from where yer feet are. Ye'll see, we'll eat dirt.

Something tears under Chotti's heart. Jejur market. Dhani Munda saying, I eat dirt, I eat th' earth of me country home. The bullet had come roaring.

Chotti said with deep pain and infinite love in his eyes, Y'all come. I"ll teach. Pierce t' target by me teachin'.

They touched his feet again and left.

The very first day Chotti asks pardon in his mind from Dhani. Ye're gone for fifteen years or more. Still me mind grieves for ye, yeah. I didn' see t' whole world so empty when me father died. When I sing it comes to mind that ye've become one with Sailrakab on a cloud's back. So many clouds in t' sky. I don' know which cloud is ye. Me lessons were with ye, but I'm not young any more. Today t' boys come to learn, even from me. I'll teach 'em, ye taught me, bless me.

Then he starts walking with the three young men toward the west of the river, where the hills look mighty close, but don' come closer. Myrobalan trees on the edge of the forest. The trees seem to bend with the weight of fruit.

Wait. Chotti whispers to them. They wait. The four of them wait in silence. The grass stirs at a distance. A bit later Chotti breathes out and wipes the sweat from his brow.

Tiger. Lyin' down. Went off.

We didn' see.

Then t' lesson starts here. Ye mus' know how ta move in forest. Ye don' see tiger. He sees ye a'right. There's eyes in his body hair, ears in his body hair. None's more careful than he.

Halfway between jungle and hill are a few flamboyant trees. Boulders below. Chotti tells them to stand there. He moves far. Draws a target on stone with hard limestone. Comes back and says, Lift yer bow. There's nothin' else. There's jes' that target. This is t' spell for hittin' t' target. Prepare yer eye.

The teaching goes on. Sukha and Bikhna are cheerful. In their own village groups they are the members who are most interested in singing and dancing. Chotti finds Dukhia a bit inscrutable. He is the most singleminded, the most skilful. But he doesn't talk at all. As if always clenched.

Why're ye so glum and mum, Dukhia?

Karmi took bangles and turmeric from him. But went and wed Kanu.

Dukhia says, I spit on Karmi's name.

Why?

Dukhia is the bondslave of the Nakata King's manager. We too. But he has nothin'. His land and all are in hock on his thumbprint.

When will't be repaid?

Dukhia says in a dry voice, Bonded labour pays nothin' back in his book. Me father's father borrowed and bound our whole line.

What'd he take?

A quarter's worth o' paddy.

A quarter's worth o' paddy!

Yeah.

A few days later Dukhia himself told Chotti, A bitta land by me hut. I grow pepper, garlic and onion there. That manager!

What's he do?

Dukhia says in a dry yet passionate voice, Father and grandpa gave bonded labour, I gie too. Don' I gie bonded work? I gie. But he calls me a cheat. A bastard! A dungbug! Why? Do I gie jest one kinda bonded work? He goes to t' King's court. We carry his palqin. There t' day goes. Evenin' time we bring'm back. All that while we sit with no food, no drink. Not e'en a bit of molasses in water does he ever gie. Says, ye're used to fastin'. Does a Munda suffer without food?

No, a Munda's no' human.

We'll sell that fruit o' t' field at market, and then get paddy. He'll lift from that too. It's old news, t' liftin' stuff at Kurmi market. For this th' Oraons have left t' village, one by one. I often think of runnin'!

Where'll ye go?

That's t' thing! Dukhia says in a burnt-out lamentation, Where'll I go? There's no place to go. But I have a mind to do somethin' awful some day! When t' manager calls names, I plead and plead in me mind, don' call names. Munda's blood boils at bad names, mind rages.

Dukhia reminds Chotti of Bisra, his dad. What'll ye do, he scolds? Dontcha think on such things.

I don' wanna think, it comes to mind.

A few more days pass. Sukha and Bikhna may be young in years, but they're wise in the ways of the world. They said to Dukhia, We agree that t' manager is a thorough bastard. But we too have mentioned takin' produce at market at t' landowner's court, we too are angry.

Dukhia shakes his head hard and says, Snatches up all t' good stuff.

Hey go to fair, play bow n' arrer, hit target, okay it's a small fair, but ye'll get a couple rupees at least?

I won' take money. I'll take paddy, he'll snatch t' money.

It's true that he badmouths ye most of all.

Ya. Does. Why does he? Why does he badmouth? There's fam'ly men to stan' behind ya. I have nobuddy. So he badmouths.

Now ya badmouth us.

How?

Ye have nobuddy? We ain't there? We're Munda-Oraon, with us behind one there's all. Dontcha see?

Okay, sorry.

If ye hit targets at arrer play—Chotti says, if ye hit target at arrer play ye'll feel good. Ye'll get a bit money, ye'll wed. Don' think odd things, Dukhia. Happiness is what ever'body does.

Chotti thought Dukhia was thinking of suicide. 'I may do somethin' someday!' This seems suicide talk. Whenever he tries to think about Dukhia these days Dhani Munda comes to mind. Why does he come to mind? He thinks that Dhani knew that if he went to Jejur he'd die of a police bullet. Yet he went. Why did he go? Why does this one thing about Dhani come to mind whenever he tries to think of Dukhia?

He said to Dukhia, If ye win in ev'n one arrer play, there'll be such joy, it'll push t' devil off yer neck.

Then t' manager won' badmouth me?

P'raps not so much.

Let's see. Ye don' tell lies.

Chotti didn't grasp what Dukhia meant by 'I'll suddenly do somethin.' There was a fair at Deo village. Dukhia did come first at arrow play and got two rupees cash. Really he got a lot of joy out of it and he told Chotti so as well. He says, Lordy! So much joy? Like stones floatin' when Chotti floods. This joy washed off all me sorrow. Me heart feels as if emptied. I've lived so long with anger and grief in ma chest. So! But I'm real happy now. Saying this Dukhia digs in the ground with his toe and says, Me mind didn' go berserk even when I saw t' manager.

Chotti was most pleased.

Then everything is quiet, quiet. Then non-violent fighters are taken off by train. But that's an event in the outside world. Paddy is ripening in Aghran, the harvest month. Droves of birds keep arriving, deer have to be chased from the field. The time is coming for migratory birds to come to the Chotti sandbanks, for finding ducks flying in the moonlight. Chotti bought a gunny sack from the market. He'll fill it with chaff so his boys can sleep at first frost. Suddenly at this time a terrible procession of many people shook up Chotti's life, indeed his very view of life. At the head of the procession was Dukhia Munda.

It was about three in the afternoon. Everyone in Chotti village saw a long line of people walking down the hillside against the backdrop of the sky. People in a long single file. At the head of the line someone is carrying something on a spearhead. The procession enters Chotti almost with a focused aim, and the man in front calls out, Chotti! Oh Chotti Munda, I'm Dukhia here.

Now everyone sees, Chotti as well, that Dukhia's holding a spear and on the spear's point is someone's severed head. His mind says this is the manager's head and it's as if an arrow has pierced his chest. He cries out in anguish and says, What's this ye've done, Dukhia?

It's as if Dukhia is drunk, drunk, as if he's free at last from the bond-slavery of his soul's thousand sorrows. His legs tremble a bit, he gives an innocent glance that holds a worldwide astonishment, and he says, Ye said he wouldn't badmouth no more. But then he comes to take his cut from t' market. I'm sittin' here with red pepper—come to take his cut why does he move me hand with t' tip of his shoe? Like a pigeon guards her young I was guardin' me basket, mate. Hittin' me hand with his shoe he says to his peon—t' peon had a spear in hand—he tells t' peon, lift his basket. He's a swelled head with arrer play, t' fucker shirks work, he's a disloyal bastard, he gives me bonded work with no will and grows pepper in his own field with all his soul. Gie a bit o' water here.

Dukhia gulps the water down. Says, Ye said, don' think on it, I didn' wanna think. But he made me do this. After he badmouth me ma, I didn' let him finish. Got his head with ma machete, speared it on t' peon's spear and came here.

Where Dukhia where?

Dukhia says, surprised, Why? In Tohri?

Ye'll go to je-hell, ye'll swing, Dukhia.

Then?

Run off boy.

Dukhia says, as if with profound knowledge, deep compassion, Where? Didn' I tell ye I've no place to run? If there's place would I gie bonded work? E'en a Munda wants to live, no? Say?

Dukhia, me heart's a-breakin'.

I didn' want to.

Dukhia looks at Chotti, this village, these fields, as if with great longing. And then he says, Let's go friends. Polis don' know nothin'. If I don' go myself they'll harass ya.

Dukhia is tried and hanged. Dukhia cut the manager down though he knew the result would be death by hanging. Then Chotti understood why Dhani had gone to Jejur. Even with the knowledge that the outcome is death, in order to remain right with oneself, the humans created by Haramdeo, having reached the twentieth century, must sometimes do certain things. Dhani and Dukhia did them.

First to jail and then to the gallows. The Tohri Daroga got all the information at the county seat and said, Some people, these Mundas. The government provided a lawyer, and the lawyer really explained to him, Talk this way. The fool spoke the truth. Hey, an interpreter explains his words to the lawyer. And interpreter tells him the lawyer's words. None of the three quite understand each other's words. Finally he says, Why? Why s'd I say 'I didn' kill 'm?' I did kill him, killed him in front of a hunnert people. I took red pepper to market, why did he push the basket with a shove of his shoe? In t' cities and towns other kinds of people kill and run. Just Munda-Oraon-Ho, I've never seen them run.

Hearing this by word of mouth Chotti smiled feebly and in pain. When a people don' know 'ye should run' why s'd a young man run? Has he done wrong, that he should fly? If he runs, wouldn't Gormen look everywhere and find him? The raja-landlords release hungry dogs in the forest to catch fugitives. The dogs tear up the forest and catch the man on the run.

No one is able to escape, and for Dukhia escape would have been more difficult. From birth he knew that he was bound in bonded labour. He could have accepted it, but the manager was his evil star. His woman betrayed him too. Dukhia was going crazy with the sense of different kinds of deception. When 'I might do something unexpected' groans in the mind—Bisra kills himself, Dukhia cuts the manager down, both are true. Chotti realized that before the law, before Gormen, Dukhia really tried to explain, with the deepest longing, the tale of red pepper, worth a quarter rupee. Perhaps Dukhia thought, I'm in je-hell, I'll hang, he knows and accepts everything. Yet, how deceptive the affair of the pepper is, will the judge understand? No doubt the judge had thought, what a weird people, they don't mind swinging for a basket of pepper. Chotti knew in his soul, until he hung on the gallows, Dukhia's eyes were full of that worldwide astonishment. Why did this happen? Why is he condemned to be hanged after a necessary killing?

Everything is inscrutable, my friend, and remained inscrutable in Dukhia's life.

Sukha and Bikhna plant a stone in the burial place of the Mundas, a Shonshan-Buru. They ask the village pahan, There they have burnt up t' body after hangin'? So we'll put a Buru?

Yeah. Pahan is comforted. The Dukhia incident is like a stone in the chest of Kurmi village. How did this thing happen. If a Shonshan-Buru is established, at least something is done for that unlucky boy. Pahan utters the appropriate words and blesses some rice and a quarter rupee for Dukhia's soul in the next world. Sukha says slowly, The basket had pepper worth just that quarter rupee.

The next manager is much more knowledgeable. He doesn't come to the village at all and his peon makes it known with a drumbeat, whether you're a bond slave or not, you must give a quarter of your produce at the landowner's court before each market day, and then sell your wares.

A manager has to keep up contact with the police precinct. The Daroga lets the new manager know the government's wish, that the government's busy with the craze for non-violent combat in cities and non-adivasi villages, the jails are overflowing. Now, a violent situation must on no account be created, not even in the interest of teaching your subjects a lesson. Finally the Police Station will have to pick up the slack, d'ye hear? Who will go to those jungle villages?

Siaram Manager lost his life because of his unwise acts, after all? The Police Station is also skilled in calming down the underclass, the manager should remember that. No action that would enrage the jungle folk must be undertaken. They do not recognize indirect exploitation. Isn't it best to follow that doctrine?

The manager is a great devotee of Vishnu. He gives a snack meal to the Mundas if they carry his palanquin. Every sentence ends with a 'dear'. At the proper time he gives voluntary food, rain loans and, as a result of his tricky ways, one morning the pahan of Kurmi holds his head in his two hands and says, This is t' cleverness of t' Diku-Hindus. What? Yesterday, found out at Court that all t' villagers, even I, are his bond slaves.

What tricks did he play?

This bond-slavery incident makes a hash out of the government census, not indirectly, but directly, but that was later. In the matter of this screw-up, the small village Kurmi shows the way to the big village Chotti. A few years later. After Dukhia's hanging, the Shonshan-Buru etc. Harmu says to Chotti one day, Father! Will ye make me a bow?

What'll ye do with it?

I do cow herdin'?

So ye'll kill a tiger if it catches a cow?

Harmu smiles forgivingly at his progenitor's ignorance. Says, Father, ye don' understan' nothin'. Do I go far? That I s'd fall prey to a tiger?

What'll ye do then?

Harmu lowers his eyes and says, Somai and Rupa now carry bows, they got their bows blessed by Pahan. And what's more, they get new mangoes from t' tree with their arrers.

Thas why!

There's no one like ye. Build me a be-u-tiful bow.

Call yer ma.

Harmu's Mother came. And said, What's up?

T' boy wants a bow. I'll make notches on t' body of t' bow. Wrap red thread in those notches, Wife.

Where do I have t' time?

Do it. Yer own son.

He's yer son. I git scared that with' a bow he'll be tied to it day n' night.

I'll gie.

If not a bow, what'll he ask for?

I tole ya I'll do it. Whate'er ye say, have I ever said 'no'?

Wife laughed and left. Never says no, Chotti says.

Why does she thrash me?

Me ma did too.

Chotti was making a bow for Harmu when Sana came along and said, Chotti! T' Daroga asked ye to go to t' station once. Said there's no rush, but he s'd make t' time to come.

Chotti went that afternoon. Market day in Tohri. By the railway line a four mile walk. His wife didn't go to market today. Chotti himself sold a bit of maize, dried red pepper. Three red pepper plants are as dear as life to his wife. And the bit of land is as dear as life to Koel. It's not easy to grow maize on this soil. Koel has asked him for five rupees. There is a big market in nearby Rye. There the wholesale buyer for myrobalan comes from the pharmaceutical factory. Koel will pay for a permanent place in the marketplace. If the landowner's Agent gets the money he'll write a receipt that the place is Koel Munda's on market day. There are many myrobalan plants of both kinds in the forest. The Mundas of Chotti village can't think of going so far to sell stuff. Koel is thinking of it. He too has a son. There are more mouths to feed now. Koel has only one concern, how to settle the family. Koel and Chotti's wife, the two have the same concern. Chotti says, Let t' time to play arrers come around. I'll gie ya money. Harmu's Ma'll raise chickens, I'll gie ya money ta buy chickens. Let t' time to play arrers come around. With these thoughts Chotti bought some red potato, a pig's hock, oil, soda. Koel's wife can't bear to see dirty clothes. Then he went to the Police Station. The Daroga's name is Nandalal Singh. Quite a solid man. In late middle age.

Have a seat, Chotti.

Chotti sat down on the ground.

What's the news?

T' days pass, sir.

How old is your son?

Herds cattle.

One thing.

Say it sir.

Chotti! I took the first statement from Dukhia Munda. He said that he had learnt archery from you. You had asked him not to raise his machete. He told you everything on his way to the

Police Station. Well I did not keep all these words in the statement. I sent the statement without your name. That's why you had no problems.

Sir! Dukhia used to say, 'I may do some strange thing.' Well I didn' understan' that he might do sich a thing. He was very unhappy, didn' laugh. I was afeared he'd put a noose round his own neck like me Dad.

By confessing to his guilt, by pouring cold water on the government lawyer's attempt to save him, Dukhia put the noose around his own neck. The Daroga doesn't say that to Chotti. You cannot explain a non-Munda way of thinking to a Munda.

Chotti! I'll be at this station for three years. You will not join in any archery contest in any fair these next three years.

Don' say that sir. From me archery earnin's me brother will get a place in t' marketplace, me wife will buy chicken. Don' say that sir.

No Chotti. This will be dangerous for me. Tirathnath says, Chotti was behind Dukhia as well. The Daroga saved him. Whatever happens your name comes up. If you don' play arrers for three years, people's attention will be displaced.

G'bye.

Chotti returns home with a face sombre with dashed hopes. Hearing all, wife says, So what? Koel will sell amlaki without a sure place. We'll buy poultry later.

Chotti says to Koel, Ye spent yer life hidden behind big brother. Ye're me brother, can't ye play arrers?

Ye and me!

Why not? Ye can only play t' drum when I play arrers?

Pain in every word Chotti utters. Koel says, Fine. Let's see. But gie yer word, ye won' kill me if I don' win.

Do I hit ya? Ye, a son's father?

Koel says, E'en now ye will if ye can.

Ye'll practice from tomorra. Sukha can, Dukhia can, not ye?

I said let's see.

Chotti's wife mixes rough molasses in water and gives it to her husband. Drink a bit, she says, cool yerself. Don' mek such a dark face. He let ye go with no more than words cos it's ye. With another Munda he would've used force.

Yes, gave me a lotta respect!

In the pain of his soul, in a night of incomprehensible grief Chotti becomes rosy rainwater, the wife became the river, spread her breast and took him into her, made a mingling. Toward dawn Chotti says, This time it'll be a girl like ye.

But name her by t' day o' t' week.

Ver' well. I keep thinkin' me ma wants to come back to t' world as me daughter. I know her hopes weren't filled.

These are Diku-like things ye be sayin.

Yes luv.

Mornin' star hasn't come up, sleep now.

Chotti falls asleep.

VI

KOEL CALLS CHOTTI at crow-calling dawn. Says, let's go.

Where?

Let's go to Pahan.

Why? Dunno what's up wit' Pahan, can't do nothin' without me. Everyone is t' same way in Chotti village. An' that's how t' Police Daroga sees me hand in ever'thin'.

Come come.

Ye too are like 'em. Since our belly's empty, like all Mundas, stay apart by yerself. 'Stead of which, big brother's all ye know! S'll I live f'rever? Sana's niece, yer wife, knows Harmu's Ma, an' ye know dada—big brother.

But didn' our ma say so when she died? Koel asks. Stay together, ye two brothers? Mother's word mus' be kept, no?

Chotti says, Mother's words're mixed with snake venom. But still ye say with ev'ry word, Ma said this thing.

Did say that thing.

Koel, ye've become more'n a jackal here.

Koel says, Right. That jackal's become too bold. T' fucker comes to catch calves. Kill that one.

Kill jackal's also me job?

Come come. It's almost light.

Pahan sat outside his hut. Saw Chotti and said, Ya Chotti. What's this that Koel's sayin'? They won' let ye join arrer play?

They said no, I got up an' left. Shall I make trouble with Daroga?

No, no, we're people of t' forest land, yes. Daroga's Gormen f'r us.

Why ya call so early?

To have some good talk.

What's good any more?

Since ye won' join, will t' name o' t' village just sink at Chotti fair?

What're ye askin' me ta do?

Why jes' Koel, teach all t' Munda boys.

All Munda boys?

Yes mate.

An' then?

They'll win in village after village, fair after fair.

So easy, eh? No Mundas in those villages? No Oraons?

E'en so.

If I teach 'em Daroga will know. An' then he'll say, Chotti Munda trains everyone in archery, they'll start fightin'. They see us fightin' whate'er we do. If every Munda did start fightin' would they've lasted?

Why s'd Daroga know? E'en now there's no one in Chotti village who'd speak to anyone if I say no. This is also about t' boys' honour.

Chotti thought a bit. Then said, Fine. Howsomever, let it be at this crow-dawn. E'en earlier. But ye do t' settin' up.

They'll give ye honour-money too, brother.

Why! T' fuckers have too much cash?

Pahan is hurt. Ever'thin' has its rules.

Why'nt ya do as ya think is good? When've I said 'no' ta what ye've asked? And hear this. Ye mus' gie a bow in Harmu's hands.

Right right. Let t' moon-phase come.

The boys from Chotti village brought a cock and a hen. Harmu's ma said, I won' let these be et. I'll raise em. Koel, raise me a hen house. Make t' walls as thick as me own hut.

Chotti smiles and says, Put 'em under t' board—under t' machan now.

Koel says, Wouldn' it ha' been nice ta eat these two?

Harmu's mother lit up the room with her smile and said, No way. T' boys've brought a pair of hens for yer brother's spell. Me wish has come true.

Chotti says, Ouf, yer son's pa knows spells. And so he ploughs Tirathnath's fields, and can' ev'n buy a brassbound comb that his boy wants and wants.

His wife says in ringing tones, We don' give bond labour and we don' borrow. Ye said t' bad, say t' good? Brassbound comb! Me dad's dad was Pahan. I ne'er saw a brassbound comb at our place? These are just city fads, one day he'll say I'll wear a shirt.

Ye too? Koel's wife too?

Eh, me Ma! I feel shame. To wear a top?

T' Munda women of Ranchi wear.

Then they have no shame. Why s'dn' a Munda lass dress up? Of course dress up. Bitta white sof' wood in ear, flowers in hair, hair oiled, an' a white cloth. Bead necklace and brass bangle would be good too. We wore wood bangles after all.

Come, tek yer hens. Jackal's gone mad. Be careful.

Kill me a duck if ye can? I'll put pizen on its bod an' kill jackal?

Koel's wife keeps cleaning the yard and says, Goes roun' lookin' ta catch t' calf. How it snarls if ya chase it! Ye're scared then.

Chotti says, Fell that one, Koel. T' cow, t' pig, t' hen, t' goat, keep us folks alive. An' wit' 'em t' wolf moves in packs, an' t'fox runs amok, bad signs. It can e'en catch yer brat. Be careful, Wife. In Kurmi a wolf came an' took t' boy from t' mother's side.

Wife said, Koel's wife puts 'er kid on 'er back an' works. T' fence Koel's put up's so high, I caint see man's head if I don' open gate.

Morning star in the sky, that's when Chotti gets up. The village youth are waiting. Walking toward the forest Chotti says, There's talk if ten Mundas're together. Ye'll come each on yer own. Even if t' tishan porters see, there'll be words.

That same forest, that same meadow. Dukhia, Sukha and Bikhna had come. Chotti sighed. He drew a line on stone. Came back and said, Raise yer bow. Ye say spell, I say practice. If ya try with yer whole life, why won' ye get it?

Koel said, If we win, ah! We'll lift ya on our heads an' dance.

Lift yer bows more. He draws a target. First prepare yer eyes. There's t' target, there's ye. There's no one else, nothin' else.

The arrows flew forward.

Go, pick up th' arrers. Raise agin. This target f'r sev'n days. I'll put target further week by week.

Arrows flew forward.

Pick 'em up. Raise 'em again. Look at me.

The young men looked at Chotti.

Day's breaking, light's growing.

Thus the training continued. Day after day. Chotti discovers that the qualities he had in archery were motivation and obstinacy. There is an especial joy in teaching them. A new excitement. If they win at the local and regional fairs, his legacy will remain with them. If one of them is truly skilful, wins repeatedly, then perhaps the young Munda men of that time will come to him. Saying, Teach us.

When they win, if they win, he will taste the joy that Dukhia tasted.

Thinking all this he recalled that he had had no news of Sukha and Bikhna for a long time. And what's going on now in Kurmi village? On the way to Kurmi is dense forest and a serried mountain range. People from that village go to market to the south, in the market town of Biradoi. Unless one makes it happen, there is no contact between Chotti and Kurmi. Sukha, Dukhia, and Bikhna made contact. But everything becomes a story in Chotti's life. Dukhia Munda's life also remained a story around Chotti.

Chotti Fair is on the tenth and final day of Durga Puja—the worship of the Great Goddess. The fair is truly big and of long standing. The fair is set up on government-owned land. The tax collector makes good money renting space to the sellers. Adivasis come of course, but others come as well. The fair goes on for seven days. People from neighbouring areas buy everything here—wooden plates, bowls, grinders, pestles, dishes, cloth, scarves, towels, mosquito nets, molasses, rice, vegetables. Wheels also are sold for ox-carts, ploughshares, spades, spatulas—all.

In the yard of the fair the adivasis dance village by village. Then the arrowplay starts. For a long time now, Chotti doesn't join the easy contests. He only joins the heavy duty ones. This time he's merely a spectator. Not everyone knows this. There is a fair on the same day in Biradoi, also a contest. Biradoi is owned by the Maharajas of Nakata. The Rajas perform Durga Puja. For that they bring troupes of masked dancers from Seraikela. The villagers come in droves to see the masked dance. Also the people from Kurmi.

Chotti saw in surprise that the Kurmi Mundas had come here to see the contest. The judges and the prizegivers were the same people. Tirathnath, the Daroga, Collector were all seated. Tirathnath smiles at him and says, This is good, Chotti. Ye win yearly. Let 'em get a chance.

The pahan of Chotti village is one of the judges as a representative of the adivasis. He came up and sat on the ground. He will watch standing at the time of the contest. Sukha and Bikhna could easily have joined. Something is wrong somewhere.

Chotti Munda is not competing. Therefore everyone is surprised this time. The Daroga became a bit grave when he sees that there were quite a few contestants from Chotti village. Tirathnath has heard the reason for Chotti's non-competition from others, not from the Daroga. So he feigned ignorance and asked, Who asked Chotti not to join, Pahan?

Pahan said nothing.

Tirathnath spoke, as if to himself, Are his powers small? He can do everything with his spellbound arrows. Seen many times.

The Daroga grew even more grave. If you read the holy Gita everyday, he said, or, say, the life of the God-King Rama, you will get such grace Lalaji, no spellbound arrow will be able to harm you.

Our land is savage, sir.

Rama's power works here too.

Many things happen in this savage land, that reason can't reckon out all. We've proof that sending a lamp on the air a distant house has been burnt. Both sons of the King of Nakata are born blind. His oldest queen is barren. She cast such a spell with the wizards that the younger queen delivered blind sons twice in her mother's house. There are many tales like this about Chotti. I'll tell you later.

Un-hunh.

Hey, Whitey turned up, Whitey. The direct brother of the Governor's Secretary. He saw his archery and became pals with him. When the Secretary came for shikar, he too had a long talk with him.

When? I didn't know? Daroga was shaken.

Tirathnath was most pleased. How will you know? he said. You have book learning, you get news from people at the Police

Station. You think we are wild beasts. And so you don't show even though we invite you again and again.

No, no, I'm initiated by a guru this year. For a year I have a restriction on even drinking water away from home. My guru is very strict, y'know?

Look, there they go.

There's a huge excitement in Chotti's breast. The first time he was himself shooting he'd felt like this, yes. Even thinking about it brings tears to his eyes. When was Chotti as youthful as they? When did his breast overflow as soon as he raised the bow?

Who are you? Collector calls out.

Koel Munda. Brother of Chotti Munda from Chotti village.

Koel is not looking at his dada. A particular excitement and resolution in his face, in his eyes, in the face and eyes of Chotti's pupils.

Ah ha! Koel has hit the target.

Uproar, uproar! A tear drops from Chotti's eye. These pupils are something, for sure. Not one is looking at him. Not even Koel. Look how Sukha and Bikhna leap. Why are they so joyous?

Chotti lights a bidi leaf cigarette. He feels quite advanced in age right now.

Chotti's students took first and second place in the easier archery contests. In the next two harder contests Rupa, Sana's nephew, and Koel took second place. Then began the hardest contest. It's as if it was preordained. Sixteen contestants from five villages shot arrows in an expert fashion. Everyone screamed as if in triumph, when Collector said 'No one won'. Gaya Munda from Tohri called out, Me children, only Chotti can do that. Don' worry if ye couldn' do it.

Daroga said to himself, Bastards! They scream at defeat, and he says not to worry. No doubt they tease us because Chotti didn't compete.

The young men from Chotti village received a grand total of eight rupees. Tirathnath said, We should leave now. Now these fellows will bring a whole pig, kill it, drink liquor and eat it, they'll dance and much else.

Is it always like this?

Always. This fair is theirs, after all. We've come later. Don't you know in their eyes we are all Dikus?

This time their enthusiasm is greater. Even the contestants from other villages surrounded Chotti. Teach us then? They urged. We'll make yer name as we win at fair after fair?

Okay, where is Bharat Munda from Komandi?

Here Chotti.

Bharat! I know f'r fact, that ye c'n surely hit t' final target, at least, yer arrers'll go near th' eye. An' ye didn' try at all?

Bharat smiles shyly, That's indeed t' thing.

What thing?

A jungle thing.

What's it?

The Chotti Pahan says, No Munda will e'en try at a target where ye aren't allowed.

What d'ye mean?

Ye don' know this, but in every fair, whosomever shoots arrer, lifts t' bow wit' yer name in mind.

Chotti was choking up. Ye honour me that much, he said.

Three years, said Bharat, we'll go on like this. Then we'll see. E'en Daroga'll be punished, ye see.

No, let that be. Just from one Dukhia, such a lot of trouble in Kurmi village . . . what's this? Wife, didn' ye go home, then?

Sure, we girls will go. Now it's yer fun. But let's dance just this once, then we leave.

The men stepped back. The women danced in a ring. Dancing, Chotti's wife asks, Ye guys dead? Where's music?

Koel and others played music. The women sang as they danced.

—'Come to t' fair, women, come to t' fair'—

—'Hey, who asks, who asks?'—

—'I'm mad with yer beauty'—

—'Step over Chotti river, hold me by hand, take me to t' fair.'

Chotti says, Look at Harmu's Mother's ways! I nev'r saw sich smiles when I came back home a winner?

Koel says, Today is a day of honour an' pride f'r us.

Pork and rice. And liquor. Suddenly Chotti hears the song that the boys are singing. Koel is hitting the nagara drum hard with his palm, keeping time.

> Ye raise t' bow, ye hit t' target
> Makes Daroga mighty afraid, mate—
> Ye go to Gormen and tell 'em our plea

Makes Daroga mighty afraid, mate—
So they didn' let ya play yer arrer.
Ye taught Dukhia Munda ta shoot
Dukhia t' bonded slave, mate—
Dukhia cuts t' manager's head off
Makes Daroga scared, mate—
So they didn' let ya play yer arrer.
Which Munda knows t' bowspell?
Only ye, mate—
Which Munda is Gormen's buddy?
Only ye, mate—
So they didn' let ya play yer arrer.

All laugh at song's end. Chotti lifts the cloth, wipes his mouth, and says, Hey, no more. I'm shamed, why all this 'bout a man ye know well? I'm shamed, no?

Then other songs, other dances. Chotti goes and sits down with Sukha, with Bikhna. And asks, Ye didn' shoot?

Sukha says, On sich a happy day we won' speak our pain. We'll come later an' tell. What did Dukhia do, t' village is in ashes.

Bikhna says, Not today. Today we'll eat our fill of pork, have fun. God, how long we haven' laughed.

The night of joy is short. The night of sorrow is long. The night passed in a flash. When the sun shone they each took the way home. At leavetaking Bharat Munda said, This word is firm now. Ye'll teach how an' as they come?

I'll teach what I know.

Also that spell? Ye say 'ya,' and I'll be yer bondslave. Hey listen. Chotti'll teach me t' spell, I'll be his bondslave.

Chotti put his hands on Bharat's body and said in a very calm voice, There's no spell Bharat. Only practice, an' practice, an' practice.

Ye're tellin' true?

I tell ya true.

Then that's t' spell!

Hey, I don' know anythin' else.

That's t' spell.

Sukha comes only a few days later. Toward night. He says, A lotta pressure on us now. It's against us if we come t' see ye. Think o' that! What a fear of bears, mate. All movin' in t' forest with t' stink of ripe sour plum.

A rogue animal. A tiger watches for humans, doesn't show himself. T' bastard bear comes and grabs t' guy and splits him with his claws, yeah.

Then how do they have dancin' bears in town, eh?

Catch 'em as cubs.

Let's sit inside. Yer lady won' be cross?

Nah. Come.

What Dukhia did do, Sukha says, It's like t' village's burnt down. Gormen forbid ye. We live on t' King's land. T' new manager has bound ever'one in bond labour. And then so many demands. Give 'em stuff right and left. If someone dies in th' office or his family then either give labour or pay tax. Birth-wedding-death in his house or t' countless pujas that these Dikus have, he raises tax for ever'thin'. We've never set eyes on t' King, yet he raises taxes if anythin' goes on in his house. He goes from one court to another. We carry t' palquin, we take an' we bring back. He walks and we must run with an umbrella. Life's hell.

What a mess!

He says, Dukhia went wrong by Chotti's lesson. Don' go near him, hear? An' from Kurmi, Dukhia's village, not a single Munda boy must join archery contest. I will break yer back.

Now what's to do?

No way. Hopeless. And . . .

What?

Sukha doodles on the floor with his nails. Then says, There's a Mission in Tomaru. There t' Mission Mundas live well.

But that's far away.

Far, yes.

Ye'll leave yer faith?

Why? Why s'd I leave me faith?

Ye must become Christians.

One can still return to faith.

Yes, many do so . . .

Let's survive now. If I go there, if I leave me faith, t' Mission Gormens will gie us land, settle us. Wherever we run, we won' be able to run from t' King's reach. He'll surely catch us and have us killed.

Then? Say ye run. Yer family?

If ye go to t' Mission t' King loses his rights.

Yer family? Villagers?

If we go, we all go. Else t' manager makes shoes out o' t' hide of whoever remains.

Everyone goes?

There's t' hitch.

Go Sukha. Wait, let me walk wit' ye a bit. Let me call Koel.

Ye'll go in this dark?

Ye'll go alone?

It's like I've forgotten to be afraid.

It must be so. How dark the soil. Nothing below is illuminated by the starlight in the sky. Yet it's the waxing phase of the moon. Sukha has forgotten fear. Otherwise how did he come? Chotti's wife gives him the hurricane lantern. They light hurricane lanterns rarely. Kerosene, ground oil is dear. Everyday lighting needs they still fulfil with lamps of mahua fruit oil.

Walking, Chotti says, Let me walk ahead with t' machete. Ye follow. Don' speak.

Chotti didn't just walk along for a bit. He reached Sukha all the way to the edge of the village. Come in t' small hours for this work, he said. Don' come in evenin'. There's all kindsa animals in forest. Tiger, cheetah, leopard, bear.

I've forgotten all that. An arrer sticks in me heart when I think of leavin' faith. Blood spills. T' joy of t' holy days!

If ye go to Mission, go. But don' get caught by recruiters. They'll take ye anywhere they like, to some distant tea garden.

No no. No hope but t' Mission. We'll escape t' King only if we go to Gormen.

On t' way back, Koel asks, S'll I sing?

Why?

Then t' bear will know many people are passin'. Be afraid.

Koel, when will yer brain grow up? Ye'll call out to death?

When the two get back, the night is darker. Cold in the frost-laden air. Fog rising from the sand banks in the river.

T' Mundas of Kurmi village did not leave easily. To set up a village by felling an impenetrable forest is a lot of work, a lot of pain. To leave that village is even more painful. Where is yer Mission? Does it have such hills, and such forests all around, like th' edge of mother's cloth?

No, but then there's also no manager.

But t' Mission life is different. Are there any holy day festivals there?

No, but then there's no bonded labour either.

Can we worship Haramdeo if we go there?

No, but we don' have to pay taxes for ever'thin'.

Pahan said, Go if ye wish. I don' ask anyone ta stay. This Kurmi was our forest-winnin' village. Mundas lived afore in their Khuntkatti village, also forest-cut. Soon's there was a crop there, Diku-moneylenders got in. An' Mundas left village. In t' same way our forefathers build this village. T' kings took this area much later.

Won' ye leave?

Me? To t' Mission?

Pahan gives a most peculiar smile with his toothless mouth. With deep conviction he says, Where'll I go at this age? Leave Haramdeo's faith? If ye want ta survive, ye go. Wit' this terror, I don' ask anyone ta stay. But—!

What?

Play t' hunt game on Holi, t' day of t' Colourfeast? Lemme fill me eyes widda sight? Young an' old from me village will run with' arrer and machete. They'll come back singin'. Then dancin' an' more song.

Pahan came to market one day. He called Chotti aside for no excuse at all and said, All these Mundas can' last here any more, son. They'll go.

What can I say?

Don' tell anyone.

I don' ask anyone to leave home and land. But this I saw that solution is not to raise yer machete and kill manager.

By 'raisin' machete' ye meant raisin' a weapon. By 'machete' t' Dikus mean ever'one fightin' together. If they could raise machete Diku-style, then it ud work. Or mebbe not even then. Lord Birsa raised such a machete with Mundas. But e'en then it didn' work.

T' Dikus and t' Gormens have lotta power, lotta arms.

Manager rides t' palquin, wears shoes, chews his betel leaf e'en after killin' us. An' Dukhia hangs if he kills manager.

T' Gormen's law!

Why no law ont' manager? No Chotti I tell 'em to go, but me heart is broken. An' see, don' tell anyone all this. They'll say t' Mundas are raisin' Diku 'machete'.

I too am sad. We've become less. Out of all festivals, this hunt game's t' best of our forefathers' festivals.

As usual, the manager made the Mundas singleminded in the matter of their departure from the village by putting them under duress. The Mundas, the Kurmi Mundas, had not been of one mind in this huge and important decision. The elders were altogether unwilling. Over eighty people forsake the village and leave? New residents brought in? To lead lives like theirs in their homes with poultry, goats and cattle? Some had said, We'll give bond labour, we'll pay taxes, but we won' leave village.

At the proper time the manager announced that the hunt festival was prohibited because the Mundas of Kurmi village are most pig-headed.

Hunt festival prohibited! The news spread instantly. Tremendous blow. Everyone stunned. Never has any Master prohibited any Munda festival.

Stay if ye wish, after this, said Sukha. We're leavin'. After this, we'll no longer stay.

At Sukha's instigation they played an un-Munda-like trick. They gave thumbprints recklessly and borrowed paddy and maize little by little. Then they all left the village one evening. They tied doors and windows upon the backs of cattle. They took their cattle, their pigs, their goats, everything with them, to sell as they walked the way. Then they touched Pahan's feet and all the Mundas left home. The village was in deep forest. The office won't get the news in a jiffy. Not along the straight way, but by the complicated forest path they left. Tomaru was two days' walk.

There's a feast for the Colourfeast at the office. The King himself will come on elephant-back. He will go hunting here this time. Bonded labour is needed. To beat the jungle. His men went to all the villages. His sepoys. Then the real news was known.

The guard said, Boss, Pahan is sitting alone. There's no one around. They even took the housedoors.

Where did they go?

Pahan doesn't know.

Search, search, was the cry. They're not there, they're nowhere. Finally it was known that they've sought sanctuary at Tomaru Mission. The manager stood in front of the King with shoes on his head. The King said, To fight with the Mission Whiteys for a little bit of my kingdom?

Sir, may I receive order to submit a petition.

What petition will you submit?

Rebel subjects have come, return them.

Do they give back? They sit in the forest to turn them into Christians. There will be a new manager, explain the job to him and leave.

The manager was burning up as he returned to the office. I must get that Pahan. He must have known everything. Knowing everything he didn't inform. Tenants left, tenants will come. But this insult! The rascals slapped me in the face as they left? Borrowed so much paddy and maize? One of the landowner's functionaries, most delighted at the manager's misfortunes, says, What can you do? The Tomaru Mission sahib is buddies with the Gormen at Ranchi. They make people Christian by force, and in this case so many people are begging to become Christian, are they going to let this go? And Gormen is not best pleased with the King either. It's difficult for him to hold on to his throne. Both his boys are blind. And he's not that sort of a King. So why s'd Gormen listen? Gormen doesn't notice these little Kings.

What will people say?—the manager says.

In response the petty officer says, in a voice as thick and tasty as clotted cream, Dontcha worry friend. You can't get things done if you thinka what people will think, will say. And we say 'people,' that's just a word. Where's people here? This jungle country? Talk? There's always talk. I heard in the palace itself? Everyone says in secret, that you cooked up this way of gittin' rid of the Mundas.

Me! Why?

Hey, everyone knows the Mundas are bastards, right rascals. Yet Manager-Sir! Such things happened for so long. The Dukhia business was just t'other day, how the police did upset the village. But still they didn't leave the village.

Because I kept 'em under control.

That's the thing, Sir-Manager, you agree yersel' that you kept control. Of course ya did. But people, I mean people here, say that to raise a kid you have to thrash 'em but also gie him sweets. You hit' em, but gave 'em sweets as well, the office people say.

How?

Yeah, ye gave them paddy-loan and explained this King's throne's not for long. The Secretary-sahib's not pleased with the King. And since both the second Queen's boys are blind, the adopted son of the first Queen will get the state. And so y'asked them to go, cos ye want this property to be auctioned, so ye can call it in.

This is the buzz?

Yes sir.

People are sayin'?

Yes sir.

Where's the people here? This jungle country?

The courtier smiles, Ye'll do things, there'll be no word? I'll say, I don' know if the Manager-Sir knew that they'd leave, but I was struck that he gave them such generous loans.

Took their thumbprints!

You've made a mountain out of these bonded labour thumbprint papers. Take Sukha's dad Sancha Munda. Sancha's grandpa gave his mark, they're still giving labour for that. Took Sancha's thumbprint again, that's good. That Sukha is today's lad. Maybe won't want to give labour on great grandpa's mark, and can be told that there's a paper with his dad's thumbprint. But why did you ask Sancha to give his thumbprint again? How many times will you bind the same man in bonded labour? There the last manager lost his head, and yet ye were so strict that we thought you had some plan. You'll buy the estate! So buy! There's no sweet in any bit of soil in Nakata, it's all salt.

So all this is your thinkin'?

Where'r the other people? In this jungle area?

The manager feels as outwitted as the tiger or the cat in the stories of the fox and the tiger, the sparrow and the cat. The courtier made this final comment, the Colourfeast day is near. The King seems ta want ta know, an' I ask too, why did ye stop their hunt game? We're very safe this year. No hunt game! If they'd lifted their machetes?

The manager realizes that for him the soil here has really become salt rather than sweet. Now he'll have to shift residence. Yet the Colourfeast preparations are afoot at the office. The King has said that he'll come hunting here. All his anger falls upon the pahan. He knew everything, yet said nothing. In a towering rage he says to the guard, Let's go to Kurmi.

They go to Kurmi. Holi is day after tomorrow. The hillside and the woods are blazing red. The flowers of the flamboyant are in bloom. Even so early in the morning Kurmi village looks scary because it is a deserted village. The doorless huts gape like empty mouths. The guard says, the village looks haunted. How empty it is!

Pahan! Are you there Pahan? Pa-han!

Calling, the manager stops, listens, he can hear singing. Songs preparing for Holi. He feels incredibly hopeful, someone is there. Elation. If he has to leave his job, he'll get even by lashing to death whoever's left. He says hush, hush to the guard. They'll run off if they hear us. They're in the village, otherwise, who's singing?

Go ahead, sir—In the guard's mind's eye there's a sudden vision of Dukhia's hand holding a spear with a freshly severed head stuck to its point. He strokes the back of his neck. If it's like that he can run. The manager can't. He's out of practice.

The manager walks in front and the guard follows. The manager is blind with rage. Otherwise the same scene would have flashed in his mind. They advance and the words of the song become clear:

> There was a tiger in th' east a male yes—
> I pierced him with me spear—
> I went to t' forest on t' day of t' hunt feast
> Ye were then at home yes—
> Ye held t' doorframe and looked west
> I was then to th' east
> I went to t' forest on t' feast day of t' hunt.

Walking up beyond a berry bush they see the singer. The pahan is sitting under the sal tree in front of his hut. A few dogs lie near him. Leaves are flying around in the yard. The dogs are weak with hunger, but they still bark and dash up to their feet. Pahan is holding a spear in his hand, and stroking it unceasingly. The pahan is singing. He doesn't stop singing at the sight of the manager, but rather goes on, On t' day of t' hunt feast—

Pahan! Hey Pahan, stop singing.

There was a tiger in th' east, oh a male tiger—

Pahan! The manager is afraid. Yet the pahan is old, decrepit, his spear is rusty, and he remains sitting. There are twigs and leaves on his body.

I pierced him with me spear—on t' day of t' hunt feast—

Pahan! The manager's voice grows weak. Why is he afraid of a hunt festival song in the voice of an emaciated old man in a deserted village?

Pahan!

Pahan finishes his song, stops, then says to the air, T' dogs! They came near me for fear of t' leopard. T' dogs!

He starts singing again and the manager and the sentry begin running for fear of the unknown. Inside the doorless huts, the wind runs around, the dry leaves fly. They run off.

Chotti see the whole scene from afar. He too came and stood breathless behind the pahan. Now he comes forward and places powdered maize, molasses and water in front of the pahan. He lowers the spear from the pahan's lap. When the song is over he takes the pahan's thin hand and places it over the ground corn. Says softly, Eat.

I will?

Yes. I didn' come before for fear of 'em. They might come again, I won' stay. I'll come again, bring again.

Pahan seems to have moved far away. He says in a weak voice come floating from afar, Chotti, Chotti Munda! Bisra's son, Etwa's grandson, Somai's great-grandson.

Eat, I'm off.

I lit t' Holi fire with Etwa long ago.

So light it today, tomorra's Holi.

Yeah. I know. Can ye take these dogs?

Will they go?

Nah! Don' know ya.

I'm off.

Go.

Suddenly, Pahan comes close and says with infinite concern, Me son, go carefully. T' manager'll do ye harm if he sees ye. All that he said in yer name!

Hearing 'Go carefully son', something tears in pain under Chotti's heart. Pahan's tone is so sincere. It reminds him of his father the suicide, Bisra Munda, a great sinner by all faiths. He spoke thus, in such a voice. I'll go carefully, Chotti says.

That evening, when in all the villages young people light Holi fires, and celebrate, and when Chotti's chest hurts because there will be no Holi fire in Kurmi then everyone screams and points south.

On the hilltop Kurmi village is burning.

Sana says, T' manager set fire to t' village.

Chotti says nothing.

Did Pahan leave?

Chotti says nothing.

The next day, on the day of the Hunt festival, Chotti gets up before dawn. Says to wife, If anyone asks say I went to t' field and I'll be back in a jiffy.

Where'r ye goin'?

Kurmi. Ta see if t' pahan's alive.

Chotti's wife's also the granddaughter of a pahan, from another village. A pahan never kills himself, she says, Why worry?

Whattya know, Wife?

Me water can's lost. Me alumini can.

Ye know this?

This I know, that he set this fire. Me mind says so.

Chotti goes off. Almost runs with his head and body wrapped up in a chador. It's as if the way is endless. Finally he gets to Kurmi. Empty, all empty. Banks of ash. Ash lying around. It is as if the earth foundations of the huts are gigantic Shonshan-Burus. He breaks off a tree branch and beats the ash heaps. Beats the ash to find the pahan's bones. No pahan, and no dogs. Did they then leave? Suddenly some dogs bark in the distance, startling him and, raising his head, he sees an incredible tableau. The hill right in front of the village has a bare head and is long and narrow. It is a low hill. On the side of the hill for about ten miles there are deep woods. On the hill top with his spear held aloft, Pahan walks, behind him a few dogs. Pahan is descending the hillside. Toward the forest. Today is the festival day of the hunt. The pahan descends, the dogs, the forest swallows them up. Chotti shakes his head. There isn't even a walking track on that forest floor. No one enters it for fear of bears.

The pahan's entry into the forest is symbolic. With it, at the meeting point of night and dawn, the tale of the Mundas of Kurmi village comes to an end. The story of Joseph Sukha Munda and David Bikhna Munda of Tomaru Mission is different. Some folktales are born. Everything is fiction in Chotti's life, my dear. From story to song.

> Dayalraj Manager was a mos' violent man.
> He bound t' Kurmi Mundas in bonded labour
> Givin' and givin' and givin' bonded labour—
> Sukha Munda went to Chotti Munda.

Chotti sent an arrer toward Tomaru Mission
And said, follow th' arrer step by step.
Chotti sent fire tipped arrers
And Holi fire was lit in Kurmi
Chotti sent arrer to Pahan
Pahan climbed th' arrer and went fa-a-r away.

About a year and a half later new folks are settled in Kurmi village. They plough the forest and build new homes. The first vegetables and maize grown in Kurmi are as nutritious as they are sizeable. Nourished by cooking ash. After the Diwali Light Festival adivasis offer the first harvest of fruit and grain to the Sun God. After that the village goes back to what it was before. Goats roam, dogs bark, hens in the thatch, out in the yard the noise of naked children. Nothing remains empty in this life.

VII

K URMI VILLAGE BURNED, Pahan left. Chotti's name got tangled with it. Wife said, Ye're like that river Chotti. Not a deed of ours's wi'out t' river, and these folks caint do a thing wi'out ye.

I see. What's that? Hangin'?

A hare. Harmu got it.

Big hunter now.

T'other day those boys killed a hyena, yeah?

Where is he?

There he is.

Harmu!

Here I be.

Whatcha got there?

Harmu's next brother Somchar laughs and says, 'Tis a hare. Soon as he ran in t' grass, brother killed it. Mother'll cook it.

Chotti was amused. Still the matter is serious. He said gravely, Harmu! That's a girl. Ye didn' know?

I saw after killin'.

Let's not see that agin. T' fam'ly of life grows larger wit' girl animals, girl birds. Why do I make ye know girl critters and birds?

I'll not kill agin.

Somchar looks at his ma and says, There's a sis in Ma's belly, no Aba?

Chotti and his wife turn their faces away from each other. Wife says, Go look after t' hens Somchar. T' fox goes aroun' in broad daylight.

Will t' fox go way if 'es shown a stick?

Ye wanna bow too?

I'll kill t' fox wit' ma arrer.

Chotti scolded him, One can't get a bow jes' like that. I'll give ye a bow when t'time comes. Go quickly! If our ma said a thing we ran to do it.

Why s'd I run? Why'll there be a sis in Ma's belly? Why s'll I sleep by Auntie then? Why will Ma not love me then?

Ma stays with girl-chile. Boy-chile stays wit' Dad. Ye'll stay wit' me then. Okay? Go now. Call yer brother.

Chotti says to wife, T' Master's killed me, plantin' peanuts. Loosen t' root soil, take good care, like a girl-chile in a Diku house.

But profit is double?

Ye're right. Before he sowed no one knew sich soil would gie sich peanuts. Now all plant this.

Tirathnath buys nothin'.

Salt and kerosene. E'en that he'da grown if it grew in soil.

Chotti and Harmu go out. Koel's gone to Rai. Goes by the morning train, it's nightfall when he returns. Yet it's in that market that the prices are high. Harmu has a bow. Once he's promoted to the bow, it never leaves his shoulder. Harmu's face is handsome. A white dhoti gets too dirty, so his mother dyes his cloth egg-yolk yellow. Station master's wife always says when she sees him, Just like King Rama. Walking he says, Aba! Is a tusked boar comin' ta eat up t' nuts?

Yeah boy.

As big as an elephant?

Is a boar ever as big as an elephant, me son?

Tell me.

Very big.

Does a boar kill people?

Doesn' it! Me dad was then young. I was a two year old kid. Me Chacha's belly was ripped by a boar on Hunt day.

An' then?

Chacha died before they c'd bring him home.

Then?

Aba said, I'll not drink water till I've killed that boar. Killed that boar wit' spear, and then drank water. But Aba didn' e'en look at pig slaughter. Such a sure hunter, but couldn' cut a hen. How me ma did laugh.

Won' ye kill this boar?

No boy, Daroga Sir'll beat me up.

His whim. He'll hunt.

The Daroga was in mortal danger attempting to kill this very tusked boar. The peanut plot is fenced, with a high cactus fence. It is Chotti and his group who put up a cactus fence, bloodied and cut up themselves with the thorns, around a square mile plot. At that time Tirathnath had the fancy to grow potatoes. It was then that the plot was fenced. In a few years the plants have grown, and new leaves have come up from the old with the rains. The bamboo entry gate is toward Tirathnath's field. Three quarters of the plot is level, and then there's a slope. Then there's a narrow canal. When God gives, he gives with an open hand. It's for that reason no doubt that Tirathnath's land is traversed by a rivulet, in their language a canal. Even in the summer the canal holds a thin flow of water. In consequence the surrounding land is fertile. In this space, where you can't get water without a well, this is a big resource. Between the high ground and the low ground, close by the canal, are a few myrobalan trees. From the shelter of these trees you can't see the other side. The tusker has broken the fence, the ferocious cactus fence at the end of the level land. Destroyed the peanut plants in a regular way. Daroga has vowed to kill it. Having taken a few random arrows the boar gets excited when he sees human beings. Chotti's lot run away when they hear his grunts. Hearing that he hadn't died with arrows the Daroga laughed and said, It's not a job for arrows. You'll have to kill it with a bullet. You can perhaps kill a bird or a hare with an arrow.

It hadn't been killed yet, the Daroga had no time. Tirathnath's mother was obstinately claiming that the animal was the 'Boar-Avatar' of Lord Vishnu. Now she is saying that, when it is killed, she will do penance at the Shiva temple in Varanasi and offer up the auspicious number of a hundred and eight leaves of the holy basil plant, in solid gold. Vishnu and Shiva—two high gods of Hinduism—are in fact one, says she.

After all this the Daroga appeared one day. Sana had remarked while working the lower field, Not a sight of t' bastard for days, yeah he'll come. Hey, t' way he'll take, he looks for roots and splits t' ground.

Chotti'd said, He comes lookin' for ya.

Why?

Ye shot an arrer at 'im and ran.

So big. I thought if I c'd kill, we'd eat a lotta meat.

So ye shot him in t' butt.

Hey he turned around. Ye didn' kill him either after that.

Daroga will git'm.

Daroga came to kill the boar.

He stood on the high ground, where the boar had broken a gap in the fence. A platform a bit away from the fence. A bit of cover on top. This is where you sit to watch out for and chase away the deer and pigs who come to loot the grain. The platform is poised on a few stilts. Chotti says, Ye're standin' behind it sir?

Daroga says, Pigs look one way as they walk. I'll hit him before he sees me. Ye leave now. Birju, ye stay.

Constable Birju holds a spear.

Chotti says, We'll stand below here sir, to watch t' hunt.

How many are you?

Six of us sir.

Have anything with you?

We have machetes, and t' weeding knife. We were workin'.

Don't talk at all.

No sir. Chotti too is very excited. He came into the low ground and they stood with their bodies pressed against the slope. Everyone's excited.

A grunting noise. Sana whispers, Comin'.

Chotti put his hand on his mouth.

Daroga had hunted before. In these areas there's still a lot of game. It's not possible to walk the paths in winter and not see a tiger from time to time. He's killed wild boar as well, but he's never killed a wounded boar. His aim is good too. He cocks his gun and stands ready. He couldn't think the boar would see him before it entered through the fence.

Foiling his calculations the boar enters, not through the open area, but, at great speed, through the fence behind him where the trees are sparse, and grows wilder with rage because the cactus thorns scratch him and draw blood. In fact he enters wild and Birju constable throws down his spear at the speed of lightning and jumps up on the platform and as soon as the Daroga turns around and shoots the boar, struck in the ribs, the boar falls on him. Electrified by his terrified cries Chotti jumps up on high ground. He's a hunter. The weapons of the hunt are bow and arrow, sometimes spear. But the hunt is in his blood. In hunting you need a quick wit just as much. The boar is splitting Daroga's left arm. Birju is high up on the platform. Chotti runs like an arrow, grabs Birju's spear. The boar gives out his bonechilling roar, Hara, hara, hara. The boar lets the Daroga go and turns to him. Chotti runs forward with the spear, plunges the spear diagonally under the boar's ear, and presses down with all his might, as if the boar is a mountain. Even fallen on his side he is getting up, up, up. Sana throws down a machete near his feet, they raise their machetes and come on. Chotti raises his machete. The tusks have raked his shin. A great hatred in his head. He starts hitting down with the machete, and then his companions do the same. The brave beast fights with great power, but at a certain point he has to die.

Daroga has to be carried to the station. A goods train has to be halted at the hospital in Daltonganj. There's no time to bring staff from Tohri thana. Tirathnath, Birju, and two coolies go with him, and the Daroga on the floor of the guard's compartment.

Chotti, you go too—says the station master.

No, it'll heal.

Chotti returns limping. Pahan comes with his herbal paste. Looking at the wound he says, T' bone's spared, it's not broke.

Chotti's foot is bandaged. Chotti says to the others, T' sonofabitch is lying dead, we'll have to cut'm up and eat'm, bring 'im.

It's a huge boar. The Mundas are almost overcome. Boar meat is shared out in the Ganjin, Dusad, Dhobi quarters, and in the coolie lines. Chotti keeps the two tusks. Says, If t' Daroga lives I'll give these to him. Wife, pickle t' meat. T' meat is ripe.

Ye're bathed in blood and thinkin' on pickles.

Hey, t' pain'll go away on its own if I eat a lotta meat and drink a lotta liquor.

Chotti's wound takes about a week to heal. Daroga's wounds take a month and a half. When he gets out of hospital he calls for Chotti. He's most pleased to receive the two tusks. He is most embarrassed to express gratitude to Chotti. And then he says, It's you who saved my life that day. I didn't expect him to come from that side.

Their devilry's more if they're hurt.

I'd've died.

Chotti laughs. Says, A very big boar.

Chotti! Can I . . . Daroga reaches into his pocket.

No sir. Won' take.

Won't take?

If I'd ha' fallen in his reach, and ye'da saved me I'd 've given ye aught?

Daroga laughs and says, I'd've taken if you had.

Chotti said, This is a lot. Ye're alive, that's a lot.

Daroga gets it said now, Join the archery games again. I lift the ban. And wait a bit. My wife, especially for your kids—I've returned alive, so there was a puja, yes—sent some sweets.

So many sweets sir?

That's not much!

Chotti ate the sweets after distributing to everyone.

His daughter was born just after this. Friday's child, named Sukhni.

Everyone is most pleased that the Daroga has lifted the ban on his use of the bow and arrow. This event also becomes a matter of his achievements and his supernatural quality, little by little. All is story in Chotti Munda's life, everything becomes a tale. Story and song. In the words of the song the boar becomes a moving mountain, and what is most thought-provoking, Chotti gets a new weapon.

> Ye picked a blade of grass
> Grass became spear
> Ye pierced t' boar
> He died right away
> And Daroga?
> He said, Go ye brave man,
> Join all games
> I was punished in this way
> Cos I banned yer play.

Chotti said to his wife, A blade o' grass turns inta spear, but if I don' plough Tirath Lala's field, I've nothin' ta eat.

Our lives pass just so. From gran and great-gran we heard legends, t' Mundas had this much and that much. But they had huts—an' f'r ploughin' an' huntin', t' forest. Ne'er did they say in storytellin' that Mundas had stone mansions. We didn' see any o' that. We saw that moneylender has a mansion, Munda lives in a sal leaf hut, ploughs t' moneylender's field. Wife changed t' subject as she nursed her girlbaby. She said, What's there in t' soil of Kurmi, dear?

Why?

Koel looked and said these very big peppers an' gourds grow there.

Soil fed with burnt-hut ash, with rottin' leaves of weed-jungle.

Keep Sukhni for a bit, Mungri will take t' goats, lemme feed her. There's no hope, y'know? Ye'll have to fetch rope.

I'll bring.

Sukhni swings in a hammock made by Chotti's hands. Pushing his baby's swing he says under his breath, Yer ears will hear songs about yer pa. Yer eyes will see yer pa livin' on three rupees daily wage and a snack, ploughin' Lala's field.

The daughter sleeps. Chotti thought of Kurmi. 'Kurmi' brings Dukhia's face to mind. That picture comes to mind. On the rim of the hilltops Pahan is moving like a moving picture with a few dogs. That wasn't the way to Tomaru. There are no paths in such intractable areas. He went down into the forest. Why did Pahan go into the forest surrounded by high hills, a forest from which there is no exit? To remain true to his self Dhani goes to Jejur, Dukhia goes to Police Station with the manager's head, and Pahan has to go into the forest? Chotti's firm belief, some day, if that forest is peeled and peeled back in a search, the skeletons of Pahan and the dogs will be found.

This very year, before Chotti had gone to any fair for archery games, four Munda youth came to him. They put down a hamper. In it were red potatoes, a gourd, coarse molasses and a lot of chickpea flour. They touched their foreheads to the ground and said, Bharat Munda sent us.

After so long?

We're much troubled with zamindar-landlord's cut on t' market.

Peace been made?

No peace will be as long as they live an' we live. We'll go under stone an' he under straw, and maybe there'll be peace.

How's Bharat?

No way he c'n leave t' village.

Why?

Every market day there's trouble over market cut.

Ye'll learn?

Yes.

When'll ye come?

Whene'er ye say.

Bharat's sent ya, I'll surely teach. But ye say there's trouble wit' market cut! If ya do somethin' I'll be blamed.

I'm Budha. Bharat's me uncle, ya. Can I say somethin'?

Say.

Ye'll teach as teacher. Dukhia didn' do't cos ye taught. T' manager heated him up with his pokin'.

True too.

E'en so t' thana folks see't as yer fault. Polis will allus blame Munda. I gave this Sugana a stick to chase cattle. He broke Kanu's head with' it. My fault? That brother-in-law of t' zamindar is our headsore. Whate'er happens will be his fault. Uncle says, Tell t' zamindar that.

Chotti realizes that with the passage of time the Mundas' way of thinking and talking is also changing. Budha's words are sharp, but their reason cannot be denied.

Still he said, T' polis torture us, so I bring it up.

Who wants trouble? But we caint tell ye what a cut he takes. If he takes ever'thin' that's good, what'll we sell, what eat?

What kinda man is t' zamindar?

Like a zamindar. He has a swollen foot, caint walk. Doesn' buy shoes, has 'em made. A big shoe on one foot, a small un on th' other.

Another young man seems the quiet type. He said, T' zamindar is in his fourth marriage. He's sent away th' other three. He lives in garden house wit' his lady. Brother-in-law oversees t' land. Wife's brother, and that swells his head.

Budha said, And what a zamindar! E'en now no Munda must have a shirt, shoes on feet, umbrella on head, eat off metal plates. If he finds fault in one, he fines t' whole village.

Gaya says, What else, ye know all. Our heart's torn with givin' bond labour. And fines for ever'thin'. That brother-in-law knows Mundari, but speaks Hindi. So tart, that we don' understan'.

In conclusion Budha says, What's to fear? T' Mundas of Kurmi have shown t' way. If it's that bad we'll go off to t' Mission?

Where's there a Mission there?

If not there, there's in Dhai? New Mission? T' Mission is grabbin' land. They'll settle us as soon as they get it.

Chotti says, come along, I'll teach. But t' fewer know t' better. Word gets around and Daroga thinks I'm causin' fight, Diku-style.

Budha said Sukha's bunch have done a bad thing. Since they split after borrowing, these people ask us non-stop, Wanna borrow? Ye'll take yer living wages and run off. T' Mundas of Kurmi village took off, didn' they?

Chotti said, Yes it was a bad thing. But t' Munda people don' know thievery, cheatery, don' do that stuff. They go and 'fess up at thana e'en when they kill. If they cheat now, it's learnt from t' Diku.

Ain't that t' truth.

Ye take ten bitsa paddy and ye caint repay in ten lives.

Budha says, They cheat cos we don' know book-learnin'. T' Mission teaches book-learnin' too.

They do, but there's never any benefit for t' village-Munda from t' Mission-Mundas, Budha. T' way we are, where we are, let's remain jes there.

This too is true.

Why just us? Dusad-Ganju in village also in t' same boat.

Let's go today.

Budha's words make Chotti melancholy. He can't imagine how long it will go on this way. Budha's words are not untrue. It would've been good to see Bharat. Pahan hears all and says, Think on another village later on. Think on yerselves.

What s'd I think?

How long more s'll I live? Who'll be t' new pahan?

Whomever ye make?

I have no male chile.

Yer brother has no boys?

Nope. These wives breed nothin' but girl chillun.

Ye'll live still.

Pahan smiles. Says, How old are ye?

From me t' Gormen's year begins.

Heard th' other day that this year is number thirty-eight. Then ye are thirty-eight years. At yer birth time I was surely two-score? Even me granddaughter is married. How much is that? Call Sana.

Sana Munda says, In two years ye'll be four-score!

Pahan says triumphantly, Then? Still live?

What d'ye ask me to do?

Will ye take me to Bhurkunda?

What's there?

Me uncle's sons. There may be someone 'mong them.

I'll tell ya, I give ya me word. Me Sukhni is a kid. Giv' her in marriage. Let me give ya some molasses, turmeric, and betel root fer t' rite, and then I'll take ya.

How much longer s'll I have to live, Chotti?

Sana says, At least ten, at least five.

Pahan calmly sat down to put up a fence around the aubergine plot in the yard. Sana says, How well yer hands do move, ye'll die after ye see our funeral, our Shonshan-Buru.

Chotti goes home and sees that Bharat's come. Telling Harmu and Somra the story of Chotti's friendship with Gormen with much skill.

I's thinkin' jes on ye, Bharat.

I knew it in me mind, then.

So ye came?

So. We're so proud of ye, but no difference 'tween this home and me home, I see. One Munda and t'other Munda has t' same home.

There's diff'rence.

Where?

We're that poor, plough t' boss's land, eat rice if we get it, otherwise boiled cornmeal. But ye, fools, make songs about me.

Let that go mate. That's not f'r ye to grab. We grab that.

Good.

That's how we're alive Chotti. Least we can boast of ya. Now there's nothin' for our pride.

No end to Munda's sorrow.

Chotti, where did this market cut spring from?

Diku import. Diku brings, Gormen supports. We know Diku-Gormen's father'n son. We ne'er saw Mundas live in Munda-property village and Oraons in Oraon-owned village, and our chillun won' either.

May they see it.

Where's there a spot mate, wit' no market cut, no bond slavery, no debt?

Bastards call for bondwork all t' time. Okay, we give. But if we caint sell grain from our fields, greens from our yard, hens an' goats reared at home, then how to stay alive? A belly must eat a bit.

They don' understan'.

Now the boys are mad. They say, Ye stay wit' yer Munda lives. Kurmi Mundas've shown t' way. We'll go and become Mission Mundas. No zamindar's brother-in-law can chase off a Mission Munda.

Fine. But is this a way Bharat? Today manager, tomorra zamindar's brother-in-law'll be on our tail, and we'll walk into t' Mission?

So what? Bharat says in the calmest voice, Think on't. It's hard to get to t' Mission, an' no joy once ye're there. No one takes a Munda to look upon his face. Some profit on't somewhere. It's fer that that king, zamindar, and Diku put up wit' Munda. T' Mission sahib will also raise profit in some way or other. But he won' take this market cut, won' ask for bonded work, won' say hard words and beat us up f'r any and ever'thin'.

Chotti smiles bleakly and says, Mission's profit comes as soon as ye are Christians.

What's puja like there?

Gormen's god, and Jesu's puja—and worship. Heard so, dunno.

Who knows! Chotti?

A lot of Mundas and Oraons went to Mission after all.

Many went.

They praise t' Gormen's god?

Sure.

But we praise Haramdeo.

Yeah.

So that brings worry.

What worry?

P'raps our Haramdeo's also old, seein' all this railway, motor-car, and pichers we hear of in town—that move, that talk—all this.

That's why he's lettin' his chillun go here and there. Thinkin' go kids go, go to tea garden, go to Mission, plough another's field, go where ye'll live. Otherwise these things cannot happen.

Bharat, will ye go ta Mission too, then?

I tell ya true brother, I dunno yet. Who wants ta leave village? A well-known land? So bondwork, so market cut, I'da stayed bearin' all, if day and night that brother-in-law of t' zamindar didn' hassle us so. Bastard hunts with dogs. Like he's Gormen already.

Then?

But yes. I dunno what ta do so I came ta say, teach t' boys arrer-play. Long as we're here we'll play arrer at t'fair. Whoe'er wins, we can hev fun with' our Munda neighbours, eatin' meat drinkin' liquor. Brother, who knows what tomorra brings?

It hurts in me chest Bharat. T' more Mundas go, an arrer goes through me heart.

No news of Kurmi Pahan?

No.

Now t' manager understands. No forcin'.

If they'd brought him before!

Hey when Diku does somethin' good, know he's scared. Tenants leave, say all at Mission, goes ta Gormen's ear, so they bring good manager.

Chotti's wife gives a pitcher of molasses-water to Bharat. Bharat drinks and says, Saved me life, Munda-wife. A long way ta go, not a little way, eh? Yes Chotti, that Budha's sharp. He learns what he learns from ya, and then teaches t'boys. So much dance, so much song in their groups, all forgotten. Now just bow and arrer.

Chotti's wife speaks up loud and clear, If them boys do t' work of ten Dukhias, me man's name mustn' come up by that, ya.

Munda doesn' raise t' name, it's Diku.

When Bharat leaves Chotti says, Why? All that pride in yer man, it's gone? Ye laugh fit to die when ye hear songs 'bout yer man?

No no, this stuff's no' good.

What he said. That Budha has some plan.

That I too know. Let it be.

What sorta thing is that?

What stuff?

If they make trouble, let 'em do it by their own wit, if not, that too on their own. Budha's aim is good anyway.

Good aim! Wait'n see what he's up to.

T' Mundas' mood is changin'. When our kids grow up, who knows what words they'll say, what deeds they' do.

Let's see! But for fear of ye, or what, t' Lala is bit softer. Doesn't carp so no more.

Don' be too sure love. Who knows when he spoils again.

There are few fairs close together before Tirathnath spoils. Chotti couldn't attend all. Sitting in his village he gets the news that Budha's group won prizes at quite a few fairs. Bharat went to two. Came first at both. The result wasn't good for him. Sana brought the news. He shook his head and said, I dunno, I didn' see wit' me own eyes. Me Dad was a young man then.

When're ye speakin' of?

Lord Birsa's fight.

To speak of that 'bout Bharat.

I'm not talkin' like a fool.

Sana, I see forever that yer bring in another thing to speak of one thing and weave a tale. Speak of root ta speak of fruit.

From root t' tree, from tree t' fruit.

So are ye in root or climbin' tree?

Was in t'root, now talkin' of tree. So in that fight t' Mundas knew, t' kingdom of god's come. They gave up sowin' and reapin', they et up all t' grain of t' field, they wore new clothes and walked about with a new soul.

What'rye sayin'? Bharat's lads do t' same?

Now I've come to fruit. Bharat's tellin' all, I cain't think what'll come tomorra boy. When I git money piercin' arrers at fair, I eat'n drink. What's t' use plowin' field, t'harvest goes ta pay yer debt. What's t'use sowin' an' reapin', it'll go for market cut?

He's lost his head?

Wit' this t' zamindar's brother-in-law is doin' two-an'-two makes four.

How?

Says, These bastards hev some plan. Kurmi Mundas borrowed a lot, et well an' took off. P'raps these bastards will take off.

He tol' us in a way that they'll take off. But Munda's stupid. They do their stuff openly, and t' Diku comes ta know.

Where'll they go?

Chotti sighed and said, Kurmi village's shown t'way. P'raps they're thinkin' on goin' ta Mission. And how ta blame them! They all go ta Mission wit' t' terror of Diku. Otherwise tea garden. Otherwise colliery. Somewhere in Bengal land many Mundas have gone off for field hand jobs.

Sana says, Where'er they go, Diku terror, Gormen terror has gone wit' them, no? When terror doesn' leave ya when ye leave yer homelan', then best stay home. No Chotti, what d'ye say?

Me mind says so. But this too I think, it's hard to swallow so many kicks mate. Sometimes ya hate it all, and t' Munda does somethin' violent. Else Manager Siyaram would've had his head on his shoulders, Dukhia woulda stayed home, Sukha and all t'others would've stayed in village. Think how much they must've hated that Sukha and t'others borrowed, gave thumbprint, and then ran off? This Diku can do, but Munda?

Violent thinkin' comes ta mind. But our village is all mixed kinds. We are minority, so I have no confidence. I'm scared of polis.

That too we must think. Violent act may be mine, but terror? Who do they spare? Didn' they fine t' village on me father's account?

Every act needs a push. After building the wax-house of epic fame the flint still had to be struck. It was the zamindar's brother-in-law who pushed Bharat Munda and his group. The landlord's Agent was elderly and wise. A Brahman. So the non-Brahman zamindar gave him some respect. The Agent himself performed the usual exploitations, but not to excess. At least as long as his word was kept, as long as the work followed his orders, the Mundas had not thought of leaving in a group. They gave bonded labour, but had time to plough their own fields. His rule regarding market cuts was different.

In this region the traditional zamindars and kings had this rule in force regarding market cuts—that the Master's manager sat in the marketplace on market day. The adivasis place some stuff in front of him and then sit in the market to sell. If someone had said, I've come to sell two hens, can't give anything, even that was accepted. This is because old-fashioned people knew that adivasis are hardly ever dishonest. By the old custom, the zamindar who is the landlord of Bharat's village sent a gift of a sheep and rice to Pahan's house on the big adivasi feastdays, for the property had mostly adivasi tenants, and the property was managed by milking them in various ways. Market cuts worked by this rule in the area. Since this was the way it was the tenants accepted it. The Agent was devoted to the zamindar. A local inhabitant. He had a certain familiarity with those he had to deal with, with Bharat and his cohorts. The advantage for Bharat was that the Agent was afraid of violence and of riots. As long as his word was good, the zamindar toured the area from time to time.

After the fourth marriage, there's no end to the Agent's mis-fortunes. The zamindar is in a separate establishment with his bride. He has given more or less every right to his brother-in-law. Childless after three marriages and advanced in age. Now he too had accepted that he is not fated to produce offspring. So his heir will undoubtedly be his brother-in-law. The zamindar has almost decided to adopt his son. The three older wives are pressing the Agent to petition the government to arrange for their upkeep. Bharat and his followers came to the Agent first in the matter of the market cut. The Agent was seriously insulted when he went to speak of this to the zamindar. The brother-in-law continues to pursue his activities, he's still at it. The Agent understands that there's trouble in the making.

In the middle of this Bharat's crowd starts a non-cooperation movement regarding the market cut.

The Agent said, What's this I hear Bharat? That ye don't come to market anymore. That ye eat yer own produce?

We usen't to, we sold.

So why aren't ye still?

What's to sell? Sir Brother-in-law rides a red horse an' takes t' good stuff. We gave a cut to manager an' then sat to sell. Give that cut, give ta Sir Brother-in-law, he has diff'ren' manager, give ta him, what's left to sell?

The market will fail.

D'ye want ta keep t' market goin'? What we git from market raises yer taxes. So thas what I tell ye sir, how many times did I tell ya. So ye say, ye have no rights to do nothin' no more. Where s'll we go?

The Agent saw great disaster for the zamindar's property in his mind's eye. He sensed which way events were leading. He said, Bharat, this guy has a foul temper.

We sell greens all our lives, we dunno how it tastes. How it hurts us to eat our goods for sale, that ye don' understan' sir.

Sir Brother-in-law has a foul temper. He'll make terror. Go to market.

When has he not raised terror?

The Agent understood, since Bharat and his people seemed reckless, they must have taken a decision. He said, Bharat! Ye see me all yer life, I know ya.

Yes sir.

Tell me the truth son, will ya take off to Mission?

Dunno sir. But this we know, we sent many a petition, sores on our footsoles from walkin' and walkin' to th' office, but no one heard a word from us poor folks.

The Agent got the answer to his question from the very way Bharat spoke. Bharat said further, Our homes, our bit o' land, all tied up in bond labour. In land held by ten generations of livin', no Munda has anythin' to call his own.

If you repay your debts, will everything be yours, son?

Sir, how much respect we give ya. What's this ye say? Bharat lamented in sorrow and despair, Who knows mor'n ye do, that Mundas' debt isn' repaid? It's not paddy-wheat-corn that we take for two bits, three bits, and four, it's as if we took gold. Lest why's our debt not repaid? What's t' price of all t' paddy an' corn that all t' Mundas take?

Bharat left. The Agent now becomes the zamindar's agent. Went to the zamindar on his pony, eight miles distance. Said to the zamindar, A lot to tell. You have to listen to this.

What's this? Why, say it to Lalmohan.

You can't let the fox do the tiger's work. The danger is to your forefathers' property, not to his. Am I bothering you for nothing?

What's the matter?

The Agent said everything openly. He said, If they leave it's a particular disaster for us. The loss is ours. They'll surely leave.

The king smiled a contemptuous smile. Tenants leave, new tenants will come.

Sir if these tenants had been mischievous troublemakers, then we'd have been able to talk to the Magistrate. Bharat and his people have never made trouble. What will you say if the magistrate asks? He will know.

That's true.

The magistrate's not pleased with the zamindars, sir.

So what can I do?

Reason with Sir Brother-in-law. If the market stops because of his terrorizing them there'll be rumours about you in the vicinity. As it is there's a lot of talk.

What talk?

What's the use listening to that sir?

What're you asking me to do?

Come to the town once. Listen to them and give judgement.

I'll go.

But right after the Agent comes the brother-in-law. Lalmohan Chowdhury. He explains everything to the zamindar. There is no truth behind the Agent's words. The Agent is provoking the Mundas out of envy at the loss of influence. There's no need for the zamindar to visit. Lalmohan Chowdhury will go himself the next day and straighten out every miscreant.

Do that. But don't beat 'em up. Then the magistrate will repossess the property, and redistribute it. This is being done.

It's the fox that's king in the forest village. Brother-in-law said, What's to fear? I'll scare 'em with guns and bring 'em to market.

Don't shoot.

No no.

But people don't shoot all the time. If a stupid villain is intoxicated it is the gun that provokes him and has some fun. If a gun follows such a person's hands, oddball things happen, and the consequences are oddball as well.

Bharat and his group didn't want to come, it is the Agent who made them agree after a lot of talk. If the master knows everything directly there will no doubt be a solution. The zamindar has given his word. The Mundas are gathered in front of the office. The Agent is there as well. Waiting, waiting. Suddenly Lalmohan Chowdhury enters the scene of action and his men start beating the Mundas right and left with their truncheons. Budha pulls hard and a man falls, Lalmohan's horse throws him, scared by the Mundas' yells. The Agent keeps screaming, Halt, halt, don't kill. But Lalmohan is all the more scared and he grabs his gun. As a consequence, a bullet hits the Agent in the ribs. Great sin, great sin, a Brahman murdered, the men shout and run off. This powerful Agent has a hardy heart. Lalmohan runs off as well. The Agent says to Bharat, Take me to the thana, and take the gun as well. I am dying for your sake. The Agent believes the words that he utters and he realizes that if he has to die by the hand of a low-caste man, the duty of the Brahman is to give as much trouble as possible before death.

Bharat's group act as ordered. Even at the Police Station the Agent believes he is dying. Weighing the Mundas and Sir Brother-in-law in the balance, he wishes to shaft the latter and he issues a report that screws Sir Brother-in-law. He threatens Daroga with a Brahman's curse and asks him to do his duty. Then the

Daroga himself puts him on a train and takes him to hospital in the county seat. There too, to police officers in higher positions, the Agent says the same thing. He thinks of himself as following the faith to the letter. He says, Yudhisthira, the great epic King, did not go to heaven without his dog. If I betray the Mundas I won't have peace even in heaven. Now I've said everything. The British government is a just king. Now let there be a good arrangement.

Even the police officers are troubled by such ill-treatment of a Brahman. The whole thing goes a long way. Because Sir Brother-in-law is arrested. The zamindar tries to escape for fear of a police investigation and cannot go underground fast on account of his swollen foot. The Mundas are subjected to heavy interrogation and the investigating police eat heavily at the zamindar's expense. Seizing the moment the three queens say to the police officers by way of the Agent's son that the Agent was a true gentleman. The zamindar is in the toils of an ogress. After the property passed into the hands of the brother-in-law the three queens have no food on their plate. He is oppressing the Mundas in a major way. The Agent was a well-wisher of the zamindar. So Lalmohan always had the desire to murder him.

The wheels of the law keep moving. Sir Brother-in-law is almost in jail, the zamindar's imbecility is almost proven, when the Agent ruins the case. He survives the operation. Gradually his reason returns. The zamindar himself comes to him weeping and the fourth Mrs. zamindar takes off her necklace of golden guineas and asks for her brother's life. When he gives evidence the Agent tries to put the blame on Bharat and company and to prove the brother-in-law innocent. The lawyer for the government scolds, You've been bribed.

The Agent gets nervous and affirms his guilt and tangles himself in complexities. The verdict is given. The Brother-in-law goes to jail. The zamindar receives a warning. The news comes this way to Bharat and his friends—the Agent has screwed them royally. He's said that it was they who started the violence. The police will plough them under.

Bharat's group is obliged to follow the example of Sukha's group. At the time of departure Sukha says, Leave now, I'll leave later.

That was the time to leave. Everyone is on the road to the Dhai Mission. They sell cattle, goats, water-buffalo at market after market on the way. Budha, Gaya and two other Mundas fire their settlement as they leave. They throw burning brands on the thatch of the office building and in the Agent's house. Bharat and his group had gone ahead by two days' walk. Gaya, Budha and all were in hiding. So everyone wonders, who lit such fires two days after the Mundas left. The event is hailed as supernatural. The Agent returned home also thinks this must be divine vengeance or witchcraft. The verdict of the government shouldn't have made the Mundas fly?

The thana's Daroga sees huge heaps of ash. He says, Making a Brahman's blood flow, the earth wouldn't bear it. Such a fire did burn.

Sounds good. But then why did the Agent's house burn? The Agent's wife said, You went to accuse them in the law courts, and for that anger they've shot an arrow and burnt the house.

Who's seen them shoot arrows?

Not that sort of arrow. They've left. The settlement is cleared out. Suddenly there was fire. It's shooting arrows of that kind. And why not? I heard Bharat's nephew went to learn archery from Chotti Munda. Chotti is a high shaman.

The Agent resigns and splits, relying on the funds he had transferred to Ramgarh.

The government's report: 'Mundas are leaving their homeland. Mostly they're going to the Mission. The responsibility lies with the imbecile zamindar, monstrously greedy moneylender and other factors. It is said that these people are excitable. But at the Mission their conduct is most peaceful and cooperative. As for agriculture, attractive Christian villages will soon develop and other Mundas will be drawn to them. Of course villages will be settled only as long as other Mundas can be attracted. Otherwise the Mission cannot have the settlement of villages as its goal. The Government's opinion on this is . . .'

At the Karam feast fair the Munda pahan of Jhujhar village tells Chotti that Chotti Munda has empowered the community by shooting arrows on behalf of Bharat Munda and his group who had left their home, setting fire to their village and the landlord's office—and thus embarrassing the Dikus some. The lying Agent is gone, that Sir Brother-in-law is rotting in je-hell, that too is a gain of sorts.

Everything is story in Chotti Munda's life. Hearing this from the Jhujhar pahan Chotti took a bit of liquor in his jar, took onion and cayenne in his hand. Then squatting and drinking he thought, What is this? Whatever good the Mundas do, why does the credit come to him? What sort of Munda is he? Is he the Mundas' wish-fulfillment? How? He's certainly not as daring as they are? All of them—Dhani, Dukhia, Sukha's group, Pahan, Bharat's group—have done something desperate in order to remain true to themselves. Chotti has done nothing. Then why this reverence? He thought, behind this there is a claim. Let Chotti do something that will make the blood flow in the dead lives of the Mundas. But what is that task? Can that task come about in a day? But the Mundas are changing as well. Sukha's group went to the Mission, Bharat's group too. But in Budha's arson the tactic of making the enemy visible comes clearer.

Chotti didn't know that in a few years he would have to assume leadership of a significant event.

VIII

A FEW YEARS PASSED with the ease of the waters flowing in the bosom of the Chotti river. The August movement did not even touch the life of Chotti's community. It was as if that was the Dikus' struggle for liberation. Dikus never thought of the adivasis as Indian. They did not draw them into the liberation struggle. In war and Independence the life of Chotti and his cohorts remained unchanged. They stand at a distance and watch it all. Harmu and Somchar grow up. Harmu marries the village girl Koeli. Pahan dies. Before he dies, he brings a distant relative and makes him Pahan. The special advantage of the new pahan is that, as a result of living close to a Christian Munda village, he too has learned to read and write Hindi. Working for certain grain wholesalers he has also learnt to reckon.

Koeli is the daughter of Donka Munda of this village. Donka has nothing, not a thing. He said, Boy and girl have gi'en their hearts, so a wedding. Otherwise, what good works have I done that I'll be Chotti Munda's in-law? And I a bond-labourer. Nothin' means I ha' nothin'. How ta feed me kin?

Chotti says, How does a body feed kin?

Can if ya help.

But I give a feast too, no?

Harmu's mother says, Times ha' changed. Town ways. That girl walks wit' her hair down I hear. I'll not gie her me son.

Wife, our words won' hold.

Why?

Lookit that straight tree in t' yard. When I swung in t'swing tied to its branch, it was young then. Now t' tree's growin' old. Pahan says me years is two score eight. Silver in yer hair, in me hair. Our lives are leanin' west now, Wife. Harmu's life is new.

He shoots a big deal at fairs, wins a big deal, so he's full of it. And ye! Say nothin' to t' boys.

There's no good sayin' a thing.

Not a good girl.

Harmu'll know.

And where's their hut?

I'll ask Lala for t' bit o' land by t' woods.

He'll give?

It's lyin' waste.

He'll give it t' Harmu?

They're two brothers. Koel has his Etwa, let 'em do what they can wit' their land? Harmu mus' raise a roof.

What's tha'? Ye didn' send yer brother away, and yer son—

Koel's wife was yer same age. This is a growin' girl, their thinkin's diff'ren. Let 'em think their own thoughts.

Hearing all, Harmu asks, Ye'll send us away? Why? S'll I live if I'm not close to Aba? Me power's his power.

Harmu raised a hut right behind theirs. Koel said, This is good. Let me Etwa an' yer Somchar go a bit far. Harmu's th' oldest boy. How kin it be that he's not close by?

Mungri sighs at this. She too loves Harmu. Harmu's Ma loves her son in turn. But she didn't like her husband's words.

Tirathnath says, Ye want land, take it.

By what arrangement?

Ye say.

No taxes fer three years.

And then?

Then we'll gie.

Why taxes? Give half the crop.

Put it in writin'.

So ye've learnt to write as well?

Don' we have our Pahan?

Tirathnath smiled sweetly. This is a matter between people who've known each other forever, he said. Who's that Pahan? An outsider. A written agreement with ye? Are ye goin' to give bonded labour, that I'll take yer thumbprint?

No, won' give bond labour. What s'll I tell ye? Debt's not repaid e'en if ye give labour fer many lives.

Chotti! Even true words spoken by the near and dear make yer chest hurt. Yeah, I take bonded labour. But I n'er forced ya. Y' only saw t' bonded work. An don' I give maize, an' rice, an' wheat at famine, at drought?

D'ye gie with' open hand? Don' we gie a thumbprint?

How c'n ye say such a thing? Ye don't give a thumbprint, me son.

That's how far the conversation goes. The case of the three-year tax-free land goes a long way, however. Before that the issue of bonded labour becomes a mountain from a molehill. After Independence.

In 1950 there's a drought. An ancient and familiar regional curse. What has never happened in a drought occurs this time. The waters of Chotti become invisible as well. Everywhere there is a lamentation for water. People stand at the station. They take water from the engine. They'll cool it and drink. All five wells in the village dry up. Processions by the station well and Tirathnath's well. Need water.

Finally Chotti says, S'll we parch to death? Forefathers taught a way.

Let's take t' way.

What way'll ye take? asks Harmu.

Come I'll show ye.

Sana says, Yeah right! didn' think on't before?

They walk along the Chotti riverbed. Where the river flows between two steep banks, the water is shaded because the vegetation from the banks leans down. Big stones on the river. And there's water caught among the stones.

Here I shot ducks on t' wing with t' White guy, says Chotti. Sana says, Here our womenfolk came to bathe on drought days. When there's water nowhere, there's here. There's always some water here.

Ye've forgotten what holds it?

What've I forgot, Chotti?

Nah, t' Mundas allus forgit their own. Chotti sighs and says, Ya
don' recall t' pahan. He came here on drought days and med us
dig deep in t' river's breast. We put baby sal trees as props so sand
couldn't fill up t' holes. I've dug so thrice in me life. Look, there's
water in't still.

Then?

So let's dig.

Washerwoman Motia is now a dithering oldie. She'd come to
see the fun. Now Motia says, Where s'll we go?

It's not my river. Call t' Dusads and t' washerfolk Motia.

Chhagan and Parosh had also come. They said, We're here.

Such a shady bank half a mile long. Ye dig holes too. Let me tell
ya somethin'. Ye hear.

Say't Chotti.

Chotti stood leaning on stone. A long time ago, ye remember?
he said. Daroga didn' call famine, I went to Gormen?

We remember. Yer kid, our kids, what do they know how much
work their fathers did when t'village was in trouble.

Gormen didn' come with aid.

No, White mission and Hindu mission came.

Who'll come here to see how we suffer. Yet we're human. We
suffer t' same thirst as ye.

There's no diffr'nce 'tween ye and we.

So I say, T' village's grown. More trains come 'n' go. T' marketeers come. A Punjabi's come to make bricks. Marwaris come from
Calcutta to see if there's coal. Howdja figure it?

Figure it?

Mebbe more ways to earn.

Mebbe.

Unless they bring outside labour.

Unless they do that.

But we must remember, we're alone for ourselves. And this too,
that we watch out f'r our own trouble.

Now Tirathnath gie's water.

We know'm. When there's more drought he'll say, Me sons!
River Ganga doesn' flow through me well. The water's dried up. I
caint give to all, but only to my bonded labour!

Yeah, that's what he says.

We won' let him say't this year. There's water below t' river. Let's dig holes, if all take shovels we'll have ten holes. No water problems then. Now it's t' second month—Jeth. I pulled wild grass, wet soil at t'roots. There'll be rain in Asharh, t' very next month. Fo' sure. When that's not t'be, ye get dusty soil at t'grass-roots.

When s'll we come?

It's t' moon phase. At dusk tigers an' boars drink water. Come after dusk? Then there's no worry.

Motia says, The girls'll come too. You'll shovel sand, we'll throw it far. They'll drink too, why drink yer hard work?

Harmu says, But Lala has seven wells, wit' water in 'em.

Why no water in our well in the village?

Cos t' water in t' river underground is low.

But Lala's wells have water.

T' river flows through his land, no? There's water there.

Lala says, good works, good works, so if he digs a well and gives us water it'll be good works. No? But he won't give.

If he gave ye'll know he has some bad plan. When does t'tiger come and kiss ya? When he wants ta break yer neck.

This tiger broke our neck long ago, says Chhagan.

Break it more if he can. Chotti sighed. Said, But ye are yer village council chief.

Only in name, hey! Dontcha see their ways? Gormen has crippled t' village councils. In th' old days we lived in deepset villages, Gormen never came to see what we did or didn' do. If there was a theft, e'en with neighbours' quarrels each one said yes to t' council's verdict. Deepset villages! Mebbe fifteen miles distant from t' police station. We all gave labour if a well was dug, and all gave labour if a road was cut. No one objected. But slowly t' village warn't deepset no more. Slowly Gormen took away t' power of t' council. So yeah Chotti we have a council, and I am its chief. However!

However what?

Today my power is to settle marriage-birth-and-death matters. To settle neighbourly disputes. Still we live well here. If there's a law court, folks sue even f'r neighbours' fights.

Motia smiles toothlessly and says, They even sue over who eats t' guava, yeah! I know me boys.

Chotti says, And why not? T' lawyer wants to make lawsuits. He puts food in his belly if there's a case.

And what were ye sayin'? asks Chhagan.

Yes. Serious stuff. So Chhagan! Our lot's t' same as y'alls. The old days wit' real Munda villages r'gone. And all t'pahan's power, gone. He too just shows how to run t' feasts, how to settle neighbours' quarrels. There's one diff'rence. Ye have caste stuff. To t' Lala, to t' Brahman, ye're low caste. To ye, Motia is low caste. We have no caste diff'rence. And I bring it up, cos t' village is now all mixed. Ye and us dies together in famine, drought and bonded work. Lala wants to decide. But if need be ye and us go together, I say.

We walk together, Chotti.

No Chhagan, for me father's sake Sukha Munda's group didn' go to work in t' fields. At t' time of t' famine petition? Yeah. Then all one.

I know Chotti. But see this too, that we give ya respect. There's not a bow and arrow play where we ain't happy if ye win.

Good. I said all this now, cos why, I fear t' drought, now what if Tirathnath raises some trouble from somewhere.

Harmu says, Aba?

Yeah?

Dig hole from today?

Yes boy.

The hole digging is like a joint festival for the Mundas and for Chhagan's crowd. The men dug up the sand, and put in planks with no gap in-between on the walls of the pit. The women threw the sand at a distance, on the bank. Gradually they dug ten pits. The water came up. They got the water right there. Don' dirty this water with dirty clothes or baths, said Chotti. Precious water.

Tirathnath says, What's up? You don't come for water?

No one spoke of the pits. They said, There's still water in the river, so we don' come.

Whyja come before?

Who knew we'd get water if we went upstream?

So good. The bonded labourers go too?

Yes lord.

Tirathnath too has to gather information. He laughed and said, Chotti is lord. You cut the breast of the river at his word.

Sana said, As ye say.

You've done well. But look boys, if the river dries up don't come to my well and make trouble.

Motia smiled a nasty smile and said, Sure we'll come to steal water. What did your papa say? There's no harm in stealing water?

Hey, hey Motia! Don't touch the well and ruin the water. I'll give water. My people will pull the water up.

Perhaps there would have been trouble if they'd taken water from Tirathnath's well. When Chotti's people and Chhagan's people took water, this was a screw that Tirathnath had on them. If one is a longtime despot in a forest area many habits enter one's nature. The servants used to keep them waiting for water and bathe cattle and water-buffalo by the well. Tirathnath used to like watching that. Chotti deprived him of that pleasure. It was as if a thorn pierced his mind. In the month of Ashadh the rains came, a tumultuous downpour. In a week, water in the wells, rivers and streams brimming, green grass in red soil and the vegetables transformed.

Now the peasants and the field hands start work in the field. There was this delay in sowing paddy seed, so what? Sowing paddy is a delightful phenomenon. Chotti's group and Chhagan's group are ecstatic as they do it. 'This paddy will enter the moneylender's barn'; these words escape all mental discipline and run off like naughty ragamuffins jumping into water.

Chotti and Chhagan went to Tirathnath. Tirathnath had not looked upon their pit digging with pleasure. For a long time this bother had ceased. The two groups had come together in the long-ago time of famine. That was a most unnatural thing. Then many trouble-free years passed. It is certainly a problem if Chotti's group and Chhagan's people work together. Tirathnath feels besieged by it. It's necessary to keep them apart. Now came the chance. Because Chotti and Chhagan wanted to borrow for meals at work. Since Chotti doesn't give bonded labour, if he takes a pound of maize two pounds are cut from his share. This is a longstanding arrangement. The majority of Chhagan's group receives the price of paddy and maize as loan. In other words, they take paddy or millet or maize. The price of these food grains is written in the book. That money amount rises in the usual way. The bonded labourers give labour, and from time to time they get some food or money. If they make a lot of trouble. Each one's reckoning is sufficiently complex. But Tirathnath says that it is due to infinite compassion that he does not repossess their huts and the little land that they have leased.

He can do so at will. In a law-abiding way. No one can do anything if he does so.

About food for work Tirathnath says, Ye'll get it of course. Come tomorrow morning. I'll give you then.

The next day Chotti went on a useless task. His cow had calved by a bush. He went to take them back up to the cowshed. He sent Harmu with the Mundas to borrow the food allowance.

Somchar and Etwa came an hour later.

Ye come.

Why?

Trouble's broken out.

'Bout what?

Come along, we'll say on t' way.

On the way Somchar says, Big Brother has got all t' Mundas together and sat down in th' office building.

What's up, tell me that?

Remember t' Mundas of Kurmi village who borrowed food and ran away? Lala hasn't forgotten, Aba. He says, Harmu! With y'all a different reck'nin'. I'll give to ye. And I'll give Chhagan's bunch. So Brother asks, and t'other Mundas? Then Lala says, First I check t' figures, then I give. So Brother says, Why? Then Lala says, Ye can be sonsabitches like t' Kurmi Mundas.

He said that? Said 'sonsabitches'?

Said. Then Brother said, Ye're givin' loans so long, what Munda's been a sonofabitch to ya? T' Lala says, Hasn't, but how long to change? Then Brother got all worked up. So Lala says, I gave to ye. So Brother says, We alone have bellies, no one else? Then Lala says, No word with ye, call yer pa. Ye're lads of these times. Ye don't understand our words.

Chotti was reminded of the crossfire of words between his dad and Tirathnath's dad. Its consequence Bisra's suicide.

Chotti says, Let's go see. What's Chhagan's people doin'?

They're sittin' down. Saying, We're at one with Chotti's folks.

Chotti sees that everyone is sitting in the yard in front of the office. As soon as he sees Chotti, Chhagan says, Make peace Chotti, we'll die of hunger without food loan.

Chotti entered. Harmu followed.

Chotti, yer son spoke rough to me with his eyes hard. And so I said to call you. Yer pahan, their village council chief, they all listen to ya. I understand what ye say.

Chotti was quiet for a bit. Then said, What shall I say Lord? Yer dad and me dad had hard words.

Why bring that up?

Chotti said, and said quite loudly, That made me dad put a noose around his neck. He who takes a noose has a peaceless ghost. That ghost roams with his hair spread in th' evil wind. I gave money, I gave clothes to bring peace to dad's ghost, and only then could I have a service.

If you'll bring up old things, I have to do a lot of penance and sacrifice for my dad as well, what's the good of talkin' about that?

Lord! After all this while those are t' words that come back? We die of shame wit' what t' Kurmi Mundas did. But how much pain pushed a Munda to act so? Hev ye reflected upon all that?

Did I not want to give you folks?

Everyone has come forward. After a long, long time Chotti has come up front again. Talking in a loud voice.

Chotti said without turning his head, Listen to this, all of ya. I knew all along that ye'd separate us from Chhagan and his people. Now I see that ye separate Munda from Munda.

How have I separated?

Chotti gives a pain-wracked smile and says, I am that Chotti Munda lord. Never done a wrong thing. Never did a wrong. Today in hard times I take loan, and those Mundas will die of hunger? No.

You're threatening me?

No lord. So much land, so much money ye have, Daroga obeys ye so, can I threaten yerself?

What d'ye say then?

Chotti says in great rage, Ye s'd take back that 'sonuvabitch' word. We've done nothin' sonuvabitch. We won' take loan with this bad name. Chhagan!

Say Chotti.

Ye want to take a loan, tek it.

Chotti, how can that be?

No Chhagan, take if ye hafta. But I say too lord, if ye don' tek yer word back I won' let anyone get down in t' field. Munda's a sonuvabitch? Chotti shouted, Munda's no sonuvabitch, Munda makes no profit. If that we knew, I killed t' boar, saved Daroga, couldn't I have taken cash? Ye take that word back. We fight for ye playin' wit' our life. No thief or thug can take a grain f'yer wheat. If ya don' take that word back life will go, but still I won' let anyone work in t' field. I'll fight alone with me bow. Bring yer polis, have me killed, but I've said me last word.

You, ye'll raise a fight?

If ye call this a fight, we'll raise a fight. Go, make a break. Let Chhagan's folks take loan. Not I.

This is yer word?

This word. Call polis. I'll show ya sonsabitches. We'll burn all with fire-tipped arrers before t' polis come.

Chotti was silent. Chhagan says, We're wit' ye Chotti. Maharaj! What's this ye've said? Tribal folks are true folks sir. Go hungry, do work, but they won' hear crazy words.

Tirathnath realized that things had become most difficult. He says, I'll give you a response tomorrow. No more words today.

Chotti smiled. And said, Say now if ye'll take this word back lord. I'll not go home. Me boy'll bring me bow an' arrer. From now we'll picket yer fields. Me boys are here, Sana and his folks are here. Kill t' Mundas. Then do yer stuff.

There was a terrible vow in Chotti's words, unconquerable obstinacy. Tirathnath said slowly, word by staccato word, The word escaped me. I didn't want to say it. I'll give ya loan tomorrer. But I'll check my books.

Chotti realized that disaster was just barely averted. Now he's the conqueror. He smiled a mild inscrutable smile and said, For us Pahan will see t' books. Chhagan will look too. It's a good thing, books. It's good for us, for Chhagan's folks, ta know who's taken how much.

Ye'll know.

Tirathnath pushed his chair back hard and left. Went saying, It's because I'm me that I'm givin' ye a loan. No one else would've.

It's for ye to give. For who else do we work?

They got the loan the next day. Pahan and Chhagan lost their way in the sea of reckoning. Tirathnath went to Daroga at the first opportunity.

After hearing all Daroga said, Walk carefully with the tribals. Now they have a minister, a ministry. Didn't you say Chotti Munda? Let me know if he commits a crime.

Tirathnath felt that ancient fear. He said with a face full of distaste, No no. Chotti is not a man to commit crimes.

You could have taught the other creditors a lesson.

They're single minded.

You don't say?

Let it go, forget what I said.

Are you afraid?

Tirathnath sighs and says, Sir Daroga! This place is a savage place even after Independence. Many things happen here, that a thana cannot figure out. Say you sit down to eat, and every time you put yer hand down on t' food, ye see that the food turns to blood. When such a thing happens who will you blame?

You don't say?

Well I'm telling you.

Chotti can do this?

Who knows? My dad quarrelled with his dad. His dad put a noose around his neck. D'ye know what happened then? We saw Chotti was still here. But my dad got his arrow and fell from the boat into the Ganga in Banaras. An accidental death. We knew all, but nothin' could be done.

Daroga says, This isn't possible.

Stay a few days. You'll say yourself, it's possible.

Then I take your word for it. Don't give it a thought. I'm doing nothing now, but I'm keeping my eyes open. I'll do what I can when I get the chance.

As you see fit. But if something strange happens, think that Tirathnath told us this.

Long before me, in British days, that Chotti Munda saved a Daroga's life, no?

Yes. He's done a lot of stuff like that.

Everything becomes story in Chotti's life. Story and song. The Mundari language has no writable script. So the Mundas tie everything up in story and song. There's unending suffering and deception in their lives. So they forget it for an instant as they sing Chotti's song. They sang,

> Tirathnath said, all Mundas are sonsabitches
> Chotti said, Take back that word
> Otherwise I'll burn yer filds wit' me arrer
> I'll light t' light of Colourfeast in yer barn
> Lala said I take it back
> Take loan take paddy
> Take loan of maize

Never will such a word come to me mouth
Hearin' all Chotti called his arrers back
The arrers were dancin', nearly ran forrard.

Chotti heard the song and said, Good. But this I tell ya, Harmu, one day Lala'll take revenge fo' this insult.

Harmu said, No won'. Else he'd a' taken. Went ta thana.

IX

CHOTTI NOTICED THAT everything seemed to be changing with the Mundas. Life was changing. Chotti station was further enlarged. Now at night a light as bright as day shines there. Chotti's people knew that they had nothing new to start in the local soil. The soil of Chotti will yield them crops only after bone-breaking toil. They'll get a quarter or an eighth of Tirathnath's crops according to Tirathnath's reckoning. The soil will give them the harvest of their own fields. But the soil has never made Chotti's people or Chhagan's people wealthy.

Everythin' is bein' kept aside for t' Diku, Chotti said to Pahan. They were fencing Haramdeo's shrine together with Pahan's hut. Cactus fence. Everyone gives labour as they can for this work.

What did they keep aside? asked Pahan.

Everythin'.

Who?

This earth.

What're ya sayin'?

No eyes? Dontcha see?

Where s'll I get eyes like yourn?

You too talk like that Pahan.

Look how nicely we fenced.

Now tell Pahani, let her put clay on t' wattles, draw designs on t' walls.

When will she do it? She's busy wit' her goats. I'll do it.

Ye?

Ye'll see. What were ya sayin'?

Come let's sit down.

Chotti sat and lit a leaf cigarette and said, Look at this earth. We serve it an' spend all our lives. But I've never seen a Munda grow wealthy, get a lotta earthly goods, put a lotta farmhands ta work.

Pahan laughed and said, Maybe gods have made Munda a holy pauper and sent him down! Why ye, no one's seen.

But Khunkatti village was like that at one time.

Who told ya about Khunkatti village?

Heard.

Pahan almost said something but didn't. He said, Go on, say what ye're sayin'.

Look now Diku knows this land. Partap Chadha's comin', he made a brick kiln. How far is Calcutta, an' from there Chiranjiram Marwari'll come and quarry f'r coal here. An' fruit orchard's a new trade. Asraf Sheikh's bought more'n two acres of land, he'll make an orchard. So th' earth kept all this brick, all this coal, all this fruit—for t' Diku?

Lala too'll make'n orchard. What fruit t' soil grows! So much papaya, so much sarifa, so much guava! Look now, we pick t' mahua from t' jungle, how much is there of that as well?

Gave us nothin'.

No.

Why not, tell me?

It's not for us.

No. Chotti became serious. It's given to them who know ta take. We're not readin'-writin' folk. Our fathers and grandpas didn' do t' new work. We know nothin'.

I hear Gormen will now make iskul for us.

Where?

Who knows?

Won' teach so we understan' our rights. And what's t' use larnin? Mundas've nothin' to call their own no more.

Ye at least get money for archery.

Yeah money.

Ye give loans to one an' all.

I hafta.

Ya get it back? From Chhagan's folk?

Yeah they give.

Thinking some thought Chotti said, Just one thing.

What?

Ye come too, Chhagan come too.

Where to?

Come, let's go to that Partap. To say, take us in th' earth-shovellin' job. Then we'll survive, and we'll be saved some from Tirathnath, whose tenants we aint, but still he treats us so.

Good thought.

One more thing.

What?

Here coal is above ground. We have to go for coal quarryin' work as well. See, I never thought I'd say such a thing.

So what if ye said? It's t' times that make ye say.

Chadha listened to their words carefully. And said, How many are ye? I'll need many people.

So there's fifty, fifty-five Munda. There's men and women. Chhagan has about a hunnert.

Good. So who'll be responsible?

Our Pahan. This Chhagan.

Twelve annas a day. No food.

Ye'll gie's a food-break.

An hour. No work in the rainy season.

We'll come get t' news.

Right.

When'll work start?

Let ye know. But one thing.

Yes Lord?

Don't let this interfere with the work ye do for Tirathnath. Now we're both here. We don't want conflict.

There'll be no conflict lord.

Chhagan comes out and says, Chotti?

Yeah?

Job sounds nice, and will gie cash?

I know, ye're bond labour, what will Lala do.

That's wha I'm thinkin', sich good luck f'rm workin' for Lala, workin' here, hard to credit. But ye thought 'f us, we're proud o' that.

Chotti smiles bleakly and says, Check it out a bit? Sit and see t'fun? What's happenin' everywhere will happen here too.

What?

Someone will come, from t'other side of forest as stonebreakin' contractor, someone as contractor f'r cuttin' forest area trees. They'll bring labour, an' we'll go too. It's like this ever'where, dontcha see how many tains are movin'? New tishans goin' up too. Here too more people more houses. Will Mundas come? Yer society will grow.

Ouf, to think it makes me crazed. Fights—disputes—lawsuits, a lot of trouble then.

But t' day is comin'.

Chotti returns home but the clouds don't lift from his mind. The day is coming. Mundas will not be able to live with their identity. In all national development work they will have to be one with those who, like Chhagan, are the oppressed of the land, and work as field hands, as sweated workers for contractor or trader. Then there'll be a shirt on his body, perhaps shoes on his feet. Then the 'Munda' identity will live only at festivals—in social exchange.

Such a day is coming. Now one must cling to what is one's own. Like archery at the fair? Where are the Munda boys? Who says, teach us how to shoot an arrow?

What Chotti thinks happens. There's no king at Narsingarh now. He's scratched the title 'King' and become a forest king. He's got connected to the export of leopard-skins, tiger-skins et cetera. Forest laws do not apply to him. He doesn't fall in the purview of any law. This dynasty is established by a Sergeant of the East India Company. The source of the title 'King' is the disproportionate devotion to the British. Some generations back the king of those days killed thirty-odd tenants at gunpoint and declared, I am of the Sun-dynasty. I do not come under the purview of any law.

In fact he was not punished in any way. From then on, whoever sits on the throne remembers he's of the Sun-dynasty. This king knows that too. He's strong in that strength, he poisons the springs of drinking water and goes on killing tigers. Other animals are also dying. The king is occupied with such tasks. On his private land there are Munda-Oraon-Kurmi and Dusad tenants. The king has no time. His Agent Tasildar Singh keeps the tenants under control in the usual ways therefore. The weapon is the same. Bonded labour on the basis of compound interest loan. These days Tasildar, if he is displeased with a tenant, breaks his home by putting an elephant on it. So there's resentment in the air of Narsingarh. Daroga and thana are quite devoted to the Sun-dynasty heir. So much so, that even the train halts at the 'no haltage' station on the day tiger pelts are collected. Now, at this time Puran Munda comes from Narsingarh. Puran's not very young, fortyish. He put down his bow near Chotti's feet. And said, Teach me.

Ye? Ye win year after year.

Come along.

If ye'd come wit' t' boys.

Oh come along.

Arrived at their destination Puran says, Me arm's off. I thought mebbe I'd get it back if I practised wit' ya.

In truth Puran's arm shakes.

What's this Puran?

Puran says in a distant voice, Me hut's been broken with an elephant's step. But can a Munda retain his wit? I leapt. Me son pulled me so I didn' fall under th' elephant. But th' arm got pressed under t' door. Caint control that arm since then.

Chotti stood with bow in hand, as if turned into stone, as if turned into a god a thousand years old. To whom for years Mundas come and sing,

They put elephant on me hut.

They took me for bond work.

He has a feast. He taxes me.

I borrowed, so he took all me crop.

As if the Mundas speak, and speak. They don't tell human beings, for they expect no redress, they tell the impotent gods. The hills remain distant, dry grassy fields, in the lee of the forest myrobalan groves shake in the wind, clumps of stone here and there, tufts of grass in between stones, somewhere the bell rings around the necks of cows, somewhere the lapwing calls.

Chotti is not a stone god. He is a man of flesh and blood. So he says, An' after that ye've come to me to win at archery?

I'm here.

Why've ye come, Puran, why?

I'm a loner, no one to stand by me.

Son! Wife!

Sent everyone to brother, to Latehar.

Where d'ye stay?

Tasildar Singh knows that I'm in Latehar too.

Where're ye stayin'?!

An old bogey by t' railway line. Forest all around. Iron room! Perhaps e'en an elephant caint break this room.

Ye're there.

Yes mate, teach?

Chotti says, Then see. Come close.

Time passes. Chotti says, Tasildar knows ye've gone to Latehar? Tell true Puran. Don' jerk me aroun'.

Puran says in the same completely disaffected and slightly surprised voice, Yes mate! He told me that, Get outa village. Then, I left and stayed wit' Dasu Munda. I was a lot scared. Next day I went to Latehar. A few days passed. Then wife says, Maybe his anger's gone, go see? What I came and saw was a strange sight.

Whatcha see?

No hut, no cowhouse, no trellis, nothing, like ploughed field. In case we return, t' hut and yard all flattened by elephants. And told th' other Mundas as he whipped 'em on t' back, sow thornbushes in's land.

Did they?

They did.

Puran said in conclusion to his narrative, Ver' thick whip. Bound in leather. Beat me once. Me leg broke Chotti, it healed only when I tied on t' paste of t' breakbone plant. Well our Mundas are not bad, so why did they still sow thorn in me plot, I ask. So Dasu says, Puran! Where they won' let ye stay, why s'd anyone else plant there? So we sowed thorn an' made t' land useless. But this they didn' see, that t' land's mine. There's even a paper wit' t' king, once he gave when there was a case with Gormen. So this t' Mundas didn' understan', t' land is mine. T' boys love papaya, I woulda planted this time.

But don' go to do that.

No?

No.

If I get t' land back?

I dunno that ye will. But e'en so I say, I'll find out and let ya know. See, I didn' hear, but Dasu Oraon heard, that in town, Gormen is sittin' ta watch o'er our welfare, tribal welfare. Maybe let'em know.

Who'll let'em know? Ye? Far from town.

Town's allus far from Munda, Puran. Don' stay near. We've gotta try and see in our need, but we caint get close. Ye can do all if ye will. Like ye came ta me?

Whate'er ye say Chotti. Ye're very close to us. In a moment t' walk's over when I come ta ye.

But there's no strength in yer arm!

Me arm shakes.

Rub with tiger lard.

Ye know, I had some at home, Chotti . . .

Come on, I'll give.

But Puran didn't come to shoot arrows at any fair. The Mundas of Narsingarh said, He's gone to Latehar.

Chotti really wanted to see the abandoned wagon. And then again he thought, Puran had not wanted to let him know about his secret lair. It'll not be right to speak of it. If he goes to see, people will know.

Returned to the village, Chotti went to Udham Singh, Partap Chadha's clerk. A goodhearted youth. By way of hunting he's even struck up a sort of friendship with Chotti. He goes to town a lot. Chotti told him everything in detail one day. And said, When ye go to town Lord, will ye ask around a bit? Chotti told him everything, just didn't tell Puran's name, the name of Narsingarh.

But the fifties belong to Puran Munda.

By then the fifties are moving towards the sixties. Early in the afternoon it was learnt that Tasildar Singh was coming back after participating in the king's hunt. On horseback. An arrow pierced his back. There was poison at the tip of the arrow. Tasildar falls. The horse lets him roll off and grazes peacefully. The entire incident is discovered late in the afternoon. By then Tasildar was foaming at the mouth. He died that very night. The Sun-dynasty heir would've been happy to implicate all tenants in this. Much to his regret, there was no one at all around. All the tenants were busy working in their respective masters' fields at midday. No one can be suspected. It isn't the Golden Age that the horse will speak and testify. Even when Tasildar's death mystery is still a mystery Tasildar's nephew runs off with his uncle's concubine. This concubine was the luscious and widowed sister of the office guard. Uncle-nephew had been in mutual dispute over her. Thus the matter is considered the conclusion of a family scandal. At no stage is there suspicion over Puran. Chotti is deeply concerned and on a moonlit night, when the station is asleep, he goes near that wagon. The wagon is abandoned. No one around. He comes back relieved. The word that Udham Singh brings back from town is negative. The official responsible for tribal welfare and development can give handicraft training to a displaced Munda, not support him in recovering lost land. The entire matter of the private property of the kings dispossessed of their kingdom is a most complicated matter. It's quite beyond the powers of his office to recover Puran's land. Apart from that, if a few from each group of Munda, Oraon, Dusad, Kurmi, Ganju and washer-caste live together, the region doesn't come under his power. If he gets a pure tribal area he can explain the importance of cottage industry to them.

A couple of months go by this way. Then suddenly an astonishing piece of news is heard. Only folks like the Mundas, whose very existence is disappearing, can send news this way.

Puran is captured. He's turned himself in.

In a highly symbolic manner he'd gone to his own village, his own yard, with three papaya seedlings. As he is about to plant the seedlings he sees a new hut on his land. In it a new Munda family.

The man of that family understands that Puran hasn't come to take away the land in a fighting mood, for Puran says to him, I had t' papers.

That paper is no' valid no more.

No' valid?

Th' office said.

Then these plants?

If ye don' mind plant 'em here. An' sit'n me room, eat. No fault of mine but guilty I am, mate. But we've come in much sorrow.

Puran plants the seedlings. And then says, Dasu! Upa! Come wit' me to t' thana, do.

Why?

These papers aren't in force no more. Then why'd I kill Tasildar? I didn' do't right?

Ye killed?

Yeah. Let me go tell Daroga.

Why'll ya tell?

What'll I do?

Run off.

Why?

Ya killed 'm, ye'll get t' noose.

I'll not get hut an' land, me heart breaks, so what'll I do wit' life? For this reason I didn' tell. And t' guy was much bad, no? Why'll I hang if I killed 'm?

Soon the Mundas find the entire affair most complicated. Then they go to the thana after all. Puran says everything in detail.

Daroga keeps him in custody. Tries to explain to him at great length that it's no use making trouble about a case that's been solved. Is this just a straightforward bit of trouble? Open the file again, set up the case again, collect witnesses again. But he cannot explain it to Puran.

Finally Puran says, Then what ta do?

Daroga is at his wit's end. And says again, The case is closed. Now you say, you've committed a murder. There may be a case over this as well. But the rule of law travels by a different road. It won't be a murder because you say you murdered. Need witnesses. Need proof. Need cause.

Broke me hut.

When? That's five months before the event. Two months before Tasildar's murder other people were living on your land. I know all about you. Investigating the people who might be angered with Tasildar, I investigated you as well. Now Daroga descends to the most familiar form as well. He says enraged, Donkey! Idiot! I'm trying to save your life. I'll have to put in a great deal of labour to make you into a murderer. I have a lot of work right now.

His work is with the Agent of the Sun-dynasty heir. The price of seven tigerskins has come to twenty-one thousand rupees. Daroga will get at least a thousand. He now has no desire to be screwed by this sort of bedraggled case, the Daroga has plenty of support in town and in the home office. He can say this only by way of his support props.

Who will give witness? There was t' horse. An' th' elephant.

Where did ye get an elephant?

Th' elephant travelled wit' him. It broke me hut.

I understand. You're crazy.

Sir, I don' understand yer Diku words.

Whose words will ye understand?

Sir! Chotti Munda of Chotti village knows ever'thin'.

Chotti Munda! He was with you?

Yes sir. He's gi'en me assurance.

Now the case becomes attractive and blooms in a thousand dimensions like flowers seen in a movie. Leaving Puran at the thana, Daroga goes to perform his important task with the King's Agent. The next day he tells a constable to seek out Chotti. Hearing Puran's words the constable says respectfully, Sir! How can that be? I saw Chotti at the market the day Tasildar was murdered. He was at the market, we talked even. The constables from this thana were there too.

Daroga said to Puran, So! Chotti was with you?

No no, went to market, but even so he sits in me heart.

Daroga scolds him a lot. He says, There was an elephant. There was Chotti Munda. Go home, go. Otherwise I'll kill ya.

Puran says in a very confused way, Then have I gone crazy thinkin' and thinkin' about me hut?

Get outa here.

I saw t'elephant, Chotti came with . . .

Chotti and his associates had thought Puran had been despatched by now. But they are astonished to see Puran coming. Puran tells him everything. Learning that the Daroga has let him go because he's crazy, Chotti says to him, Come, sit. Tell me everythin'. First have somethin' to eat.

Puran eats maizeflour stirred in water with salt and cayenne and says, Daroga didn' credit that I killed Tasildar.

How's that?

I couldn' understan'.

Puran said everything. I'd see th' elephant, ye were in me chest a-a-ll false?

Puran t' way ye were saved today no Munda was saved that way ever, ye haven' understood what a savin' was yers.

Pahan said, Keep him at home. Then find out who's where of his and let 'em guard him.

Chotti kept him in his own hut. The next day he and the pahan went to Latehar with him. By train. Sitting in the train Chotti said, Ye put us on t' rails e'en. I n'eer thought I'd be on t' rails.

Railway's good. I used to live there.

Shut up now. Forget that.

Hey Chotti, is me chest empty. I don' e'er see t'elephant? I used to sleep in t' train car, and I saw th' elephant all t' time?

The elephant became a duck and flew away, okay?

They laughed a lot all three. The load on their mind lightened with laughter. Three smiling Mundas got off at Latehar. They said to the porters off their own bat, First time on t' rails mate, so we feel like laughin'.

Puran says, Chotti, Let's buy liquor.

Let's go home first.

In his hut Chotti explained the importance of the entire incident to Puran's sons. And said, Don' let 'm go anywhere.

How long s'll we remain here?

Where'll ye go?

Contractor says fellin' timber.

Where?

Oh somewhere. In t' Gormen forest.

So go. But don' let 'im go.

Puran says, Ye won' drink?

We'll come later an' drink.

They returned on foot. Returned late at night. Pahan says, Chotti? What's that? Elephant? Have I turned Puran?

No no. That's a she-elephant. It's th' elephant of t' god's temple in Tahar. T' driver goes around with it.

Say that! Who knows what's wrong with Puran's head. Hasn't yet understood what a terrible fate he's avoided.

I haven' understood yet.

Why did this happen?

It's t' Daroga who knows.

Everything is story in Chotti's life. All said, ye sat in Puran's chest and brought him courage?

Puran's lost his head.

Puran's entire family leaves with the contractor. Walking and walking they come to the colliery of the king of Ramgarh. There they merge into another life. There's no joy in that life. But there's no Tasildar or 'elephanth' either. The son of Motia, the washerwoman of Chotti village, sells parched chickpeas on the bus route. Seeing him Puran sends word to Chotti, Everything is unknown to him here. He doesn't like it. But they've all got jobs because there's a unine. But the contractor who brought them takes a lot of money.

Chotti says, Let 'im. Let 'em live at least.

The Puran affair is settled. Puran doesn't have to go to jail. But Chotti couldn't keep jail at bay for his own son Harmu.

X

TIME HAD GONE ON. Chotti didn't stop going to the archery play at Chotti village fair every year. He didn't let anyone else win the contest. The boys who learnt from him have won in fair after fair. Partap Chadha has gone toward Bokharo, to open another brick kiln. Harbans Chadha looks after the brick kiln here. He manufactures hollow bricks. He likes to give the work to the villagers because their rates are extremely low. Chotti's group and Chhagan's group save Tirathnath's labour and work there. They don't get porter's work at the station any more. The contractor brings porters. But it's the villagers who get the jobs of illegally killing trees, deforesting the hills, and breaking stones to make morraine. Everybody gives the twelve annas daily wage announced by Pratap. Chhagan says, We are now the twelve-anna soliders. We fight where'er there's a job, any sort. Whate'er the job, twelve annas'll not grow a rupee. Hey Chotti howsabout goin' and talkin' once?

What'll ya say?

Gie's a rupee.

Won' give.

Why not?

Ye're a booklarnin' guy, don' ye see?

Ye say. Yer head's stronger.

Tell me why they'll give.

Say it, say.

Chotti smiles faintly and says, There are countless people to do t' job. An' there's little work. If we don' do folks'll come fro' all aroun'. It's a land of drought and famine. All t' work caint be done by us alone. At famine time Harbans's giv'n four annas and Gormen relief Milo.

Say that then. That's why they don' let's work with' outside labour. An' so they don' mix with' us neither.

Yeah. Take a look how t' place is bigger now, so many typesa folks now. So many diffren typesa jobs too. But we remain where we were, us. I see one good thing. Before we couldn' eat if Tirathnath didn' give loan. Now we break stones, we shovel earth, we take less loan. And I see that ways are changin'. Harmu wears shirts, and t' girls e'en wear blouses. It's not our old ways.

No. How'll they stay? Now at every market there are cheap shoes and sandals, many kindsa shirt-ribbon-bangle-forehead dot an' so much more? Our blood-earned wages spent on that stuff.

Why don' yer kids go to school?

What school! First we're not school folks, ye've to hit 'em hard ta send 'em to school, and then t' schoolmaster says, What'll ye do with school? Go herd cows.

If they see Munda boys they chase 'em off.

Readin' and writin's not f'r us.

By law it's f'r ever'one, but not in fact.

Oh let t' Brahmans', and t' Lalas', and t' caste-Hindu kids go to school.

Chotti laughs and says, I'm not in pain, Sana's sister's son has seen that in Ranchi, Munda girls and Oraon girls go to Mission schools and still don' get jobs. Work construction, go to cut coal.

Even that brings in money.

Money there. Not here.

Chotti went to Pahan. His wife's sister's daughter's going to wed Somchar. Somchar's first wife is dead. They must find a day for t' wedding.

Pahan said, Ye were right.

'Bout what? Ye see all me words as 'right'.

What ye said at t' fair? At t' time of t' feast.

What did I say?

Ye said t'Munda would never get anythin' his own way no more. To survive he mus' work at odd jobs bein' one wit' Chhagan's people. Th' archery game's also over. Ye caint beat t' bushes durin' t' hunt game and get a hedgehog. Now Munda'll be Munda at festivals, and for community things like weddings. Bow 'n'arrer are now toys to win at games at t' fair. What used to be a weapon's now a toy.

Chotti sighs and says, Let it be a toy. Puran survived by great good luck. Otherwise if they'd caught him they'd ha' broken down every adivasi hut in Narsingarh by elephants. Whenever somethin' happens, if Munda is oppressed, then Munda leaves home, leaves land and goes away.

They don' go to t' Mission no more.

Mission! With Sukha's group t' joy of t' Mission is over. T' Mission no longer gives land to Munda and Oraon, and makes him a farmer no more. Go to t' market town, and ye'll see Mission Mundas wanderin' around like us lookin' fer work, driven by hunger. Before Gormen and Mission was like father- an' son-in-law.

Why don' Mundas return to their religion even so?

They forget all in their belly's worry.

Still, religion's not nothin'.

We're in our religion, and there we'll stay. But we don' get off from belly's hunger, bond work, debt's lash?

Ye have yer little plot o' land.

It's Harmu's, it's Somchar's, and Etwa's. For Koel and me just t' littlest bit from our dad.

Harmu's land is good.

I say, Sell that land's harvest and buy e'en more land. Otherwise everyone's family's increasin', what'll ye eat?

After all this time unexpected trouble arose with Harmu's land. In this year of 1961. Another newsworthy incident this year was the behaviour of Chotti's son's father-in-law Donka at the Chotti fair. At the close of the fair, at the archery game he said out of the blue, Chotti's arrer play ain't right no more. Spellbound arrer, so it hits t' mark. Not right.

Chotti says, Ye caint do it, so ye say it in rage. Ye're younger to me. Me years are three score an' one. Right. I'll not shoot. Gimme yer arrer. Gimme everyone's arrer.

Everything is story in Chotti's life. He hit the target with every-one's arrow. The eye-target was full of pierced arrows. Then Chotti said, I've won for two score and five years, done a lot, I'll play no more.

Daroga says, What're ye sayin'?

Harbans Chadha says, Yer shooting gives a name to the fair.

Pahan says, Then let me say a thing. Now that ye've spoke, ye won' take yer word back, I know. Then—Pahan says to Daroga, to Tirathnath, and Harbans—then why can't he be a judge? I'm a judge cos I'm Pahan. But th' arrer's in his power. So he'll be a judge?

Why s'd we object? But at Chotti fair it's t' pahan of Chotti vil-lage who judges, that's become t' standin' rule.

But it's the Chotti village pahan who's himself givin' up t' seat, an' also givin' Chotti Munda an order.

Chotti smiled, Whate'er ye say.

Sana said, Hey Donka whatcha do?

Chotti said, He's right. An old man now, and still I had to show ye, that Chotti's spell's in 'is arm, not in th' arrer. Yeah, I do have that one arrer, yeah. For long I hold it in ma breast. I bring it to fair, I tek it back. That arrer is not for winnin' at target. It's to keep close by. Yeah, an old man now. Archery ain't me property that I'll hang on to it. Let t' young 'uns see. I've to let 'em play, no? No, I'm not sorry at all.

But who'll do it, say?

Chotti laughs and says, With practice me Somchar, yer broth-er's son Jita, won' they do it? That Harmu gets worked up. He has no quiet in 'im. But before his hand was very calm, ye know. As a kid, he's shot a lotta yellow-green doves from behind green leaves. Now that land has become his life. His ma says, He loves his land more than his son. His land's his life.

Looking at his field of grain in the eighth month of Aghran Harmu had said, Land's me life—this is me life.

Tirathnath's Agent heard everything quietly and said, The land belongs to Lala. Ye've ploughed it fer a long time. Raised a lotta grain.

Grew a lot of harvest! Don' I gie Lala half?

Hey, shame on ye! Did he say such a thing?

At harvest time his man is there. The weighing takes place in his presence. We gie half of straw, half of chaff, of everthin'.

Sure ye do.

Then why does he want t' land?

His land, he can want.

He's gi'en his word to Aba.

Hey, look here.

What'll I look? Isn't it a standin' word?

Go tell 'im. Who'm I? Obedient servant. Got an order, told ya. Now do whatcha like. Ye'll bring the produce. Then talk to 'im? I'm off.

Harmu charged his dad, Why dintcha get it written with Lala, Aba? Now t' land's about ta be lost?

What d'ye mean?

Go talk to 'im. Great distress in Harmu's voice, don' ye know why Lala wants land? Ye know so much?

Whatcha think?

It were bad arable land. With' our three brothers' labour it's now bearin' fruit. It's like t' land is laughin', wit' fruit, wit' grain. When t' paddy's ripe, it talks to me. I giv'm produce, huge big grains o' maize, big thick paddy. So he's jealous.

But Lala's gi'en me t' land.

Greatly troubled, Chotti goes running. Harmu and other Mundas are with him. Lala says, Are ye gonna beat me up?

But first tell us lord, ye want t' land back?

Yes Chotti.

But t' land is mine.

If it's yours then why do ye give me half the harvest? Tell me that? Do I give the harvest of the lands I sow to anyone? The moment you give me harvest it proves that I've given you half-share.

Dintcha take land tax?

Yup.

Whose name did ye deposit?

My name. The owner pays tax.

But lord! Take t' case of Maniram Chhatri. He ploughs yer land, gives ye half his harvest. He gives ye his land tax, and ye deposit it in yer own name. But ye don' tek his land. Ye follow t' rule of half harvest, half right in his case alright?

He's a Hindu, man of my faith.

Then whyn't ye let me have it in writin'? Whyja lie? Whyja say, word o' mouth is all?

When I said—

Harmu said, Then ye didn' think that yer throwaway land ud bear fruit. That's what ye thought lord.

I've nothin' ta say t'ye Harmu.

So speak ta me, says Chotti.

What s'll I say? I've spoken.

Why only Hindus? Dontcha give to adivasis? Gave to Bhikan Oraon, and to Burha Munda. Who's got a reckud of land grant? And lord, youse takin' half crop fer so long. So that also proves that y'accept this way. If no, youda taken t' land, or made some other rule. Ye get a right if ye keep a place up.

Chotti, why talk more? I give the land one way. If it doesn't suit, I give it another way.

Why dintcha let us write down th' agreement?

Chotti! Truth ta tell, I didn' know before that the land would bear.

T' land wouldn' bear. Three brothers put rotten leaves from jungle on shoulder yoke, wit' so much trouble they sweetened t' land's sulk and made it smile. Then land smiled. An' tell me true, ye knew this, no? Tell me.

Ye don't understand, Chotti.

Chotti said with the intense heartbroken passion of ruined hope, insult, and pain, So ye're our lord, no? We never hear that we understan'. So lord, make us understan'. Let's see if Munda understan's Diku-talk. Tell, tell me? Nothin' written down, taxes paid up, and still say adivasis, say Chhagan's lot get half right in land. Many times it's written, many times not. Many things are done wit' worda mouth. Ye say I've borrad so much, worda mouth. Ye say I've harvested so much, worda mouth. Make me understan', Munda doesn' read, so how does he know worda mouth won' stand true?

Tirathnath was realizing that he was not acting right. It's true that bosses of his sort and he himself never gave these folks good land. By shares they are given stony land, barren land, dry land, distant meadowland, land by the borders of the forest. Given half harvest, half right. For these people nourish even such land with their heart's blood, thinking of it as golden. They raise crops on land that has never yielded anything but thorny rush and coarse grass. Poor quality. That bit is the landowner's profit. They too know that this does not mean that on this soil, upon this foundation some continuous tradition of half harvest half right can be built. But the right does not disappear as soon as the person who took the land dies. Everything is the landowner's whim. But because it's an established practice even the landlord recognizes the right in the case of unproductive land.

Bad land has never become productive in this way. There is no precedent and for this lack Tirathnath is trying to establish a precedent. This is profitable for the landlords. Thus from this precedent a custom will emerge. If he had seen feeble and undernourished maize and paddy Tirathnath would not have wanted the land in this way. This too Tirathnath understood, that he's possibly wronging the worthy and honest Chotti by ignoring established practice. But can Tirathnath stop to think if Chotti is being wronged?

Listen Chotti—

Tell me, tell me.

It's no use fighting. Let me take this land and mebbe I'll give you land on the Kurmi side? The fallow land?

Yes lord. Ye'll give that land, I'll make it bear fruit with me heart's blood, and then ye'll tek it. And then where will ye give Chotti land, lord? Have ye bought all t' fallow land in t' world?

Tirathnath realized that he was talking to Chotti, to Chotti Munda. The Mundas of the area hold Chotti to be a god. He gets a lot from Chotti, from adivasis like Chotti. Chotti has a spellbound arrow. That arrow has great powers. Still Tirathnath couldn't turn himself around. He's a landowner-moneylender. If he doesn't do as he says he'll be cursed for the crime of leaving a bad precedent. Now India is independent. Absurd botherations like kings and zamindars have vanished. He's no more than a middle farmer. But farmers like him and farmers-landowners-moneylenders like him and bigger-than-him and smaller-than-him are a great source of strength for this Gormen. At the last vote he gave two rupees per head, and then they gave their votes as he said: it's most regrettable that Tirathnath is a landowner and moneylender of a forest area. Neither educated nor sufficiently organized. Now the vote is next year. If he were rich and organized enough Tirathnath would have a truck. Chotti and Chhagan's group would have had money in hand. Then Tirathnath's own people would have gone by truck and cast their votes. But is it correct for him to treat Chotti thus? It was because of Chotti that, at a very young age, Tirathnath had received the title 'Raisaheb' from the English Gormen. He and Chotti are about the same age. He should definitely not be like this with Chotti. But it's now beyond the point of no return. And what's there to fear? The office of the Gormen party is just three stations away. Support will surely come if he goes there. Tirathnath said, That's it then.

Th' end, lord? All finished?—There was a dry lamentation in Chotti's voice. What was all finished? Some tremendous event? Why is Tirathnath uncomfortable? What has he done? Why are there so many people in the room? Chotti's group had come, the Mundas. When did these ones come, Chhagan's people? Why is everyone looking at him in silence with inscrutable eyes? What has Tirathnath done? Once he'd told a Munda I give you this barren piece of land for half crop half right. No need to put it in writing. And today he's saying I'm taking that land. What's wrong with this? Tirathnath realized, his own mind is saying there's something wrong in this. He realizes that when the people of the town areas say about him that he is a 'jungle moneylender', they're correct. You need a greatly strong heart muscle to aim a kick at the business of lifelong familiarity. Tirathnath is neither that strong nor does he have that much spirit. When the coward does something wrong, he becomes savage. In that savage mode Tirathnath said, That's it then.

That's it?

Yes. And, and listen here, you don' have to give any produce this year.

So this time it's t' full crop and rights lost? No lord, Munda doesn' understan' yer rules. We'll give our crop.

Tirathnath screamed out, You see a wrong in everything I say. I'm bad! Do you know who's called a bad man? You can find out for yerselves, no other landowner, no other moneylender, is letting the Munda-Oroan pleat their dhotis like Hindus, eat off metal plates, wear shoes on their feet.

Harmu was looking at Tirathnath with an unblinking stare. Now he says, What'er ye say or don' say, that's our state.

How? Hey Harmu how?

No money to buy dhotis, so we tuck up our short dhotis into loincloths, and no money to eat on metal plates, to walk about wit' shoes on feet. That's how.

Go, go now all of ya.

Returning, Chotti says, Gie him his share tomorra.

An' then?

Harmu! To remain true to yerself ye sometimes hafta do various things, no need ta talk about it.

What d'ye say Aba?

I'll say . . .

What? Say . . .

The talk was wit' me, but t' land's yers.

Me life.

Lala's said what there was ta say. We'll do what we have to do. There'll be trouble between him an' me. I know he tells t' thana ahead o' time, that's his strength. I'll go tomorra.

What'll ye say?

What's t' use tellin' ya? Oh me heart's burnin' up. What pain makes Munda leave home, what pain makes him go elsewhere?

Harmu says, Git up, wash up, eat.

Today I eat, tomorra?

Eat.

One thing t' Lala's done well.

What? Whyja laugh? Aba? Whyja laugh?

Lala's done a lotta good. Dontcha see? Our state's t' same as other Mundas. Cos we had that land we had sump'n ta eat and we forgot that as Mundas we had no right ta happiness. Land's gone, now we'll be like all others. This is good.

Whyja say land's 'gone?'

Harmu! Ye're jesta kid. E'en ye have children! But where'll ye get me eyes?

Raising his finger Chotti points at the dark and says, I won' give land fer nothin'. Such insult! Won' give fer nothin'. If life goes let it go. But Harmu! Then polis-law-go to court. Me, Munda, will die agin after turnin' all t' turns. Is't jest landowner and moneylender that kills Munda? T' law kills. T' land's gone Harmu, I can see wit' me eyes. There's an offsir now ta look after tribals and e'en he says, Sit home and weave rush mats, and cone baskets, I'll give help. I c'n do nothin' me son if ye speak of land. Then go to Court. Laws! Law courts! Never felt trust. Where'll we get lawyers? Lawyers will tek money, but what he says Munda doesn' understan'. And he don' understan' what Munda says, for lawyer understan's B when Munda says A an' explains t' contrary ta t' judge. T' judge judges contrariwise. But—

What 'but' Aba?

But if there's trouble o'er land, t' trouble will roll inta t' lawcourt's hole like t' loose wheel of t' buffalo cart. Then will t' land be there f'r us? Lawcourts hev nev'r seen t' Munda, an' will nev'r.

Will nev'r!

No Harmu. Ever'thin' is Gormen's. If Gormen looked after Munda rights wud Munda be beggar like this? Leave land with Diku's kick? Will nev'r look out fo' us, Harmu. Harmu! Son o' mine. Yer wife's waitin', go, eat sump'n, sleep. Lemme sit a while. Darkness seems nice, me boy. Darkness's like mother, ya don' feel no shame with it.

Aba! Ye allus talk ta Chhagan?

What s'll I tell Chhagan wit' this matter? This is a reckonin' of one Munda wit' one Lala. Why s'd they come into this?

Won' come?

No. Lala hasn' raised trouble wit'm, with other adivasis? When there's polis-thana-lawcourts, we s'dn' bring them into it Harmu.

But t' blow c'n fall on them too.

Fo' sure. But Harmu. There'll be trouble wit' t' boss. We go forward knowin' that. We know there's no oth'r way. If we go like this, there'll be a lawsuit, we'll be kicked there too, we know, an' yet we go forrard. When ever'one understan's like this in t' blood's fire, go forrard that way, then we can be together, move as one. C'n say come all of ya. Who'll go forrard like that?

They're cowards.

No son! Don' ever blame hungry folks, sick folks, folks who's kicked around. No one behind them, no one to give advice, no money anywhere, who'll ye blame son? Go eat somethin'.

Ye?

Didn' I tell ya, sit in t'dark.

Harmu left. Chotti's wife came and stood beside him and said, I'll open t'window, see t' dark lyin' in bed. Now eat, lie down. Tomorra ye'll go t' thana, ye've work to do.

Ye've heard ever'thin'?

Heard. Come.

Chotti got up and went inside. Harmu's mother brought the plate forward for him. Lentils and starchy rice. Now there's no game in the forest. They eat lentils and starchy rice, thin gravy of boiled tamarind-leaf, occasionally pork bought at market. When the mission people come to give aid at drought and famine, they say the adivasi seldom dies of hunger because they are in the habit of staying alive on food with very little nutritional value. If their bodies had been coddled, more would have died.

After eating Chotti says, I'll be back.

Where ya goin'?

Gimme t' machete.

Who're ye gonna cut?

No one, jus' habit. No fear from humans, and those happy days are gone that t' tiger'll leap.

Chotti grasped the machete and went out. Open land past the hill. If you cut across it's his land. Now deer don't come drawn by the smell of ripe paddy. They're not there. Everyone, hunting in any fashion, has killed them all off. If there are any animals left, they've gone off into deep forest for fear of the human. Chotti stands still for a bit when he reaches the plot. Fenced in with cactus. Birds see the paddy and come flying in. Koel's son Etwa and Somchar scare off birds all day.

The paddy's bent over. Just a bit of land. The paddy'll be cut tomorrow, and taken to Lala's office. Half portion must be measured and given.

Who's this? Chotti hears footsteps.

Dada, it's me.

Koel? Ye here?

I heard all as I returned from Rye.

How d'ye know I was here?

In t' mind.

Stay home tomorra. I'll go to thana.

What use, dada?

I dunno. But I see that t' Dikus let t' thana know as soon as somethin' happens. If somethin' happens later it comes in handy.

They'll take yer word fer it?

Dunno. Daroga speaks well to me otherwise. Only th' other day he told Sana, if anythin' happens let thana know. Don' start fightin' yerselves. Sana said, Willya lissen if we tell? Daroga says, Fo' sure. All tenants are same in Gormen's eyes.

Come, let's go home.

Come.

The next day Chotti goes to thana. Told Pahan, and Koel, and all of them to go with Harmu when they give up t' portion of paddy. He told Harmu before leaving, Don' raise trouble.

Don' worry Aba.

Everything becomes story in Chotti's life. Someone else was chatting with Daroga. He saw Chotti and said, Look now! The man I was talking about is here. This man is well-known to my father-in-law. Tribal welfare officer. Lives in town. He's come on tour here, but he's also getting news of the tribals. I was the one who was saying, There's an adivasi here, our pride and joy, a magician with the arrow, knows everything about all the Mundas of the region, and that is Chotti Munda. Saying this I took a sip of tea, and you arrived.

The tribal officer says, We were talking about you.

Lord! I was wantin' ye, and ye brought me in mind, and so connection was made.

What's up, tell me.

The tribal officer saw, hard to tell the man's age. Slim build, vigorous skin. Ancient and much-laden eyes. But there's dignity in his speech, in the way he sits straight on his haunches. To look at him one knows he's used to respect. Awakens curiosity.

Chotti said everything slowly, with pauses.

Daroga says, But Chotti, the land is Lala's.

Lord! There is a practice of half crop half right for tribals in barren land.

True. The tribal officer agrees as well. Said he, The landlord doesn't usually break this agreement. For they give the kind of land where you don't get more than eighty-odd pounds of paddy per a third of an acre. And bad quality paddy at that.

But I'd never heard of this?

You haven't heard, sir, because the adivasi and other castes live together in peace in village after village.

Is this custom only for the adivasi?

No, no, sometimes other lowcastes get it as well. But they usually haven't the courage to take absolutely barren land.

Chotti, what d'you want to say?

I understan' lord, that this is a question of right. It's true that not too many tribals have such land. P'raps about ten people, among tribals and other castes, in yer thana. But after this who'll have any confidence lord? I said, let's put it in writin'. Lala said, word o' mouth's okay.

Does the land yield much?

Lord! Land was stony, stones if ye dug. Barren land. No one ever put a plough there. Us two brothers and two sons moved all t' stones. No water buffaloes lord. Borrowed Pahan's buffaloes an' got t' job done. Some years a hunnert an' twenny pound paddy. Forty pound arhar lentils, ne'er got more. Land didn' smile. Then t' sons bore rotten leaves from forest, water from t' spring, on their shoulders. Workin' like that t' land smiled. For t' last five years it's givin' two hunnert pounds paddy. Now that Lala wants this Lord, will he put in so much work? This time t' land'll become barren agin.

Daroga said, I'll go tomorrow. I've some business as well. I'll say something. I'll explain. Chotti we must come to an understanding. I'll do all this because you are asking. I haven't forgotten that if you hadn't saved the day the thana constables would have had their heads bust open when the constables fought with the Kunjaras.

The officer says, Who're the Kunjaras?

Wholesalers of fruit. They come to buy myrobalan and mustard, and they'll buy all the fruit at the lowest price, and they'll thrash anyone who tries to sell fruit from their own orchards at market. They'll come from Ranchi and Gomo. They are from other districts. They'll feel up the women. I have a bad name. I look out for the poor. And that's why they've sent me to this abandoned thana.

So ye'll come lord?

Yes, Chotti. And look, you don't have to think about protecting everyone's rights. When I hear such things I feel that you're planning a machete show. You people have an ancient relationship with Tirathnath.

Lord, we keep his paddy, his wheat, his maize with our lives. If we weren' there e'en his office would ha'e had armed robberies. Ye know how many offices've been hurt by armed robbers.

I'll come.

Lord, may ye be blessed. Who wants to fight, lord? We've ne'er done it.

Chotti left. The tribal officer said, The government wishes the tribals well, otherwise they wouldn't have opened an office. But the landlords and moneylenders are mostly uneducated. They won't give up their old ways. If we want the welfare of those whose arms and legs are in hock to the moneylender we have to give them other powers as well. When will they do cottage industry? They'll give bonded labour, they'll work in the moneylender's fields? Can we easily teach handicrafts to farming folks?

Hey, don't I know it. But—

What?

I must go tomorrow. Moneylenders like Tirathnath are my curse! Look how much land he has. They give a damn for ceilings. All the gods in Tirathnath's house have land dedicated to them. You became crazy when you saw bad land turn good, what's the consequence? The tribals will go crazy. When that happens, they won't understand that only a few will lose their land. Didn't Chotti speak of 'rights?' Tirathnath doesn't know that not only from the Mundas, Chotti gets respect from the Hindu lowcastes as well? The police will surely come if there's trouble. Then it'll be cognisable offence. And if you do that the government will catch you, Why're you hurting the tribals? This is a tribal vote area, and the voting's coming, in 1962. If I don't raise the vote, they'll say I support the machete men everywhere. Then I'll definitely be suspended.

What will you do?

I'll explain to Tirathnath. I'll say, Don't take Chotti's land, I'll tell the government you're a very good man. You do a lot of good works. You got a 'Raisaheb' under the British Raj, let's see if this Raj gives you a Padamsree.

Will he listen if you tell?

Has to listen. If it were anyone other than Chotti I'd have caught him on the charge of rioting. But the Munda community obeys him to the word. If I try to do that I'm in double jeopardy. Ananda Mahato of *Adivasi Samachar* is a real dog, and he has lotsa power. If he hears at all, fire ta kindling.

Will Tirathnath listen?

He has to listen. Will I place myself in harm's way for his little bitty land? What can I say! My job will be in trouble. Let me tell Chotti as well! The owner of the land wants his land, so why won't you hand it over?

How to say yes to this? You've no idea how poor the adivasis are. This is their right.

Let's see what I can do.

Daroga had the good intention of going the next day, but he knew nothing of the angry scorpion in the crack in the cistern when he was washing up after his meal. The scorpion doesn't come out in cold weather, loses its strength even. So he didn't burn with scorpion venom for two days, as expected. He suffered abominably for a day.

Just a day was needed for the explosion. The day Daroga was laid low with the pain of poison, that very day Chotti in Chotti village is burning with another fire. Daroga didn't keep his word. He didn't come. Harmu lay in bed all day. Even his father seemed to be on the enemy side. The land was his life. Tirathnath waited this one day.

The next day Chotti went to thana again. It was still just daybreak. He sat and waited. Daroga came after nine. Said in an irritated way, Come on let's go. Said to the tribal officer, Ye come too sir.

How shall we go?

There's a train at ten.

How far?

Four miles.

They're getting ready to go, and Sana and Pahan appear. What they say panting is roughly this, Harmu went to his plot in the morning. When Tirathnath's people came to get possession of the land, there was fighting between Harmu, Somchar, Etwa, Jita, Budhna Munda on the one side and Tirathnath's ten men on the other. The fight is in progress and Mathura Singh, the doorkeeper of Tirathnath's office, has gone to get his gun. Lord must come instantly.

Daroga proceeded with the thana police, and with constables. The adivasi officer also came along. Chotti and his folks also got on the train.

The train arrived. Arrived at the designated place, Daroga saw a terrible scene of violence, and a gun in the hands of the guard.

The sepoys and the constables raised their truncheons and joined the fray to keep the peace. Come out of it, Harmu, shouted Chotti. But there was the sound of a gunshot. The bullet hit the constable's arm, a loud scream, and then all quiet. It was seen that Harmu had wounded three of Tirathnath's men with his bow and arrow. Daroga was furious. To wound police? Seeing the seriousness of the situation, Tirathnath too came running. It's not an arrow that has pierced the constable's arm, it's a bullet. Great pity! It's not possible to cover the matter up because of the tribal officer's presence. Tirathnath was ready to play the old one-two with both Daroga and the wounded constable. But the money in his pocket remained in his pocket. Harmu, Somchar, Mathura Singh and Tirathnath's men were all transported to jail. It's the unwelcome presence of administrative officers that lead to such disturbances. The adivasi officer's a witness, the inquisitive station master is also a witness. He'd given someone else the responsibility of moving the trains along and come to see the fun. He is annoyed with the Daroga after the Kunjara fiasco. The Kunjara's daily bribe is his rightful due. Daroga has turned the Kunjaras' head. He said with a highly worried look, Transport everyone to je-hell. He feels pure joy in closing the passageway between Tirathnath's money and Daroga's pocket.

The case goes to the court in town. Somchar and the rest are freed for lack of evidence. Harmu gets two years' prison sentence with hard labour. Five years for Mathura Singh. The unlicensed gun is confiscated, but no one mentions the fact that it belonged to Tirathnath. Chotti is obliged to come to town. The tribal officer behaves extremely well with him. Lets him stay in his house, wants to arrange for a lawyer. Because you're asking for it, he says to Chotti, I'm looking for a lawyer. But will you be able to pay a lawyer's fees?

How much will it be?

At least a thousand rupees.

A thousand rupees! I don' have a hunnert.

Then the government will provide a lawyer. I'll see that you get a good one.

By luck he gets a good lawyer. A young lawyer. It'll be good for his career if he pleads a good case. But if you put an adivasi in the witness box, he won't say what you've taught him, he will tell the truth. Knowing all this, he took up Harmu's case. He doesn't try too hard to save Tirathnath and Mathura. The entire thing becomes a nightmare to him now. When Chotti realizes that his son will go to jail, he doesn't stay at the tribal officer's place any longer. He stays under the tree in front of the courthouse. Until the verdict is pronounced in Harmu's case. The unbridled urban renewal of the county seat does not catch his eye, he keeps thinking of Harmu's face. Two years will pass, me son, says Chotti.

Harmu shakes his head.

The lawyer says, Two years sounds a lot, but they will pass.

Chotti shakes his head. Then he gets on the bus. The bus leaves in the afternoon, and gets to Chotti at eight o'clock in the evening. He sits silent throughout the journey. It's Harbans Chadha's bus. On weekdays the bus travels this route. The conductor knows Chotti quite well and, surprising Chotti, he buys Chotti food when they get to Behut, gives him a bidi, and says, Tirathnath has a lot of grief coming. Getting off at Chotti, Chotti sees a lot of people waiting for him. Pahan gives a questioning look.

Two years' jail sentence.

Chotti says this without being asked and everyone remains mute. Came and went with ye at that time, Chhagan says. S'da gone now.

No, I had no trouble.

Came back alone.

That tribal offsir's a good guy. Gave good evidence too. So Daroga couldn't say somethin' funny. First time I saw a Diku tell t' truth fer Munda.

Mathura Singh?

Five years. Mathura's sent word to me, Chotti don' shoot yer arrer, I used force by order. I think he's afeared.

Could be.

Feared of what? What I understood, t' lawyer knows Mundari, he tol' me, that he was punished cos he shot a policeman. E'en if Harmu had died by his bullet he'd not ha' bin punished. Harmu lost his cool. Otherwise—

What're ye sayin' Sana? Harmu has saved me face. If he hadn' raised his, I'd have had to raise me bow, and I'da felled a few.

But Somchar an' th'others came back th'other day?

Not much of a case fer them. Why s'd they stay?

I wanna talk to yer, says Pahan.

What about? Let's go home. They're worryin'.

Thing is, ye'll not have to give a puja when Harmu comes out. He's not sinned.

Let's see what Lala says, says Chhagan. We too feel strong in our hearts Chotti. Reason why Lala is mighty afeared.

Don' take his name.

He'll giv ya back yer land.

And who'll take it? Harmu's in jail.

Go home, said Pahan. For so long ye've been comin' and goin'. An' this time so long in town.

Come.

Walking home Chotti says, I were in town, but I noticed nothin'. I'd think of that Harmu. But this is true, it was a two year stint cos 'twas Harmu. I woulda bin for t' noose. Cos why, I'da killed a few. That Mathura.

Chhagan hadn't lied. From that time on the Lala had many tribulations. Daroga says, On yer account the adivasis have gone awry. You brought a riot during my tenure. My constable's right arm was cut off, he became useless. And ye did this bad thing before the vote.

What does Lala say?

Why d'ye bother? Then the flag babus came from the Gormen party. Lala asked them to sit down, they didn't sit. If the vote is spoilt because of yer bad ideas, then we'll take it back by breaking yer neck. The vote comes next year! Ye'll give us fifty thousand rupees. Lala says, Forgive me boys. I caint dispute with yer. They said, Our people win by twenty-five hundred to three thousand margin. Votes cost a lot. Cos of you four thousand Munda votes'll be spoilt? We don't understand this land stuff. Settle your dispute. Otherwise the people of the other party'll win by harking to this case. You sit in water and make a hole in the boat? This was their talk. That's why Chhagan said, Lala will gie ya back your land. If ye take t' land he'll get his release from t' flag babus. He won't win if he disputes wit' t' flag babus. Otherwise he'll lose fifty thousand rupees.

It's a funny situation now.

Ye kin say that.

Not funny? We get half-bearin' land. His own land is in such arrangements. There'da been no trouble if he accepted me right. And now he wants to give t' land back! Why? Disputed land. E'en his own men will fear goin' ta that land past t' Munda quarters. The flag babus ha' spoken of votes, ha' asked fer money. That too's a reason. Daroga also is angry. He too will get off if I take t' land. The flag babus take him in his lap, and Daroga is happy too.

Ye won' take t' land.

Haint thought.

Here, ye're home. Our hearts are heavy. What happened in a moment!

Go home.

Chotti enters and says, Call everyone, Wife.

Everyone came. Don' anyone weep, Chotti said. Harmu's in je-hell. Two years' hard labour in je-hell! Then he gets out.

Won' weep? Wife asks.

No.

Why not?

Munda in court! He coulda got ten years. T' lawyer was good, and t' tribal offsir a good guy. So he got a break. Otherwise who knows what coulda happened?

Got a lawyer?

Gormen gies. Th' offsir did everythin'. Do I know where to go, what to do, what to gie?

No money?

To eat, jest a bit. Fed Harmu.

Two years.

Harmu's saved me face. If I'd raised me bow I'da killed 'em, I'd be hanged. Where's Koeli?

Harmu's wife came forward, restraining tears. Now ye're me son and daughter, both. I'll look at ye an' fergit me pain fer him. No weepin', is two years any time at all?

Beat 'im in je-hell.

The Lawyer said, adivasis work well in je-hell. He kin get out fast that way. No beatin'.

Shackles on feet.

No no, I found out everythin'.

Won' feedum.

Twice a day. Eat better'n at home.

Koeli shakes her head, says, Fine.

Harmu's real sad? asks Koel.

No no, he's a big boy. Come on, let's eat. I'm sleepy, no sleep fer so long.

For a long time now, Chotti's family is adrift, confused. At first Chotti went to town with Koel. But when he saw that everyone at home waited without food, wondering when they would return, he didn't let villagers or Koel accompany him. He went alone. This time he didn't even come back from town. Everyone felt their purpose come back when they saw Chotti was so composed. Koel looked with sharpened glance. His brother can become as unknown as he is intimately known to him. Now Dada's face is quite unknown. Dada's head seems higher after his son went to jail.

Dada?

What?

Lala wants to give up that land.

Heard ever'thin'. Koel?

What?

T' fence is crooked, there's white ant in yer hut's stoop. Ye were at home, so many of ye, what were ya doin'? Get to it tomorra, s'dn' keep work waitin'. If ya don' sew up hole in yer cloth, it widens, and t' same fer t' household. Right tomorra ye must pick all this up. Where are t' boys?

Somchar and Etwa stood by with head lowered. Tomorra I must see fence mended, says Chotti, See t' roof up straight, good sense in every task. Have ya given up t' job? Is there someone ta feed ya?

Chotti's wife said to Koeli, Oil yer hair tomorra, wash yer clothes, if ya stay like this Harmu is harmed.

Harmu's youngest is four. She said to granny, Whyja say Harmu? Eh?

What'll I say?

Say Aba.

And if not?

I'll hit ya.

Everybody laughed. The atmosphere of the room lightened. After they lay down, Wife asked, Where were ya?

First at th' Offsir's. Then when I knew he'd surely go to je-hell I stayed in front of t' courthouse, under a tree. From there I saw him when he was brought to Court, t' police din' say no. I'd gie him a bit ta eat. Otherwise all day in Court.

High price for ever'thin'?

Yeah, a lot.

Didja feel lonely?

Hey you see Mundas goin' and comin' in town. They'd come talk. We're okay even in such bad luck. They have no joy.

Dintcha sight see in town?

Chotti knew that Wife was willing herself not to talk of her boy. Her fondness for the eldest is greatest.

I'd see town sittin' under tree, he said. I never thought of sight-seein'. And then I'd walk.

In town?

Yes dear. When me body was tired wit' walkin' around I'd come back. Then sleep came to me eyes. An' walkin' an' walkin' . . .

What?

I saw that madman one day. Puran Munda. He put's arms aroun' me. Town's close ta Ramgarh. He comes and goes. He took me aroun' for two days.

Whatcha see?

Nothin. P'raps I saw all, but in front of me eyes was polis and Harmu. No other picture could get inside. Saw a lake as big as t' sea, so much water! I walked cos me mind was burnin' up. T' madman walked wit' me two days. And then one day—

What happened?

It was night time. T' town doesn' know darkness. Ever'thin' crackles wit' light as if. So one place I see they've made a man with copper and iron, looked like! So high. I'm sittin' under t' man. And then a beggar comes an' says I sleep here. Give up me place. Gave up. So I say, Ye're from aroun' here? He says, Yeah. I say, Who's this man? Good to look at an' I think he's Munda. So t' beggar says, he was a Munda all right, Birsa Munda. Many said god Birsa even. Me mind took a turn hearin' that, Wife. Look! A Munda man, but in town they've cast his likeness moulded in copper an' iron. By day we know t' town is Diku's. At night it belongs to him, seems like. 'Twas 'n town they put 'm in je-hell. And y'know Wife, Harmu Canal's also in town.

Chotti sensed that his wife was asleep. Long days of worry, sleepless nights, pain held tight in the breast. Chotti sensed that he too was sleeping. It's as if he can't fall asleep if he's not touching Harmu's Mother. Again he thought, Harmu'd saved his face. Chotti fell asleep.

XI

SENDING HARMU TO jail had multiple consequences for the area. The entire incident makes Tirathnath's face crack a smile, and Chotti's people win no ulterior gain. But their honour is enhanced.

Chotti means storytelling.

Harbans Chadha becomes Chotti's people's helper indirectly, unawares. He says to Chotti, My cousin, my mother's brother's son, is now a forest contractor. For six months the timber's felled, and it'll stop when the rains come. Now the trees are getting marked. You have no way to join that work.

Why lord?

Chotti always makes the signs of respect when he speaks, but there's no timidity in him. This Harbans likes a lot. Tirathnath's wealth comes from farming and the moneylending business. Harbans is somewhat modern. He's heard that places like Bokharo, Chas and Patratu will be developed, and he wants to be involved in it. He keeps up a good front with Tirathnath. Yet he finds Tirathnath and the matter of his moneylending medieval. A man who doesn't buy a motorcar, doesn't play the radio, doesn't run to the county seat to roam the moviehouses and the hotel-bars—who wears a knee-length dhoti, a coarse kurta and sturdy cobbler-made shoes—whose idea of entertainment is to listen to the 'Feats of Rama' sung by the village bards—seems in Harbans's eyes a country hick, somewhat uncultivated. Only philistines gain from moneylending, according to Harbans. Bonded labour and making the poor work for lower wages also seem to him to be philistine behaviour. Harbans sees no fault in himself, although he does not give Chotti and his people more than twelve annas wages and in bad times makes famine-struck folks dig hard ground at no more than four.

Harbans said, He's a contractor. He'll pay rupee a day as wages. The timber will go to Tohri. The splitting then takes place in his factory. Over and above the wages they'll give four annas for tif-fin. It'll be good for you if you can get it. They need about a hundred people. But don't you have to give bonded labour at Lalaji's fields? That custom is stupid. In my Punjab state farming is well-advanced. But this idiot custom does not hold there.

Lord! A word.

Say it.

Ye know what tuk place.

Of course I know. Most unfortunate. I don't understand what he thinks he's up to. Such temper over such a little piece o' land? Hey his wits are ancient. Why all this trouble? Cultivation too must be modern. Drive a tractor, raise your crop threefold.

Chotti thinks the poor will be unemployed if tractors are used. But he said nothing. Just said, I'm not a bonded worker. There's more folks in our village who're not bonded labourers. Will ye take thirty-plus people? Why so few? Say fifty-plus.

There'll be no trouble?

I gie ye me word for t' Mundas. Chhagan'll give his word too, I know. Ye'll benefit, me lord.

Day after tomorrow, Harbans says, We'll let you know.

Chotti came to the village. Said to Chhagan, Come to our pahan once. Importan' stuff ta discuss.

Came home and said to Wife, When I see no way anywhere, a way appears. I was thinkin' and thinkin', I won' do that job of Lala's so how to fill our bellies. But there might be a way.

What way?

Let's see. I've asked Chhagan's bunch to come.

Why be together wit' them?

What other way is there today? We'll do t' same work wit' t' same boss, and all other work is also all together. We are few, they're on t' rise. We don' know what it is to be kicked for caste. They are kicked for it. Don' ye see how few Mundas there are now? We can last if we bite th' earth together. Otherwise we'll have to leave all and get on t' road.

Chotti sat in front of Pahan and spoke at length. And said, I like this idea cos why, t' contractor gives work fer six months. If we can show work he'll take us where'er he goes. True too that t' contractor works to see how low he can get labour. For him five quarters are t' dust of his feet. Fellin' trees is hard labour. But for us folks that's best?

How shall we manage the bonded labour? Chhagan asks.

How many people are there who're not bonded labourers? We're thirty-plus? Listen to me plan. Ye have ten in yer fam'ly. Eight go for bonded work. Four go, and four stay? We too have bonded labour in ev'ry fam'ly. We'll split it like this? See, our women will go too. Ask yer women to go as well. Those of ye who are bonded, stay that way. If not a one gives new thumbprints, ye'll live. We haint many ways to live. Let's live whichever way, or is this wrong?

He'll give five bits.

Yeah, four bits—a rupee—is wages and t' last bit for food.

Lemme tell'em all. Take it that they'll all agree.

Pahan said, Lala'll let ye?

'Slong as his work gets done? Yeah, we must keep an eye that his work gets done right. Then he won' be able to raise his voice.

He'll raise it.

Then I'll see? He's made me Harmu a je-hell bird, I'll never fergit me anger. But everythin' is his, so we must have strategy. There's tiger in t' forest, but also hare an' hedgehog. No? They live by strategy. We'll live like that? Lemme tell ya 'bout strategy, fer Mundas. I don' feel good 'bout nothin' no more.

Lemme go, tell everyone. Knew we'd get strength when ye got back. 'Slong as ye were in town, we were like dead.

Won' ye go ta see Harmu? Pahan said.

Yeah. Lemme get this done first?

Thus do the Mundas and lowcastes of Chotti village enter the national economic pattern of independent India. The state has left no spot for them in this pattern. The majority of the population in independent India is low caste, and a significant percentage is adivasi. Therefore they are excluded from the national economic pattern. But even the excluded must live. By that necessity Chotti's group and Chhagan's, without support from any group or organization, attempted to and succeeded in weakening Lala's group the slightest bit. As a result further complications arise and increase progressively.

Chotti and his folks go to fell trees by the contractor's decision. Tirathnath takes a look at the folks who have come to take care of his spring crop and asks, So Chotti didn't come? I don't see Koel, I don't see Somchar.

Chhagan's son Parsad says, Gone some place.

Tirathnath had thought Chotti wouldn't come, but he was still disappointed not to see him. We want to give Chotti the land again. But Chotti's not here. Then should he go to Chotti? There was considerable menace in the words of the Congressi party boys. If Chotti doesn't take the land, there will be an effect on the minds of the tribals. The affair of the vote is imminent. The tribal vote will decrease, be divided. The boys will mark Tirathnath as the reason. And fifty thousand will also disappear. If the wilderness had remained wild, then Tirathnath would have set fire to the houses of Chhagan and his people, evicted Chotti and his clan. The place is not 'far far away' any more. Ananda Mahato has reported Harmu's fight for land in the newspaper *Adivasi Samachar.* There Tirathnath has been unreasonably called 'the enemy of the adivasi', 'bloodsucking moneylender', 'the cause of adivasi eviction', etc. All kinds of people live in Chotti now. Among the moneyed folk Harbans Chadha thinks of Tirath as the most backward country hick. Tirath thinks of Anwar as 'cow eating infidel'. Why did so few people come to work in his field?

Washerwoman Motia said in her rapidfire way, Ye're crazy. When did more than fifty-odd people work on yer farm? Just fifty-five people have come, they're working.

True. But where are the others?

Let 'em go.

Why do I see women in bonded work?

But the work's not behind?

Not behind, but . . .

If ye like to look at our faces so much, give us a feast one day, Motia said, laughing. There's a barb in the suggestion. After long years of silence Tirathnath has just a few months ago fathered a son in the womb of his washerwoman beloved. They'll sing about the entire event at the Colourfeast.

Tirathnath digested the barb. Now the problem is his. D'ye know where Chotti is? he asked. I need to talk to him.

Gone some place.

Ah Motia, what are ye up to?

Whadja mean, up to?

Ye walk with the Mundas, go to their pahan.

Live in t' same village, so we walk together? Pahan's yard is neat an' clean. It's nice to sit there and talk, so we go.

They're a rough crowd. Ye're Hindus.

They're not rough on us.

In the evening Tirathnath walked to the trader's shop. Sat on the cushion there. In the evening the villagers come to buy. Chotti came. Bought a hundred grams of oil, two seers of rice.

Chotti, how're ye doin'? said Tirath.

As ye keep me, lord.

As I keep you.

Chotti smiled sweetly and said, In me old age me staff of life Harmu is in je-hell. An' so I say I am as ye keep me.

It's as if t' house burnt up in a dead fire. Such a to-do otherwise! Chotti, I have somethin' ta say.

Say it.

Let's walk off a bit.

Coming to a less crowded spot Tirathnath says, Ye take that land. Word of mouth no more. I'll write it up.

No lord.

Don't speak while ye're angry, think on it.

Chotti smiled just as sweetly and said, I'm not angry. I'm thinkin' on it. No more land, no more writin' up, no more nothin' lord.

Yer hard life would have been eased a bit with the land.

Since I'm born Munda, a hard life is me birthright. I won' let it go.

Chotti went home. Tirathnath returned to the store for his walking stick. The trader said, Chotti doesn't go to yer place?

No. What does he do now?

He cuts trees in the forest. Many villagers go.

Who gave the job?

Chadha's cousin's a contractor. Chadha gave.

The next day Tirathnath tied up some mixed nuts in a kerchief and went to Harbans. Praised the brick kiln profusely and then said, Is it true Harbansji, that you are thinnin' out my village workforce?

How's that?

They're workin' with yer cousin. And gettin' five bits wages. Brother, we must look out for each other in this wild place. Twelve annas, just three bits, would have been right. Two bits wages and one fer food. They'da worked fer that. It's not right ta raise the rate. This'll make us lose out in the end.

Why should the rate go up wit' this? Let'm give what he gives. I won't go above twelve annas, they know. There'll be no trouble with that. For they know, there's countless labour here, no work. Why should they make trouble?

Brother, whyja tempt them?

Harbans lost his temper. What sort of talk is this? he asked. Fifty-five people worked in your fields, and that's firm. Who'll give food ta everyone? You or me?

Brother, you won't understand.

No, an' I don' want to.

But ye must try. Tirathnath said in a hard voice, hitting the ground with his stick, Not everyone works. Those who don't stand and watch. They know I'm their only hope. And they stay disciplined. If they're not under control how'll I last here?

Harbans is a bloodsucker but he's a small industrialist, and his way of thinking is more modern than Tirathnath's. In the coming five-year plans he wants to be a middle industrialist from this area. Tirathnath's land-centred mentality is altogether repugnant to him. He strongly wants to be more powerful than Tirathnath. He said with some asperity, The time of kings is past Lalaji. You want to remain the master of law and order, but that's not possible.

It's possible if you support me, Harbans.

Arrey! Are ya dreamin'? You won't give work, and they won't do work? If ye're too pigheaded about this I'll be forced ta let the Congressites know that ye're deliberately picking fights with the adivasis and the untouchables. Then Congress will have problems at the votes. You're fighting unfairly with Chotti. These villages are ten miles, twenty miles apart, it's hard to bring in other people to cast votes here. How're you going to make these people cast their vote on the sign of the twin bullocks? And Congress's goin' to leave you alone if there's trouble with the vote?

Tirathnath gave up and got up. At the time of harvesting the spring crop, he said, I'll just take bonded and outside labour. I'll show 'em.

Do what you like. Ye don't understand yer own future.

Does Congress want that I remain under their feet?

Not at all. Whatever their law, when it comes to enforcement, Congress looks the other way. Go ahead and forget the ceiling, keep more land than it allows, carry on with bonded labour. Kill 'em with high interest, you'll get backing. One thing, keep the vote solid. They're not yer tenants that ye'll terrorize them into voting. Use money to secure the vote. And this time the candidate contesting Congress is lowcaste. He's got the backing of Anand Mahato, Swami Shuddhanand, the anti-casetist monk, and people of that ilk. The lowcaste vote will be divided. Remains the adivasis. Ananda will make lowcaste and adivasi the same issue and carry on his election campaign. Now if the vote is screwed because of your pigheadedness or mine, Congress control will falter. Then will you get support from the lowcaste candidate?

Tirathnath sighs and says, This looks very complicated.

Even if Congress wins on the state level if non-Congress wins in the area, the area will not receive support. Then will there be anything in it for us? You want bullock cart, I want aeroplane. We need a connecting road here. I want to have a bus running seven days a week. Industrial townships growing up all around, this is the moment.

I don't want all that though. My life will go on wit' land and bonded labour and moneylending. Industry is just for today. Land is forever.

So why don't you farm with tractors?

Why should I? Their labour's cheaper.

You and I will not understand each other.

Tirathnath doesn't like the times. Anand Mahato calls a campaign meeting in Chotti with all the Mundas and the untouchables. He explains that tribal and untouchable are equally oppressed by the depredations of the caste-Hindu moneylenders. He makes a false promise, that his candidate will look out for the interest of the tribal and the untouchable. The meeting is very successful and Chotti's people join in as a group. The vote and the spring harvest are synchronized. The untouchable candidate wins by a large margin. Tirathnath is abused by the Congressis in spite of giving them fifty thousand rupees. He goes to get outside labour to take revenge, but Chotti says to his middleman Govind Karan, Go ahead, bring labour, but you won' stay alive. I'll finish you off.

Ye'll kill me?

Chotti says, enjoying himself, I'll sit in thana. There'll be nothin' in me hands. But me arrer will search ye out and pierce ye. You won' bring labour, an' if Lala knows this I will too. Then look out. Lala's pa couldn' escape even in Banaras. Kurmi village burnt up with fire-tipped arrers.

Govind says nothing to Tirath, takes a hundred rupees as advance for bringing labour and takes off. Tirathnath gives him the money. And then, to thicken the plot of the storylines about Chotti, armed robbers arrive. This is indeed the season for such dacoits. Tirath's estate is robbed clean. Like armed robbers in the movies these dacoits stop a cargo train and travel north in it.

Tirath realizes that his misfortune is a result of making Chotti angry. Daroga can't help him at all. The usual folks turn up at the time of the spring harvest. Tirathnath gets the spring crop home with their help and for the first time opens an account at the bank in the county seat. Harbans mocks, Money in the bank?

Different times, different rules.

So ye're with us now?

Whate'er you say.

For the Mundas all this is Chotti's personal success and the events proclaim Chotti's glory through the medium of songs. After a long time one hears music at the Sohrai festival of the adivasis and of Chhagan's clan. Listening, Chotti says to Koel, D'ye hear what they say in t' songs?

C'mon, let me hear.

> Ye took away t' land of half-right half-crop,
> Sent our golden boy Harmu to je-hell
> Who talks to th' arrer at home?
> Chotti Munda talks t' talk—
> Th' arrer swims thru' th' air
> Now all seem crazed and crazy
> Else why is Bidur Mahato t' vote-winner?
> Why does Govind Karan run away?
> Why do dacoits fall on yer estate?
> Hey hey hey what's happenin' to ye?

Chotti hears and says, Oof. They know just Chotti Munda. So powerful that he keeps his boy in je-hell and sleeps at home.

C'mon, let me hear!

So t' stories build up again. Songs. For everything is story, mate, in Chotti Munda's life.

Chotti sighs and says, they make songs cos they need to. Ever'thin' runs away like water through fingers. They look for hope when they make songs.

Who'll go to see Harmu tomorra?

No one. Lotta pain doin' five bits' work, but t' work mus' be done ever' day. I've tol' Harmu ever'thin'.

What's that offsir say?

Says, Why come? It's a lotta money.

But we do earn some.

Not a pice mus' be wasted, Koel. We'll take that land. In writin'. Harmu'll get t' land when he comes. He's gone to je-hell with t' land's loss in his heart. He'll come and see t' land there.

T' trader's land's barren, dada. And t' forest's not close by neither.

Who gives good land to Munda?

He'll write off t' whole plot?

Yeah. What'll he do?

The land is dry and stony. The trader had bought it cheap. Five bighas of land. He doesn't make enough money from his small shop to make that land bear fruit. Eleven years have passed thinking maybe I'll make enough, now I'll make enough. Tirathnath has had two of his kinsmen open stores last year. The time has come for the trader to shut shop in Chotti. He has no customers but Munda and untouchable. Tirathnath has built a row of rooms on the long arcades behind the station and set up two stores and a flour-grinding machine. It's impossible to compete with Tirath. Mundas and untouchables have little buying power—spend on oil, salt, cayenne, molasses, lumps of washing soda, soap, matches. Even that in tiny quantities. It's not possible to keep the shop going on such custom. The trader will go to Tohri. There he will test his fortunes! This land is rough and dry. No one one wants to buy his five bighas even for five hundred rupees. Far from Chotti river, in a stony field. Now if Chotti buys it on an instalment plan, he is relieved. He says to Chotti, Take it all.

Caint.

Then you look for someone else.

The trader is a timid and simple soul. He says, I'll give t' land on your word alone. Adivasi doesn't cheat.

Let's see who takes it.

How'll I take it, says Chhagan. All my income goes to repay Lala. Else I'd a taken fo' sure.

To Chotti's amazement Sana comes to his room. I'll tek it, says he. Fix that land for me.

Ye'll tek it?

Not in me own name. Ain't I bonded? Work it in t' name of me nephew Jita.

But t' money?

I've heard. Fifteen rupees a year per bigha. Do ye give half, an' me half. Thas enough, no?

Ye have money?

Chotti, I buy wheat, put it in hot water an' eat. An' puttin' by money fer fellin' trees. See here—

Sana pours coins from a hollow bamboo. Twenty-two rupees I saved, he says. Won' this do? Tell me?

Chotti says, Let's see.

The trader agrees. Chotti goes to Udham Singh, Harbans Chadha's accountant. A one-rupee legal form is purchased in Tohri. On it Udhan Singh writes, I, Sir Puranchand Bania___village Group___Revenue Sector am selling Plot no.___to Chotti Munda and Jita Munda on an instalment plan. I will keep ownership of the land. Chotti and Jita Munda are liable for an annual payment of thirty-seven-and-a-half rupees to me. If they are unable to pay I can hire out my land to new clients.

No one has ever heard such a lease document. But Chotti and the others still think this was an achievement. Tirathnath asks the trader, Sold it dirt cheap?

The trader says, Nothin' but thistles grow there, lord.

I'da taken if ya'd told me?

It's the roughest and driest even 'mong the barren plots lord.

Harbans Chadha says to the trader, Ye've done very well. No one would have taken that land. Chotti's crowd lusts after land. Otherwise even they'd not have taken.

Says to Chotti, Should one take such land?

Chotti says, What d'ye do, lord!

How to explain to Harbans? Be it barren, be it stony, a bit of land means tying one's drifting existence to an anchor. Chotti doesn't have the power to run to the law courts. That bit of paper is his hope. The trader will come take the money every year and write a receipt in Udham Singh's presence.

Like Tirathnath Harbans also disapproves of the matter and asks, Will you be able to do outside work after this?

Sure. T' land belongs to our sons, lord.

Yer two sons?

Also Koel's son.

Where's that written down?

We don' need to write down.

Ye're crazy, Chotti.

No lord. I tell ya true.

What's that?

Papaya seed lord. Weren't ye speakin' of it th' other day? And this papaya has no grains inside, t' pulp is thick, t' fruit so sweet. Ya kill so many snakes ever' year. Bury 'em at t' root of this. Ye'll see how sappy t' tree will be with that food. There's no plant food to come near't.

Both Tirathnath and Harbans remain dissatisfied with Chotti's acquisition of land. It's not correct that Chotti and company should own even stony land. This might alter the balance of their mental make-up. They may get a sense of property rights in land. This is not desirable. They should be kept like spectres without any recourse, without any materiality, forever dependent. Like those who are kept apart by earth, by water, by air. Unknown to each other, they both look at the matter of Chotti's land in their own self interest. In deep curiosity. Those who have nothing but themselves and their rags—what will they do with this ghostly stony land?

They do not take into account Chotti's sharp intelligence and sensitivity. His mind is marinated in deep distrust of the Diku-Hindu. He says to Sana, That Chadha, that Lala, those bastards don' like our gettin' land. They buy t' whole earth, that's justice. We take two and a half bighas of stone, thas unjust. Now whate'er job we do for them, we must do right.

It's against Sana's nature to think anything from bottom up. Many of them are like that, Chotti will do the thinking. The leader of the hopeless. They'll just obey orders.

Sana says, We'll do that fo' sure, but what's this Chotti? I'm a landowner.

Tek care what ye say. Not ye, it's Jita's land. He's not e'en an owner, it's a lease. Jita took it.

Jita an' I's t' same.

No, don' mek that mistake. If yer name comes up Lala will grab't. What s'll I say to ye! We've got out jest a bit from under Lala, got jobs in t' forest, jobs wit' Chadha. Done nothin' wrong, still I walk caref'lly. We were in Lala's bite, I've moved his teeth a bit. He's mad angry. And now ye talk outta line. Me land! So Sana, ye're bonded wit' yer debt load. Nothin' can be yer own. So ye put in Jita's name. And ye've told this to a lotta folks? If Lala hears this he'll show ye t' capital city, me boy.

Haven' told.

Don'. Ye're old, hev some sense. Keepin' youse in line I haven't t' time to cry fer Harmu.

Why s'd ye cry? Hasn' he saved yer face?

Dontcha hev anythin' to say. That's me stuff.

Okay, say what ye wantcha say.

Chotti lit a bidi. Then said with fitting solemnity, Howe'er stony, there's land now.

So all Mundas will be thrilled wit' this.

Yeah, and lease stone. Munda can do anythin'. I took, so they're all thrilled.

Okay, tell me.

We've taken land, but there's a lot to do.

It's as if the Mundas have won some wager because Chotti and Jita have leased land. Chhagan too comes by and says, Done good. We'll dig up the stone wit' shovels. When t' moon changes phase we'll come on t' quiet and gie labour. It's yer land, after all. We do feel hope wit' this.

What hope?

We know we too can have land.

There's only one tiger. Tirathnath. D'ye think he'll let anyone else lease land? He'll cast his vulture eye and lease up all t' barren ground. He'll not let barren land give fruit in yer hands 'n' ours. Ye know how?

How?

They, the Tiraths, want little land to bear, and that land must be theirs. If more land's barren, t' better fer them. Then we remain in their bounty. We're tied up. Now they know that if we get barren land we get crops. So they'll buy up barren land to keep control.

They'll farm?

'Course not. Then too many folks get day work.

What'll they do?

Keep barren. The more t' ground is barren, t' more youse and us take loans, give bond, eat kicks.

Ye understan' so much, not us.

But what can I do, if I understan'?

Ye're our eyes, our life, our arms too.

Uh, ye dumb Diku.

Dumb Munda, ye.

They both start laughing and Chhagan says, We'll gie labour.

The matter becomes most significant to the Mundas. Tirathnath fulfils Chotti's predictions and starts buying up barren land. Because of ancient feuds the fruitseller Anwar holds on to his plot and lets Chotti know secretly that his thirty bighas he'll distribute later.

Pahan divides Chotti's and Jita's plot by throwing a rope down and putting up a cactus fence. Cactus fencing goes up around the whole plot. Then the ground is blessed with a puja and a sprinkling of the blood of a sacrificed cock. Then for a few months the work of removing stone and gravel goes on during the phase of the waning moon. Paddy is sown after the rains. Chotti puts up a bamboo platform and since he identifies with both plots, he watches over both with an eagle eye. Jita stays up with him and now all those memories of staying up with Dhani crowd Chotti's mind. He says to Jita with Dhani's enthusiasm, If ye wanna learn to shoot an arrer, sharpen yer eyes. Look, deer.

Nah, they've killed all t' deer.

Look more.

A spotted deer has come with the smell of paddy. Jita says, Kill it? Oof, so long we ha'n't eaten deer meat.

Nah, that's a doe. I too feel like shootin', but they are bein' killed off like we are. Way in t' forest mebbe there are some. Now comin' out. There'll be increase if we let t' doe live.

Chotti claps and the animal runs away instantly. Sleep, says Chotti. There's no sleepin' for me.

Ye won' sleep?

No.

Jita sleeps. Chotti loves this solitude, the spreading horizon, the night chill. Then he descends from the platform. He walks around and inspects the entire field. The paddy has come up. Not so very bright, but still paddy. Suddenly he recalls something. He says to himself, Yup. An unbroken field gets no shade. Now during rains I'll bring seedlings of straight growin' trees and plant them all around. It'll get a bitta shade.

Sana goes crazy toward the harvest month of Aghran: Hey, hey, hey, t' paddy's ripening, he says, and comes to sit on the platform. Once he sits, it's impossible to get him down. He says to Chotti, I won' go fer bonded labour no more. I'll stay here.

Chotti scolds him and sends him to work. After the harvest they go to Khublal, the coal merchant. They get the paddy weighed. Just measure. Two and a half bighas land, two and a half maund paddy.

Chotti goes quiet when he sees the weight. He'll get one and a half maunds—a hundred and twenty pounds—paddy. And chaff. He sighs and buys a sack from Khublal. If he fills it with chaff Harmu's boys will sleep. Khublal doesn't worry about land. D'ye know the pond in the railway compound?

T' scummy pond?

The same. Tishan-Sir will now get it dug. Dig-up that mud and pitch it on t' land. This paddy is sick like. T' land had no strength. What a crazy, ya leased stone.

Hey, that's good talk!

Chotti goes to the station master instantly. He says, I'm goin' to have it dug out, yeah. The last time the station caught fire, and the fire spread before they could draw up water from the well.

T' pond was good before.

So you want the mud, take it. So why don't ye dig it out yer-selves? We'll give twelve anna wages?

Okay, we'll dig it. But look out fo' a good time. We can' hurt Lalaji's ploughin' work. This work'll get done wit' ten men and ten women. Let's do it this way.

Now?

Ye can start now. The spring crop is being sown in t' field now. There's not much work right now. But can't t' twelve annas be a rupee?

No Chotti, that can't be.

Then that's t' deal. And, if there's fire in t' villages do we get water?

Why not? Government property, is't mine? But only if there's fire. Won't let you use it all the time.

So that's fixed up. Khublal hears everything and says, Tishan-Sir had submitted a tender for this job in false name. Ten thousand rupee tender.

What's a tender?

Rail work is not done in any old way. First Tishan-Sir explains to Company that this pond must be dug. Then Company calls for tenders, who'll do t' work fer how much. Tishan-Sir oils t' machine, and the Company's ready t' gie him ten thousand rupees. Now even if ye work fer two months, he won't put out more'n a thousand rupees. So nine thousand rupees profit. Then he'll sow fish in t' water and sell fish. Talk of water made me think this. I was walkin' around the other day, saw the pits ye've dug. Crystal clear water. Tis a good thing ye're doing. Ye cut a pit in t' river bed year arter year—ye get sand, ye get water. Chhagan's folks come as well. Otherwise we'da felt t' well-water too dirty to drink with' all th' untouchables crowding for water.

Are ye high caste too?

Sure. I'm a Kurmi. Not a Dusad, not a Ganju, not a Dhobi—washer caste. Hey Chotti, why do ye folks have no caste?

Who knows?

Hearing of this, Chhagan's group says, What're ye up to? Picked up this job as well? Who knew there'd be so much work in Chotti?

Sure there'll be work. Times are changin'. Now we've to mek sure that we get all t' jobs ever'where after Tirath's work is finished.

Won' gie more than twelve annas why?

We'll have ta learn.

Learn what?

Chotti smiles weakly and asks, Why s'd they gie, tell me? Chadha give twelve annas, he'll gie t' same. Otherwise by their count t' rate goes up.

True.

No use thinkin' on it. Feel dizzy to think on it. How much money in t' world! Chadha's made so much money sellin' these hollow bricks, that he now says he'll buy two or three coal quarries. Here t' coal is above ground. Givin' us twelve annas. Lala's made so much money farmin', wit' loan interest, that there was t' robbery, and he gave Congress fifty thousand rupees, and he didn't feel a scratch. He's givin' yer t' dust from his shoes. T' tishan master is takin' ten thousand rupees to dig this pond. And he'll giv' us twelve annas. So look, they won' giv' us a cut on t' ten or fifty thousand. Let's take what we get.

Whate'er we get, ye're right.

We'll take it. Put food in our bellies and live.

True.

But ye call me a god, I'll tak an' offerin'.

What'll ye tek?

When ye dig t' pond each one put that scummy mud on t' land, carryin' as ye can. T' land's cryin' like a babe sick wit' hunger.

We'll give, we'll carry.

Thus all the discussion happens and Chotti's people and Chhagan's people take atom by atom through tiny holes from the national economy. The national economy is not thereby disturbed and they get food to eat. One thing everyone accepts in the life of Chotti village and station. It's the locals that are showing their faces in the labouring jobs. This too they accept, that it's best to speak to Chotti about labour. He is old, a man of experience, a man known and respected by all. If he gives his word the work will go as promised. Chhagan's group will also honour that word.

When the pond-digging starts Harbans laughs and says, Now be a labour-contractor Chotti.

How so?

Ye're giving everybody jobs, take a cut.

No lord.

You can but. Everyone does.

No lord.

In time the pond is dug and algae-rich mud falls on the land of Chotti's people. Pahan is a citizen of these times. He squints at the land and says to Chotti, if one can go downhill, cross t' river, climb t' bank, walk that far and get t' scummy mud, then ye can walk on flat land and bring rottin' leaves from t' forest.

True nuff.

Ye know a lot of folks. Gormen gives crop food. Go to Tohri. Ask for it from Biddibabu.

But will they give, says Chotti. There'll be words.

Three most unusual things happen to Chotti and his people at this time. Each is suggestive enough to be captured in song and story. Behind the first the excuse is Chotti's land and the first incident is one of a kind.

Tirathnath is a local resident and this place is in his blood. After his hostility, rage, anger, he has a sense of proprietorship somewhere about Chotti or about all Mundas, or about all low-caste folks. It's not the feeling of proprietorship of the creditor toward the debtor. It is the proprietorship bound to an ancient relationship. Sure Tirathnath takes bonded labour, but he wants that they should say without hesitation, as they used to, Hey lord, ye're goin' to eat all this papaya alone? Gie us one or two, yeah?

Lord, yer cattle's gone strange. Let's call t' shaman lady, let her do an offerin' in the cleaned-up cattle pen.

Tirathnath and Chotti. He used to call Chotti's father 'Uncle'. That Chhagan's mother made some herbal paste, and cured Tirath's mother's menstrual problems. Now the thing is to go to the doctor, but Tirath has never seen a physician like Chhagan's mother. As long as Chhagan's mother was alive no one in Chotti village worried about the health problems of women and children.

Everything is out of joint now. Tirathnath had said to Harbans, You are breaking up my labour force. There was special emphasis on that word 'my'. They are 'mine'—Tirath's. Tirath will kill them or keep them at will. He won't kill them. If Tirath was such a killer, Mundas and untouchables would have fled Chotti village, no? Is Tirath like other bosses, other moneylenders? Japu Singh keeps the rhythm of the Gormen's five-year funfairs and finds an excuse to burn down the fields and homes and paddy stacks of the untouchables right after elections. If I don't do like this, he says, the bastards will want to be the Berahmin's equals.

Why doesn't Tirath burn down the homes and hamlet of Chhagan's folks? Why doesn't he? Because adivasi, untouchable and other folks are a mixed lot there? No no. Tirath may be old-fashioned as compared to Harbans, but he is modern as compared to Japu. The Japu matter is either very complex or very simple, who knows? It's true he burns up untouchable quarters. He doesn't stop the police from coming either and says, Right, right, do yer duty, brothers! That's why Gormen feeds you, no? Tell me, tell me.

He does not bribe the police, and he goes around with the police. The oppressed homeless human beings do not open their mouths in front of Japu. Japu is infinitely delighted by this and says to the police, They love and fear me like a father. Then, truly amazing, Japu goes one better on Gormen aid and gives them money for housing and food. Gives means donates, not as loan. Japu says, Tirath Lala is a Lala—trader. I'm Japu Singh. Rajput by caste. My forefathers were rajas—kings. What does a king do? Take life, save life. Where will Tirath get my temper? It is also true that, because of such insane behaviour the people have a kind of devotion to Japu Singh. Japu Singh is most exceptional among the regional moneylenders and bosses. Today's bosses and moneylenders carry on the imperial tradition of the Tughlak dynasty inherent in the pre-British king-landowners. Tirath had once said, Have you ever thought on one thing, understood one thing?

What thing?

The human body. You too are seventy. Suppose it happens that you burn down the huts, and die before you can give aid?

Ho, ho, ho, that caint be.

Suppose the police catch you one time?

Ho, ho, ho, what a joker. Laughing and coughing Japu Singh had poked Tirath in the belly and said, I do yoga and body culture, iron fingers, see? I won't die like that and Gormen won't catch me.

Tirath doesn't burn down huts like Japu Singh. He doesn't do holy festivals twelve months of the year and raise taxes from his creditors like Ramsaran Mathur. What wrong does he do? Take interest on loans? Take bonded labour? What's wrong with that? There can be no wrong in the longstanding ways of the world? That out-of-joint mindset in the people of Chotti, is it cos of loans? No no. Yet because of bonded labour and moneylending, that upstart Harbans despises him. Is it good to despise?

No no. There's more reason behind the out-of-jointness of the people of Chotti. Before there was just them and Tirath. Now for day-labour they go to all kinds of people. Tirath doesn't want it. Tirath doesn't want violence either. In fact, during the land riot, Tirath had told Mathura Singh repeatedly, don't shoot. Terrorize. But stupid fool fired left and right. Who can be more ignorant than a man who shoots police in front of Daroga, Tishan Sir, and Adivasi Offsir—Three Gormens?—Actually Tirath has thought it through, everything went wrong from the time of the difference with Chotti. Was Tirath possessed? Why was he set on that piece of land? Harmu went to jail. Chotti is now shooting arrows into him in many ways. Otherwise why should there be armed robbery on his estate, Congressis ask for fifty thousand rupees, why would an outcaste candidate win the elections, and the thing that he can't tell anyone, why would his laundress beloved go against him? Tirath wants to make up with Chotti. And that's why he asked Chotti to take the land back. Chotti didn't take it. Hearing all, Tirath's wife said, Why should he? He's casting spells on you, his arrows won't work if he takes your land. Everything became confused. The holy man whose blessing Tirathnath received in Tohri was caught by the police as a marked criminal as soon as Tirath returned to the village, these are called bad times.

Thinking all this Tirathnath was walking in the strip of land beside the railway line, as indeed he does every day. Every day his mother says, You don't hear good after that fever, and you don't buy a hearing aid, you're going to be run over or be pushed around by a train one day.

Hey, do I go at train time?

But Tirath hadn't reckoned that in independent India the trains are also becoming independent. A cargo train leaves Chotti station and comes forward. Tirath doesn't hear the whistle. Chotti was bringing the cows home. He sees what's happening and starts running, climbs the embankment on the run and pulls hard at Tirath's leg. Tirath slams down on the stones. Don't hit me Chotti! he screams and, raising his head, he sees the cargo train stop. Chotti directs a stream of unrepeatable invective in the Mundari language at the driver and says in Hindi, The lord is deaf, doesn't hear a word. When ye saw that he wasn't moving from t' line, s'dn't ye stop t' train?

The train leaves. Chotti says, Get up lord. Ye can hear soft words, couldn't hear t' loud whistle?

I had that fever three months back—

Get up.

Tirathnath gets up and in the shock of relief at this rescue from a great danger tears stream down his face.

Go on home.

I've dirtied my dhoti.

Tirath's body was bruised all over. His cap had fallen off. Chotti sees that Tirath can't control his limbs, he's dazed. Chotti sighs and says, Get down. Wash yer dhoti in t' river and be clean.

What shall I wear?

Spread t' dhoti out on t' bushes, it'll dry.

Stay here awhile.

Wait, let me bring t' cow.

Chotti gets the cow. The difficult operation is performed. Washing his clothes in the river, putting it out to dry on the bushes, Tirathnath stands naked. He's in a bad spot. Chotti sits to the side, lights a bidi.

Chotti!

Yeah!

Forgive me.

Why?

I thought ye'd kill me.

Chotti has always been a free spirit. He feels even more free in spirit after giving up Tirath's job. He says, Lord! My head is not like yours, it doesn't think those thoughts. Ye woulda killed me, right?

Me?

An' I saved ya.

But my misfortunes come from yer arrow.

How?

This armed robbery, Congress taking fifty thousand and neither you nor Chhagan obey me after Harmu went to jail.

Lord, since ye think I'm doin' pierce-arrer wit' ye, I won' be able ta get that thought outa yer head. But if I do pierce-arrer, I'll shoot straight, own up in thana and swing on a noose. Yes lord! Chotti is me name. Ever'thin' ye say is mad words. But I'll answer t' last thing.

Now even Chhagan's folks wear shoes, carry umbrellas. Didn' before. Tell me if I lose face wit' this or not?

So someone puts on a rupee an' half flipflop slipper from weekly market, puts up a bamboo umbrella on a rainy day. Where's yer face there?

This is not good Chotti. Here ye tek the land—

So?

That's not god's law. The land belongs to bosses and moneylenders. The Lord above doesn't wish that Munda-Dusad should own land. If He had, they'da got land.

Ye've become t' Lord above. Ye tek all t' land, let it lie still so we don' get it.

Haint I saved ye all these years? Where was Chadha, where was his brudder? Where was Tishan Sir?

Ye saved us yeah.

If ye're there would anyone rob my goods?

Ye never understood it lord.

You won' come any more?

Nope. Would ye have?

Lordy lordy.

Here, yer cloth's dry, put it on. What'll I say more? Ye reckon God's law one way, we another. Like two steel rails run side-by-side, they never meet, then t' train would topple. Maybe this too is t' god's wish that t' two of us—ye and we—don' understan' each other. If we did there udn't be so much fightin', so much starving, but yer god woulda been scared, if t' train turned over. Go home now, go.

Then ye have no curse on me?

No curse, no word. The boy's in je-hell, can I fergit that pain? No, I won' lie, I don' fergit. I think lord, ye woulda don' that, when ye walk along t' line, lemme shoot an arrer.

Hunh? Whaddya think?

Chotti got angry. What is this cravenness? If paddy grows on me land ye think let's grab t' land. If we take more land ye think let me buy up all t' barren land cos otherwise t' nekkid beggars'll know t' taste of land. Then if ye put me boy in je-hell s'dn' I think that when Lala walks around alone at sundown, lemme hit 'im? I think, but I don' do it. Me blood is not that way.

Oh God—and Tirath started crying—lemme go, he says. Don' kill me Chotti. I beg ya.

Tirath ran. Chotti called out, If I wanted to kill would I hev saved yer life? Tirath didn't hear those words.

Hearing all his wife said in great and explosive rage, He's put me boy in je-hell, ye kept his life?

Even if it weren't he but Mathura, I'da run. I didn' think who he was. What came to mind was that a life was gettin' lost.

Why dintcha break his head on a stone?

Don' say that, Wife, Chotti roared out, In me mind I split his head on stone ten times a day, ten times at sundown I pierce his ribs and put a hole in his heart wit' me arrer.

Why dontcha?

Wit' Harmu, t' Gormen offsir was witness, so Daroga didn't feed us to t' dogs. If I kill 'im polis will come and burn down t' Munda hamlet. Then? The Mundas adrift for me sake? I'll be t' cause? Tell me will that be a just thing to do?

I know. Come on, drink some molasses-water. Sit with yer grandson. His ma's gone to t' far forest to gather kindlin'.

How'll she pull it?

She knows. Pull on a rope?

Gimme.

Taking Harmu's boy in his lap, Chotti says, Oh Harmu'll come back and see how much his boy talks. Left 'im a bitty baby.

When'll he come?

Now he'll come.

Tirathnath undergoes an astonishing transformation. He no longer goes walking that way. He considers every villager a possible assassin. He no longer squabbles with Chhagan's people and because he has avoided the misfortune of being hit by a railway train he sends a portion of the offerings to his household god Narayan to Chhagan's quarter.

This is the first unusual event. Chhagan says, The lord's gonna die Chotti. Else why's he turned so good?

Fears ghosts.

Whose ghost?

Chotti spits on the ground and says, He sees ghosts all t' time. I'm killin' him, that's t' ghost he sees.

Whatever, he's given many sweetballs, much ground chickpea.

So eat up.

The second unusual event happens around water.

Surprising everyone immensely, and how strange, before the elections come around again, the untouchable candidate comes to Chotti and declares that, because of the quick population increase in the Chotti area, a health centre will be opened there. Without delay. Everyone should avail themselves of this health centre. Then he informs that this is a drought area. Therefore a huge government well will be dug between the settlement of Chotti's folks and Chhagan's group. He says in fiery tones that he knows that caste-Hindus are so narrow-minded, superstitious and prejudiced that they don't let adivasis and lowcastes take water even from government wells. This too he knows that they are reactionary to the extreme and real obstacles to India's development under Jawaharlal's leadership. But the adivasis and the untouchables should remember that they have demonstrated good sense by electing him. That's why there's going to be health centre and well. If he wins the elections again he'll pave the dirt road to Chotti and connect Chotti to life on the move—Saying all this, and picking up and patting Chhagan's sister's grandson on the back he climbs on the train.

Even more surprising, the health centre is built, and the well too is dug. You can tell from the well that it'll dry out in summer. Still it's their own well. Both Chhagan's and Chotti's people are utterly delighted and Chhagan's group sits by the new well and sings songs in praise of the mythic king Rama and just has a good time.

Tirath says to Harbans, A lowcaste man, he'll look out for the low castes. So he dug a well.

Hey he won the elections because of you. The trouble you raised over claiming barren land! And now only thistles grow there. You gave a blow to the Congress for the sake of a tiny bit of barren land.

The elections will come again.

Then you'll raise some more trouble? And you'll become the opposition. You'll be able to say, I've kicked out Congress from this area. Harbans begins to enjoy himself and says, Then you'll become Comnis. If you're not Congress you're Comnis. You'll go to jail.

What's all this? What's opposition? What's Comnis? I haven't heard these words in my entire life.

How's that, don't you read the newspapers?

Papers? Why, why should I read the papers?

To know national and international news?

No no, I don't follow such fashions.

Then why do you turn on the transistor?

I listen to music.

Not news?

Why should I listen to news? You people need all that. The news I need, I get sittin' home.

The MLA was right. India is so backward because of people like you.

What d'ye say? I don't understand.

What happens is most startling. One evening Harmu descends from Chadha's bus. Chotti sees that all the women, men and children of the village are coming toward his home. He takes it for granted that there's some misfortune. But as the crowd comes close, one person starts running. As he comes forward Chotti cries, Harmu!

A huge tumult arises. After mother, wife, father stop talking Harmu says, I lived well, I worked, so they let me go four months short. That offsir fixed it, sent petitions, otherwise it wouldn't've worked. So many, so many Mundas are there, and there's no one to speak fer them.

Howja come? Bus fare?

They made me work in je-hell, didn' they give me my wages when I left? So I raised t' fare.

Chhagan shouted out, We brought him from t' bus, now ye put Harmu in t' hut, ye don' know us? Come outside, we'll dance, we'll sing.

Where is Chotti?

Chotti comes out and smiles. Everythin' tomorra. Today he's tired from t' road, let'm go today.

No, we won' go without a drink?

Hey crazy, where's so much to drink?

Say yes t' liquor will come.

Okay, yes.

Ye said?

I said.

Look then.

Chhagan, Parash, Sana, Donka, all brought out bottles.

Yer brought out ever'thin' ye had at home?

Sure.

Harmu's mother brought puffed rice and hot chilli peppers. Harmu's wife has instantly oiled and combed her hair into a bun. She brought onion. Koel went shopping. Said, they sell crumble fried yam wit' red pepper, lemme get some.

Chotti's yard is full of noisy joy.

The next day on his way to work Tirathnath says to Chhagan's son, Bishua! Chotti's boy came home so you too got drunk with the Mundas?

Not a lot lord, just a little fun.

Ye're throwin' away yer caste-laws.

Nay lord.

Whate'er ye say! Yer poverty remains because ye don't take good advice.

Gie's some rope lord. Let me bind t' fence.

The very next morning Chotti goes with Harmu to show the land.

This is our land?

Three brothers'.

Harmu lay prone on the ground, touching his father's feet. A little later Chotti says, Why d'ye cry? Aren't ye a man-child? Let go of me feet. I'll go ta work.

I'll go too.

Now do what ye can wit t' land. I can't any more. Now me mind wants a bitta peace. I don' like bother any more.

I'll come right away. Why dontcha rest?

I'll eat yer wages?

Doesn't anyone?

Now I'm workin', I'll work. Whyn't y'all polish up yer arrerplay? The winner can get more wit' his money.

There's a lotta land.

No, where?

What d'ye say, there's a lack of barren land?

When I got land Lala got scared, if we get a taste of land. In case someone else takes land. And right away he took all t' barren land. He couldn't get the fruitseller Anwar's land bits.

He's farmin' them?

Would he ever?

Why'd he take t' land then?

Less land will be farmed, more people will starve. Then he can give loans, and bind t' free ones in bonded labour.

In je-hell I heard a lot from a lotta people. It's not enough to put it in writin'. Ye have to take t' paper to court and make it legal.

If not?

If not t' paper ain't good an' true.

If I go to court, t' lawyer will cheat me.

If ye take Chhagan or Pahan with ye?

Let's see. But I say let's see for a few years. T' land is a wasted lass, she's given us scrappy paddy. When she eats yer sweat and gets stronger, when t' crop is better, then we can make t' papers legal. Else I'll try to get Anwar's land too an' make it legal.

Let's see. I'm here now.

I'm old Harmu, me mind wants peace.

And the Mundas, Chhagan's bunch also said on the way home, They too hope, they too wanna try to get Anwar's land.

Good news. But what'll happen?

After hearing all later Pahan says, I don' know. But this I see, what ye do, all do.

Whatja see?

Munda dies of drink, and of buyin' colourful things. Before t' Munda people didn' drink so much. At fetes, on holy days, they brewed, they drank. Now it's t' government toddy shop, they e'en buy an' drink. D'ye know t' name of Birsa god?

Yes?

He didn' believe Haramdeo, didn' believe Pahan. But said one good thing, Munda won' drink.

The Birsaites don't drink.

That's good. V-ery good. Ye drink I drink, from time to time. But what's this? Pour out t' money earned by t' body's sweat?

What were ye sayin'?

That ye tuk t' land and they came one by one askin' me, Then we can tek land too, let's get t' land written up? So I like Sana eat boiled wheat an' save money in tin boxes, in hollow bamboo. On lord's day ye giv me yer account, who saved how much. I'll write down. That giv's 'em a bitta good sense, I see. Yer son's father-in-law, that Donka, is bone silly. E'en he obeys me.

Pahan!

Say.

I thoughta somethin'. Ye know a bit of Hindi, even Math. The whole day goes in labour, but if ye teach t' Munda boys a bit in th' evenin'?

They'll learn? Don' they go to t' government school?

A Munda'll go to government school here! Diku boys won' study then, and t' master chases off even t' boys of Chhagan's caste. They say, Low caste, do low work, why d' ye need ta study? But it comes to me mind that times are changin'. Munda won' do book learnin' work. Girls are learnin' from t' Mission in town and doin' construction jobs. Now there's good money in construction work.

But that's in town. Here their gods, their Kishna-Mahadeo-Kali tell 'em, don' go over twelve annas.

Town rules in town. But if one Munda boy learns a bit, he can reckon, and write too.

T' boys'll come?

That t' dads'll see.

Can be Chhagan knows too.

Let 'em teach his boys? If our boys go to Chhagan, or theirs come to ye, Chadha, Lala and all will talk, that they'll join up and raise a revolt Diku style.

Well, ye see. They might listen if ye say't.

Another thing.

Ye're givin' rice?

It's rice from t' grain in Harmu's field. No one et it. T' paddy was husked when he came back. The first I gie ta ye.

Pahani said, Ye don' bring birds an' rabbits no more?

Where do I get it? They've killed all.

They didn't get Anwar's land. Finally Anwar used Chotti's folks to dig the soil and to plant papayas, guavas. But the Mundas hang on to the habit of saving. By way of Pahan's infinite perseverance, Harmu's eldest boy and three other boys learn the alphabet, and learn easy addition and subtraction by counting the seed of the myrobalan. This seems a great gift to Chotti. Chhagan also becomes inspired to teach, but his students run away because he's too violent. New tales spring up about Chotti. And finally, when during the famine year there is a system of giving aid in exchange for labour, Tirathnath himself and Harbans say to the officer, Call Chotti Munda and tell him. The work will be done if he's in charge. The road will be built. Just repairing a dirt road, that they can do.

Why only Mundas?

Others will also listen to Chotti.

To say this about Chotti is to acknowledge that he is equally important here to Mundas and to Hindu outcastes.

The officer asks, Is this a leader?

Not a political leader, says Harbans. But an elderly man. I don't know about Lalaji, but I like to work with him ahead of me. Let it rain, let it scorch, let it frost, Chotti will keep people busy and get the work done.

Tirathnath sighs and says, Yeah.

Thus day by day Chotti ages. Somchar marries a second time, Etwa marries. Chotti's age comes to mind on the day when Koel says, Dada? Me head hurts so, me body's burnin' up as if. It's pullin' an' pullin' inside, and ever'thin' seems dark.

XII

IT WAS EVENING TIME. Darkness was descending on creation. The season was rainy. A torrent was roaring down Chotti river. The year was 1970. Chotti lays Koel down on the bamboo platform and asks that his head be washed. Koel shakes his head from side to side and says, Dada, Etwa has no sense, look after him.

Shut up Koel. They're wettin' yer head.

Why does me head hurt?

Yer head'll be comforted when t' fever goes.

Ever'thin' is dark like.

Drink some water.

Koel vomits up the water, suddenly screams 'Dada', and loses consciousness. Now Chotti feels he is quite helpless, his age is three score and ten.

Harmu says, Go to hospital?

Let's take'm. But keep 'is head wet.

Pouring water on his head the floor melts into mud. Koel doesn't regain consciousness. Now Chotti shakes off age from his body. Says, cut down t' hammock. Chhagan's age-old mum came back healed from t' hospital.

Doctor'll want money Father.

I'm comin'. I'll gie money if he presses.

Mungri swallows her tears and says, He'd fever in t' mornin', he went to market. I begged an' begged, he didn' listen.

Did I know? Cut down t' hammock, come along boys.

Chotti bends over the unconscious Koel and says with passionate concern, Let me take ye t' hospital Koel, I'll bring ye back healed.

The hammock's cut down. Chotti lays Koel down and covers his brother with the quilt. It might rain, he says. Hold 'im down wit' one hand, all of yer, as ye walk. He'll startle if he comes back to 'is senses all on a sudden, he'll fall.

They start off with the hammock and walk with care. Chotti says nothing. The health centre is a mile and a half from their place. Harmu's son goes with them, holding a lantern. Chotti's wife calls out, S'll I come?

Chotti says, No no, hold t' fort.

The doctor has to be called from home. The doctor's face falls when he sees that Koel's neck is stiff. Chotti, he says, Koel will have to be taken to a big hospital. I have no medicine, no injections.

What's he have?

Meningitis, I think.

Are people cured of it?

Take him to the big hospital.

The sons look at Chotti. Now the rains come, symbolizing their inner turmoil. Chotti thinks for an instant and says, So I take to hospital in Tohri but t' train's in t' mornin'.

That is so.

Chotti is suddenly galvanized and says, Bring 'im along. I'm off. Don' shake him.

Where're ye off to, Big Aba? asks Etwa.

Lemme halt a goods train. Ye can't give 'im a needle to keep 'im alive till t' hospital? What kind of a doctor then?

The doctor is young and still has a feeling for people's pain. I'll give you something, he says. You go ahead. I'll come with them. I'll give a letter to the hospital as well.

Chotti runs to the station and gets hold of the station master. At last a miracle happens. The goods train halts to take up Koel Munda. Koel is placed in the guard's compartment. I did it because you asked, says the station master. I wouldn't have done it for someone else.

Yes lord.

Sitting in the train Chotti says, They stop t' goods train for Lala all t' time, and now 'e says I stopped t' train fer ye.

Guard says, But he did stop for ye too, no?

Sure. I'll not fergit.

A good man.

Yes lord.

Hospital at Tohri. Admission on the chit from the doctor. The doctor takes a look and says, Another epidemic case. Chotti's heart sinks with just a look at his face.

Will he live lord?

Go away, let me get on with my work.

Chotti's group sits outside and now Chotti says, Listen Harmu.

What Aba?

Ye go now to Etwa.

Now itsel'?

Ye'll have to go me son. Dontcha see, Koel won' rise no more? I got it from t' doctor's face.

Let's see what 'e does.

He knew only his big brother.

It goes on raining. An intolerable night of waiting. In the morning Chotti learns a lot from the ward orderlies. There's a lot of this disease going around. Seven cases have come to hospital, not one returned alive. Now it's Chotti's luck. How's the patient? Alive. Unconscious. The doctor is trying.

Koel dies in the early afternoon. He knew nothing but his big brother. Ma said two brothers stay put together. Only the other day he danced when he won in Chotti fair. He bought a kurta at market, pushed by Donka. Never wore it thinking his brother might comment. He worked like Harmu's mother's right arm because he wanted to shore up the household. He ate nothing for two days when Harmu went to je-hell. In hard times the two brothers split one cloth and each wore half. All times are hard times, in fact. Gathering the harvest from their own field, he'd asked, T' hard times are over, isn't it, Dada? He only knew his Dada in the whole world.

Harmu and Somchar go back to the village. Dusk falls by the time they return with the Mundas. Etwa cries and cries and at last falls asleep. Chotti stays awake. What will he say to Mungri? Weeping for Koel she might say, He died after all? So why'jye take him to hospital? What'll he say then? Chotti can't sleep. He doesn't even remember that he got up at dawn yesterday, and hasn't closed his eyes today at all. A terrible urgency below his heart. Chotti knows, he won' feel sleepy until he has buried Koel. Now he has a lot of work ahead. Sana and the others arrive. Donka says, Ye go off by terain. Let Etwa go. We'll carry um.

No, let's walk.

It'll be long.

There's no rush now. What's t' use savin' time now?

Seeing Chotti so calm Sana says, This heart is under stone. Chotti smiles gently at this and, buying a palm-leaf, makes a three cornered roof like the roof of a hut. He puts it on top of Koel. And says, If t' rains come t' water'll flow off this. It'll be heavier if it's wet.

It starts raining on the way. A dark path, but known. The known path is endless today. They see their way by lightning flashes and reach home near dawn. A tired keening greets them. Setting Koel down Chotti says, It's smellin' now. Smells stronger than t' med'cin smell. Call Pahan.

Bathed and dressed in new clothes Koel Munda goes to the Mundari burial-ground on a new string cot. For his funeral service rice and corn and a new washcloth go with him and he is buried with the pahan's help. Back home, Chotti says, Go away ye all, I'll cry for Koel now. Mungri don' mind me, ye're now me child, but me soul has slipped fro' me body like, if I don' cry me cryin' I'll die.

Everyone cries. Harmu's Ma says, Bout t' same age as me, never said a rough word. Ne'er slept away fro' home, ne'er et but me cookin'. E'en a fox don' go out in such rain, why does he lie in t' ground?

They fall asleep weeping. Chotti still can't fall asleep. He feels he'll not be able to do anything any more, any task. He's grown old. Now he recalls that when their father hanged himself Koel had said, We're not orphans, ya? Dada's there, ya? He says, half to himself, Ye had a lotta faith, but yer Dada couldn't save ye. The tears come rushing now. The noise of rain outside. Half to himself Chotti says, I'll do a proper funeral when our community settles. Koel is now altogether close to him. Dense and wet and all over creation, like the rain. Don' worry, I'll keep Etwa, Mungri, all of 'em in me arms, says Chotti to Koel. Etwa has as much right to t' land as Harmu an' Somchar, says Chotti again. Now one suddenly hears a long drawn out keen of someone's suppressed lament. Chotti loses his reason, opens the door in piercing expectation, Ye've come Koel? The old dog enters the hut. It was getting wet outside. Lie here, are ye wet? Chotti pets the dog and suddenly falls asleep like a child. The next morning a bright sun bathes the wet world. Waking late, Chotti's heart breaks as he sees the trees' bathed leaves, bright sun. He holds the bamboo supports of the hut and weeps shouting in grief beyond consoling. Koel's not there. All the emptiness is in Chotti's family, there is no gap in the universe. Everything is the same as before?

Pahan said later, Chotti took straight to hospital. Maybe an ill wind struck 'im. He didn' show me once.

How many died in hospital, Chotti told Sana. Then he says, Now we see magic spells at t' hospital. No more smallpox, a body dead of cholera comes back alive. Didn' tell Pahan, not cos I don' respect'm. I thought I s'dn' waste time, at that time.

The ill wind theory is blown away. For Tirathnath's manager's son and the station master's daughter Khublal's wife, died in the meningitis epidemic. Sana says with an air of wisdom, Not a good disease.

At Koel's funeral the memorial stone is set up with the appropriate ritual. Chotti says, Harmu, bury me here when I die. By Koel's side.

The burial-ground is lovely. Shaded surrounded by piyal-nut trees.

Everything is story in Chotti Munda's life. Now these stories are reaching the supernatural. In every area Munda men and women say when they put their children to sleep, There's a man called Chotti Munda. He's taught his Lala a lesson with arrers. Gormen is scared of him and lets him have land with paperwork. When his brother took ill, Chotti stopped t' train with an arrer. He can do anything.

For a long time after Koel's death Chotti remains emptier than anyone. Mungri oils her dry hair one day, boils her quilts and cloths in washing soda and goes to wash them in the river. Harmu's mother gets busy looking after the pepper, brinjal, squash plants in the yard. Harmu, Somchar, and Etwa go to the field. Harmu's daughter takes care of Etwa's boy. Etwa's wife cooks. Harmu and Somchar's wives herd goats. Harmu's boy herds cattle. Chotti has a lot of work. It's work in rain and shine, he has to tie the wicker umbrellas, get the lantern soldered, he has to have handles made for the two scythes. The rains are gone any day now. He must go out to work again. But everything seems empty at all times. All this was his brother's work.

The warp and woof of daily living continue unbroken. Chotti's wife says at night, Mungri has a sense of self now. She thinks of herself.

How?

Says lemme tend poultry, sell eggs now, keep money. Gotta think of mesel' from now on. He's gone. T' boy's a fool.

Let 'er do what she wants.

Who's tellin' her things? That Etwa's wife.

What's she tellin'?

Her father's got land. She's her father's youngest girl. No brother, t' two girls have rights. Says, Maybe we s'd go live there.

Ye or I won' tell her to go. She'll go if she has to.

T' home'll break up?

If it breaks, it'll break.

Ye won' say nothin'?

No nothin'. After all these days of joy and sorrow spent together if she thinks, it's t' boy's in-laws' house that's more er own, ye think she'll listen if I talk?

But not two months ha' gone by.

Yer heart is in sorrow?

A lot. Can' have chickpea paste, he loved it.

Sleep now.

Chotti thinks it would've been better if he rather than Koel had departed. He's uneasy at Mungri's news. He believes that Mungri did say these things, since Harmu's Ma doesn't lie. But whatever she says from time to time, you can't see the difference in Mungri's work. She took the task of tending poultry long ago. Chotti doesn't ever ask if she keeps the money she gets selling eggs. But one day to his great surprise Etwa brings a tin can full of coins. Says, Ma says to get more land. Here Ma's saved seventeen rupees and ten annas.

Ma said get land?

Mungri comes forward. She was twisting straw rope; if the rope is wound round a clay barrel and sprinkled with water, the water in the barrel stays cool; the rope is needed to bind thatch, also to make looped stands for clay urns. Twisting straw she raises her calm and patient, slightly sorrowful eyes and says to Chotti's wife, Three sons at home. He'd said, We'll tek more land.

Koel said?

Yes. Mungri shakes her head like a dumb beast, and Chotti now sees in her whitish eyes a deep startled pain. Mungri says, looking at Harmu's mother she says, for she doesn't speak directly to Chotti unless absolutely necessary. Mungri says, He said, When Dada and I are no more, who knows how much love there'll be 'tween all of 'em? Maybe they'll leave home, driven out by want. So, if each of 'em have some land, there will be no worry.

What land there is will keep 'em worry free, says Chotti.

That Somni, Etwa's wife, speaks of her father's land.

I'll speak to Etwa.

Mungri now says, very clearly, Etwa has no brains.

I'll talk to 'im.

He said to hold on to Dada.

Chotti says softly, We'll look for land. Now I see no land anywhere, keep t' money. Let t' money build from poultry sales. I'll tek when I need it.

Harmu's mother takes the can in hand and takes Mungri to the other side, holding her hand. Chotti realizes that Mungri is still in deep mourning. He calls out, As long as I'm here we won' go by Etwa's words. I'll speak to his father-in-law.

Hearing all, Pahan says, Why is't so bad? His father-in-law Parma has four bighas of land. If Etwa doesn't tek it his nephews will. If ye say no, Etwa won' tek it. And later he might regret, he coulda have land. I coulda settled, me uncle didn' let me.

Chotti sees the truth of this. He lets Mungri know this very thing but Mungri shakes her head in defiant obstinacy and says, I won' let it be.

The question remains unresolved. Life goes on. Somchar, Etwa, Jita and Dukhan start going to fair after fair again. Sometimes they win. Jita says, I'm not leavin' this work. Chotti Munda's raised up t' name of Chotti village, now if no one wins, the name'll sink.

So the days pass. Now the work of felling timber is in far forests. Going to these areas to cut trees Chotti meets up with the Narsingarh Mundas. He's most astonished and asks, Y'all here?

There's little diversity in Munda nomenclature, but because of his birth during the First World War, and being named by a bad-news reading schoolmaster, one of them received the name German Munda. He's kept the name 'German', and renounced the name 'Budhna' which indicated his Wednesday birth. That German Munda says, Why?

Cuttin' down trees?

We were saved by yer advice.

How?

Ye showed us t' way. Had no spunk before.

So tell how, come on.

Ne'er thought afore that we could do other work arter doin' t' boss's. Keepin' ye in t' lead Chotti village showed t' way. Now in ev'ry village all t' Mundas gie bonded labour, and watch t' boss's field as well, in bits and pieces. On top o' that, they're doin' t' cuttin' work. Five bits a day, money's comin' in too.

Mundas alone?

The others too are workin'.

Good.

Some of our boys've gone to t' log splittin' factory of t' contractor. They make e'en more. Two rupees a day. T'contractor's happy too. For why, cos adivasi don' know how ta cheat at work. We's happy too.

This makes Chotti strangely happy, and his great sorrow for Koel lessens some. German Munda says further, Ye showed other ways. Our Bhagat Munda and Nagu Munda have taken barren land, and done paperwork. We're hopin' t' same. There's land inside o' jungle.

They'll gie?

They say they might fer five years.

An' then?

They'll gie only us. But we'll have to lease it agin, wit' more money. But t'land is fertile.

So take?

Now t' boss's a bit soft.

Can't trust 'm. But still.

Let's see. Ye did a lot fo' us.

What'd I do?

It's ye who did it. Bhagat's made a great song in yer name, yeah. I'll tek ya one day, let ye hear.

I'll hear.

A few months later Bhagat and Nagu come by and give Chotti some maize. Our field crop, they say.

Ye're crazy. Why give ta me?

It's good for us if ye eat it, yeah.

In this way Chotti reaches the age of three score and twelve. Etwa's father-in-law dies and Chotti visits that village. He explains everything to Mungri and himself sends Etwa there. He s'd visit now, Chotti says. Why s'd his wife be cheated out of her father's land? Ye must do things ta fit t' situations as they change. Otherwise life makes a fool out of ye.

Etwa is most dejected and says, Big Aba, are ye pushin' me away? Me boy won' grow up in yer shadow?

Chotti says lovingly, Are ye crazed, m'boy? Ye're me Koel's boy, can I push ye away? Where'er ye are is me home. I'd no place to go but Chotti village, an' now I have another. Ye'll come, we'll go. Yer father-in-law has water-buffaloes too. We'll eat curds.

Mungri doesn't want to let go. Finally Chotti says, Go there Mother and Aunt. Go'n put t' house together. T' boys' wives are at home, they'll cook, they'll serve.

We won' stay.

Mungri says we won' stay, but in the event she and Harmu's Ma stay three nights. They get served like gods as Chotti Munda's wife and brother's wife. Etwa's mother-in-law says, Me mind really wanted ta bring this son-in-law home. If he comes, his uncle comes. We'll get good karma, yeah. He's everyone's hope now. If ye come to holy days here ye'll see how many songs be sung in his name.

They ask Mungri to stay put, but, says Mungri, Caint stay away from home dears. If Etwa's aunt don' cook I caint eat, and Etwa's Dad said nev'r leave home. Ye're speakin' of someone whose sight brings life to yer body. He said, when Etwa's father died, Mungri! Now ye're me daughter. So does a widowed girl stay away from her parents?

Yer boy's here.

Let 'm be. I'll come 'n' go, I'll see 'im.

Etwa weeps when Mother and Aunt leave.

At first there's a lot of coming and going. Then gradually Etwa's heart is caught in the new place. When he has no farm work, then he too comes for forest work. But coming to the village constantly doesn't last. Mungri goes now and again, but returns the very next day. She says, Their place is not by a hilly river like here, t' wind doesn't blow like here, I'm outta breath, like, there's no sleep in me eyes.

It's Harmu's youngest son who visits all the time. He's always been more drawn to Etwa than to his own uncle. One day Chotti goes and visits Etwa's household. He sees, comes back home and says, Etwa is as happy as Munda can think to be. T' soil bears well, t' buffalo gie's milk, and 'is ma-in-law lives on th' oldest daughter's crop returns. She doesn't come 'tween 'em fer ever' little thing. She e'en gie's Etwa t' curd-sale money.

The wife asks, Munda girl sells curds?

She's learnt from t' dairy folks. I think tis good. Ye must do t' job that's needed when tis needed.

Etwa's too soft. No one bothers him I hope.

No no, he gets a lotta respect fer me name's sake. On feast days and holy days they keep him in front and do their feastin'.

Well here t' wife was in our shadow.

But she did a lotta work, no? She's doin' all that. Hey she binds her boy on back and reaches Etwa to t' river and then goes to market. P'raps she's learnt from t' Hindus. She poured water on me feet and washed 'em.

Well good's good. Still t' hut feels empty. He sang such songs, like his pa, playin' t' tuila. E'en Harmu's boy's not like that.

Harmu's Ma! Those days're gone. Not for a Munda boy to dance at our gatherin', to sing with t' tuila. What used to be t' daily round in Munda life is now put away for feast days and holy days. How ye used ta dance at fairs!

Hey! Don' mock an oldie.

I don' see ya old.

Hey, me back allus hurts.

There's tiger fat in store.

A bit. How ye called to people and gave it out in th' old days.

Then I didn' know there wud be fightin', and then this Independence! They've shot 'em from jeeps and made t' tiger vanish.

Yeah. T' joy of eatin' meat is gone. No boar, no deer.

There's nothin'.

So I feel sad, that our grandkids'll come o' age at such a time, that we'll not be able ta show them somethin' and say, we've seen this too.

They'll see river, mountain, forest.

Forest! T' way ye're fellin' trees.

But timber is in much demand now.

For what?

Now many places 'tween Gomo and Daltonganj are gettin' bigger. So many houses a-buildin', so many doors, windows, bedsteads.

People have a lotta money.

If ye have money, yes. We'll wear ballbags, eat mealie, watch from afar, come away. Nothin' will change for us.

Least we're alive.

Gotta stay alive. E'en if all Mundas died, Diku-Hindus don' gie a damn. They'll be happy. They're surprised that we don' die after all this. Think we're made of stone. Gimme a bitta chickpea paste, do. Sana's mum lived then, but mebbe she's on her way out now. Fever, arms and legs swelled up. Lemme go look at her.

In a few days Sana's mother dies. She's given last rites. At this time lightning dazzles the Chotti area. Special Police come by train, they get down at Chotti. They spread out and look for some group and, giving the essential news to the station master, they instal two policemen at the station and leave. Nothing remains secret in Chotti. Everyone whispers to everyone else. The station master calls Chotti and Chhagan, two gentleman boys have fled to this area from Durgapur. If they are seen they must be trapped.

What have they done, Lord?

Hey, they're Naxal boys.

What name didja say, Lord?

Naxal.

Chhagan says, I know I know. They cut down contractors and bosses, grab guns, fight the polis. I went to thana to sell eggplants th' other day. I heard about 'em there. But Lord, they're not here. That trouble happened in another place.

No, no, they're hidin' in t' hills and forests when they can. If ye grab 'em ye'll get money from t' thana, ye know that?

Polis waitin' to catch 'em? God their guns! Ye shoot and people die.

Catch or kill, what's it to ye? Ye too are t' head of yer community, so I tole ye.

Coming out, Chotti says, They cut down contractors, bosses? They've cut? Ya know?

That's what t' thana sipahis said, cut a lot.

Where?

Do I know?

They'll kill 'em if they catch 'em?

Do I know?

Chotti says, Know nothin', how many lands are there, hey. Then bosses and moneylenders everywhere?

Whyn't they come and kill our Lalas? Chhagan makes such an irresponsible comment and departs. Chotti sees his grandson on the way and says, Tell 'em at home, I'll sit mournin' at t' burnin' place and then come.

He sits often at Koel's last resting-place. And so he went today. A solitary shadowy place for the dead. Only the huge stones are standing. It's as if Chotti finds Koel again when he sits down here. Everything is at peace in his heart. Chotti feels good.

It's there that he sees the lad. Thinking nothing of who lies under, the boy leans against Donka Munda's father's stone and stretches his legs on his mother's stone. Emaciated in appearance, bespectacled eyes. Bare feet, trousers and shirt on his body. It's impossible to imagine that it's possible for him to sever anyone's head. Of course who'd say to look at Puran that he'd killed the estate manager. The young man is startled to see him and is instantly cautious, fierce.

Chotti says, Get off of there.

Why?

It's our burial stone.

The boy gets down.

Where's th' other one?

The young man is silent. He watches Chotti.

Whenja come?

I'm here since last night. What is this place?

Chotti.

How far is Ranchi from here?

Ver' far.

If I could get there somehow . . .

Polis at t' tishan.

Police!

Yes. Money if they spot ya and turn ya in.

I see. You?

I'm Chotti, Chotti Munda. I'll not turn ya in. But what to do. Whyja come here?

I jumped off the cargo train.

Where's th' other one? Ye were two.

He didn't get down here.

Whyja come here, ye? Here any outsider stands out. Whyja come, why?

Police will shoot me at sight.

Chotti keeps thinking that he is too old. Just as it's impossible to give up someone to the police by his own hands just to be shot at sight, so is it not possible to get him somewhere safely. What to do? Chotti thinks and thinks, and finally decides.

Darkness come, he says. Ye wait.

What'll you do?

Keep ye at me place.

And then?

I'll see ye a bit o' t' way.

Where?

On t' way to t' county seat from Tohri. Ye'll hide. Timber trucks go by, ye stop 'em an' get on. Truck goes to county seat.

Ranchi?

Yeah.

Where are you goin'?

I've work.

Chotti strokes Koel's burial place. He says in Mundari, I'll sit by ya another day, Koel, today I have work.

Are there other people at your place?

Yes.

They? If they talk?

No one will talk.

Dusk falls. Darkness gathers. Chotti brings the young man along and sits him down close to his hut. He goes inside and calls Harmu out. Harmu says, Why s'd ye go? Lemme tek him on t' way?

Chotti says to the youth, T' truck'll take money. D'ye have any?

Some.

How much?

About two rupees.

Chotti says, Ye cut down bosses and sharks, so take a bitta their cash? Seein' that ye hafta be on t' run.

The lad smiles. Chotti says, Harmu, if ye go yer wife and boy'll ask. Yer ma won' ask. She's ne'er asked. When I went at night to save Puran? Did anyone know?

Thas true, yeah.

Come, let's go home. To the young man Chotti says, I'll tek ya when everyone's asleep. Now ye sleep on these stones.

No one'll come?

No.

But . . .

I'm givin' me word, no?

Are you t' headman of t' village?

Harmu says, He's t' head of all t' Mundas of this area.

Chotti says, What does he know, come on. Maddened by t' polis chase. What's t' use tellin' 'im all this?

The boy says, No harm in sayin' it either.

Ye're speakin' Hindi?

I've learnt speakin'. Can you give me a drink of water?

Now drink from t' river.

They go off. At a certain point everyone goes to sleep. Chotti calls the sleeping youth. His wife says nothing, just feeds him priceless rice, smoked eggplant, pickle. She's heard all from Chotti. No mother at home, she's asked. And then she brings bland maize powder and molasses, bound up in a clean rag bundle. Eat on t' way, she says.

They speak in whispers. Chotti says to the lad, Sleep a bit. I'll call ya when that star is in mid-heaven.

The lad sleeps. His clavicles push out. He looks unwashed. Chotti can't think how this boy will get to the county seat. Aren't

there police in Tohri itself? The wife gives him a plan. After t'
bridge t' cargo train goes mighty slow, and climbs. Harmu and t'
boys got Sana and others on to it when Koel was sick. They
weren't runnin', says Chotti. If he's caught?

Scorpio climbs the sky. Chotti calls the lad. Then the two step
out. No way to take a lantern. They walk in the dark. Whyja cut off
t' bosses' heads, asks Chotti. Do they bother ye?

No. You're a tribal. You know well that they terrorize tribals and
peasants.

Fo' sure. But why y'all?'

This is our fight.

Fa what?

We'll finish off the contractors and moneylenders. The land
will be in your hands. Everything will be new. No one will oppress
anyone.

Good words.

Do you accept this?

Yeah. But do Mundas an' low castes get land where ye kill t'
bosses? They're now landed?

No.

What's happenin' there?

Police have entered the village.

An' a lotta ye'r also dyin'?

A lot.

That's t' problem, says Chotti. Me boy, that Harmu, went to je-
hell on a land fight, an' I still didn' shoot an' arrer. Cos why, cos
polis woulda come and burnt our corner. If a Lala dies, 'nother
Lala will come. Knowin' that I didn' raise me bow.

But we must fight the police.

Is't easy? I'll fight if ya tell me? I'll fight when I know it's me
fight too. Ye're a Diku. Our Birsa lord fought with Gormen f'r our
good. An' look! How long will ya keep yer land if ya fight t' polis?
Gormen has polis, has law courts, has je-hell, we don' get land.

No one will give anything if you speak softly.

So ye speak of that fight, t' polis catch ye too. Ye're runnin' too,
an' I see that here too, if ye kill t' boss ye run.

Perhaps we didn't have that power.

If not, what's a fight! Then t' polis come in, that's all. Burn up
our neighbourhoods, beat's up, put's in je-hell.

All must join the fight.

An' there will be sich a fight?

All must be convinced.

If ye die, who'll convince?

There'll be more of 'us'.

Whyja come? Stay, I'll build ye a hut, turn Munda.

I knew Santals.

They raised their Hul.

You know of it?

Chotti Munda knows ever'thin'.

You're a great guy.

So they say. But if I'm great why wear only a ballbag, why no rice ever' evenin', why so much pain, eh?

The same story everywhere.

Diku doesn' grasp our sorrow.

We grasped.

An' so ye run?

And so.

Why does polis chase t' man who grasps our sorrow? All I've seen all ma life.

The young man gives a lovely smile, and says, That's the job of the police.

No more talkin'. Villagers here.

They walk in silence. The youth follows Chotti and Chotti goes on saying, Here's bump, here's rut, here's flat path—and the lad walks accordingly. Keeping Tohri on the left they gradually get to the bus road. Hide here, says Chotti. T' truck'll come from way back there. Raise yer hand an' climb. Chotti opens the fold at his waist. Keep't, says he. 'Bout two rupees in change.

The young man takes the money in boundless amazement, returns the cloth-fold to Chotti and says, I won' take this. If I'm caught, perhaps I'll be caught, then who knows what they'll think when they see this.

Who knows if polis is warnin' all trucks or no. But at this time Lal Singh and Jamdar Singh drive trucks. They're dead drunk. They take persons if ye give a bitta money, this I know.

You're leaving?

Yeah. Hafta go a long way. Me wife'll stay up.

The young man says with youth's passion, Why did you save me?

I dunno if I saved ya yet. Lemme know when ye get to town.

Why?

Jus' like that. Polis will chase ya with dogs and kill ya. Mother's son.

You are a strange man. If you gave me up—

I spit on such cash. So I'll become a Lala?

I didn't get to know you at all.

What's there ta know?

Perhaps a fighter.

The fight ya talked about, is good, but it's not to be. Be equal to polis and then fight, no? Else in th' end it's t' polis wins. Thas what I allus see.

But one must fight for the work that one feels is right.

Yeah. That's true too. Ta stay true ta yerself.

This you understand. Don't you?

Sure. I know of such persons. Dhani Munda went to Chaibasa and died, he'da lived if he hadna gone. That Dukhia cut down t' manager hisself.

I learnt nothing at all. I'll come again.

I'm off now.

Chotti comes back. Boundless worry in his mind. Astonishment. Why is Diku getting chased by police to do the tribal good? He constantly remembers the lad's face. From time to time he raises his face and looks at the stars. Keeps walking on the familiar path. This day is most peculiar. The experience splits Chotti open with amazement somehow. When he reaches home, Scorpio has inclined even further. His wife opens the door. Anxiety in her face, her eyes. Gone? she asks. Ye put 'im up on truck?

No. They'll notice if I help 'im up.

Then?

I tole him to go on.

I'll breathe when he reaches Ranchi.

Got water?

There.

Chotti washes his hands and feet and lies down. I'd ne'er known, he says, that Diku comes to do good for tribal and runs away from polis chase.

Where's t' boy from?

Who knows what land.

What'll they do if they catch 'im?

Kill him mebbe.

I can' think.

Sleep.

Nothin'll happen ta ya?

No no. Sleep now. No one knows, hunh?

No. Harmu asked me and e'en that was long ago.

At last Chotti falls asleep. His wife sleeps as well. And dawn breaks.

Next day they go to cut wood in the Dhai forest beyond Tohri. While they're felling wood, they suddenly hear an unfamiliar voice, Halt.

Everyone stops in place. They are all familiar with the word. Whenever the police come to a scene they say to the assembled people, Halt.

They keep standing still. Then they see an unusual and un-believable sight. Three policemen are dragging along a young man. His face has caved in, his body has come loose. Yesterday he had eye-glasses, not today. Chotti covers his own face. It is as if someone is breaking stones on his chest. The police drag him along, they drag him. Suddenly they push him ahead, out of sight of Chotti's eyes. Then comes the sound of a gun.

Now everyone comes out of their trance and starts to run. Chotti can't move, can't look that way. Then the police come back. They have tied a rope round his ankles to pull him forward. They pull him along. Something pierces Chotti beneath his heart, it pierces him, pierces him forever. He couldn't escape, then.

Getting back to Chotti they hear the official version. A man hid in the bushes beside the way to the county seat, says the station master. He had bombs and a revolver. He attempted to kill the police with those arms. The police fought him hard and then killed him. Who knows where the other Naxal went.

Sana says, No, no, he didn' attack t' polis.

Who said so?

We saw.

Forget what ye saw, boys. Ye won' understand all this with yer jungle brains. Say what t' police say. If ye want to stay safe.

The contractor also scolds Chotti's group. Not a word about this, he says.

Chotti's wife cries out when she hears. Chotti says to Harmu, If yer wife or son ask, say ye're grievin' fer Koel.

Chotti can't bring himself to eat that day. The experience is so massive that thinking of the young man his heart wants to break.

Yet he can't lighten his load by telling anyone. Harmu also is completely shut in himself. They did one thing, he says to his dad, and said another. The boy was doin' good killin' such polis. What bomb, what gun? Had nothin'.

Shut yer mouth, Harmu. There'll be more.

The police keep searching for the fugitive youth. He can't be found. The Daroga tells all of them at Chotti, Send news immediately if you see an unknown boy. You'll get a hundred rupees tip.

Tirathnath also says, Yes boys give 'im up if you see 'im. They don't give time to say 'boo'. They cut down moneylenders on sight. Who knows where he's hidin'.

Where s'll we see 'im?

Hey, if you see 'im turn 'im in. A Naxal boy. A venomous snake.

Sana suddenly plays the fool and asks, Lord! What do I hear that a snake bit ya, and then it died?

A big slippery snake, yah. I stepped on it and killed it.

We heard that it was a poisonous snake and died when it bit ye. That's just a story. So, nothin' happened to ye, eh?

No no. What's ta happen?

Then Tirath thinks perhaps Sana'd made a jest. He says to his manager, Harbans has spoilt them rotten. Venomous snake bit me and died, is there poison in me blood?

The police resumed their search in a few days. More fugitives are on the run from trains. The police stick the notice announcing the reward on a tree by the station and the old crone Motia gets a tongue lashing from the station master because she spits red betel leaf juice on it. No one is caught, but as a result a pent-up tension enters the area. Now everyone talks a lot about the official account of the police killing and face-to-face combat. When they see police repeatedly that past event creates an even greater excitement in their minds. But they put detachment on their faces. Seeing this, even the station master says, These are pig-headed folks.

XIII

A T THIS TIME, in Chotti's three score and twelve years, the elections come again. Just as the murder of the young man and the forest search by police brings the turmoil of the outside world to Chotti, so do other patterns of the outside world invade the Chotti area. By such erosions do the geological layers of the mental world of the Chotti area begin to change their appearance. The patterns of the outside world are of a mixed-up type. For instance, the planned bauxite mine starts operating on the streambed of the River Shone and an aluminium factory starts up in Chama, sixteen miles from Tohri. Harbans, Tirathnath and others of that ilk become vigilant about the mines and the factory. They have a summit meeting at the tea stall at the station. It's a complicated matter. If things of this description become operative then labour will feel the pull. Everyone will leave in a hurry for more money. So you kept saying, says Tirath, that bonded labour is bad. And now what? See, it's the old things that are best. Why in the outskirts, even if in Chotti itself there's a factry which pays ten rupees a day, even that my bonded labourers won't be able to take. They will see it happen, but give me bonded labour. That's the fun of keeping land.

I'm thinking the opposite.

What?

Harbans says with dreamy eyes, Lots of houses will go up if there's a factry. Then they'll need hundreds and thousands of hollow bricks.

So why's that the opposite?

And if factry after factry goes up all around, then outside winds will blow here too and all these folks will scram. Will you be able to do anything if they go?

How'll that be?

Why not. I have Chotti Munda. If he says these people will stop work sir, then work will stop. And Chotti doesn't work for you since that Harmu case.

Won't there be a problem for you if labour runs off?

Lalaji! Harbans Chadha is Punjab-born. Punjabi folks know how to march with the times. My dada didn't look for farmland when he came to Palamau, just because my grandpa did. He could've. But he built a brick kiln.

So what happened?

Hey I'll raise their wages.

Hey hey Harbans! Don't do suchlike stuff, brother mine. You spoil the rules. There's folks here that are not bond labour. They too'll want higher wages. Don't take suchlike steps.

Don't do! Won't they split if I don't? Lalaji the times have changed! Now many people come from Calcutta and buy surface collieries for fifteen-twenty thousand rupees. There'll be labour shortage, do you follow me?

No no, here there are people as many as insects.

You stay in your satisfaction.

Bro'! Why not buy an orchard? Lotsa profit.

So I'll make a guava-custard apple orchard like Anwar and sell fruit to Kunjara? I'll buy later if I buy. When there's a road, we'll send the fruit directly to Bokharo-Ranchi-Dhanbad. Then we'll be able to can the fruit at the factry. Then a small industry can come out of the orchard.

If you'd bought an orchard you could have got rid of the Muslim.

Lalaji! I have no love for Muslims. But I don't like yer rules for touchables and untouchables.

Tirathnath sits and waits to see what Harbans does. Harbans raises the wage to a rupee. So Tirathnath too has to give his bonded labourers a rupee. To the labourers' amazement he gives each a quarter for food.

This is an event.

But the second event is altogether strange.

A certain Anathbandhu Pal descends upon Chotti with a travelling cinema. In the open fields by the station he shows a picture called 'The Conquest of the Nether World by Lord Hanuman'. Both Chotti's crowd and Chhagan's are new to the bioscope. They are delighted to see the film. Tirathnath bows down again and again after he sees it and he says, I'll give money, there'll be a show tomorra as well.

Everyone is delighted again at the pictures. Then Anathbandhu Pal leaves by train with his cinema. Then there is a great to-do all over Chotti. Tirathnath's manager's son has stolen two thousand rupees and left. He's left a letter saying this world and the manager's job are poisonous to him. So he's renouncing the world and becoming a monk. Tirathnath is furious and runs to the thana. There are no results. Daroga learns through his network that he's gone to Ranchi and become Anathbandhu's partner.

The third event is totally different. In 1962 and 1967 the aforementioned candidate, sympathetic to tribals and untouchables, won the seat. This time suddenly the Youth League party are intent upon winning the Chotti-seat and threaten the candidate. They come to Chotti, hold a meeting and threaten that if they vote for him the village'll burn. Behind their threats lies drunkenness. Then they ask, Who is Chotti Munda?

Me?

Heard that tribals and the untouchables here respect your word. You must tell everyone to vote for us.

They don't wait to hear Chotti's response. Then Chotti's group and Chhagan's group meet. Chhagan says, What to do?

But he gave us a well, and this hospital. And pavin' t' road as well.

We say the same.

But thas not ta point. I don' find t' signs good. Never saw a vote meeting with thugs, eh? Then they came and went with Lala. I don' like this.

Tirathnath informs them, This time it's better that you vote for the new candidate. Problems otherwise.

They can't imagine what problems might arise. But the elderly candidate goes to Dhai to hold a meeting and is suddenly wounded and killed with a bomb. The assassins leave by jeep. Who knows what directives the Daroga receives from where. He's quite unable to come to capture the assassins. From Chotti the eyewitness account comes from the washerwoman Motia. At that time Motia was in Dhai at her sister's house. A vote meeting is not much for working people but for Motia and company it's a great fête. Motia comes to Chotti and gives everyone a detailed account. Everyone goes to her to hear and they do hear. The candidate was popular and had done good work. Everyone is curious about his death.

Next the Daroga goes to Chotti. He gets off the train and steps briskly to Chhagan's neighbourhood and says, Now we know that the candidate was killed by people of his own party. Those low-caste folks become members of the legislative assembly to get hold of money. He embezzled funds, and problems at the time of dividing the funds led to great dissatisfaction in the party. Anyway, I hear the washerwoman Motia is spreading many stories. Tell her not to spread silly stories. There'll be trouble if she tells tales. I don't have the power to stop that trouble.

Motia say, Now what did the polis say?

Chhagan says, Times are very bad Motia. What ye see is not true. What they said is true.

Hearing all, Chotti is even more stonefaced. This is not a new thing, he says. Then they killed t' boy, and they said, t' boy threw bombs at t' polis. This guy was doin' good and they kilt' 'im. Motia say nothin', there's a whirlwind.

But Chotti! Daroga wasn't there.

Motia! If anyone comes to judge t' words it'll be some Diku or other, and who'll be believed?

That Daroga.

Now ye know. Go home.

Then there was another vote meeting on the public stage. Everything is possible in this kingdom, according to the needs of the ruling class. Therefore the train comes in the afternoon, with the candidate and his followers, and stops for half an hour. On the station platform itself the candidate gives a speech and decorates the deceased candidate with adjectives like Naxal, thug and the like, and then gets on the train. Chotti does not attend that meeting, but Motia comes to his room. She sits down with a thump, Oh god!

What happened?

I'm scared.

Why?

Dintcha go to the meetin'?

No.

What I saw Chotti!

Whatdja see?

T' guy who came will take t' votes?

What about 'im?

That's the one I pointed at th' other day. Of all t' people who came, that's t' dwarfish guy who threw t' bomb. These are t' ones who killed 'im. What did I see Chotti.

Chotti says, Stop. Don' say any more.

D'ye know what Lala is sayin'?

What?

No money this time, they'll not let us go to vote. And still the votes will come, and why, cos this guy doesn't need the riff-raff's vote.

I see. Now go home. I'll walk ye.

Chotti goes to market after taking Motia home, to get the kerosene by permit. There he sees Tirathnath. Tirathnath says, Chotti you didn' come to the meeting I think?

No.

Who'll you all vote for?

Let's see.

Tirathnath smiles as if held up by some invisible power and says, There's another lowcaste candidate. That bastard doesn't come near us for fear.

Chotti says nothing. Just looks.

You'll see this time the place will get better.

Chotti doesn't answer, he turns his back.

A couple days later Tirathnath doesn't smile so much. Says to Harbans, And took fifty thousand rupees again.

I gave ten thousand rupees as well.

You gave!

Sure. And the agreement for supplying bricks to factry housing contract is also firm. That's it. This will be the party and we'll benefit.

And what about me?

Be good for you too. You'll see.

How?

This bastard also keeps the touch-no-touch rules like you, yeah? A big operator. You know what party?

No.

Arjun Modi's.

So what?

You are incredible.

Oh say.

No I won't have to say anything, you'll understand. In five years that fifty thousand will come back as five hundred thousand.

Come back?

Sure. This is the new sun for India's future, no?

This brash young guy?

Vijaya Modi.

When Chotti and his people go to vote, they see that their votes have already been cast. There's fighting at the booth to hold back the voters. Armed Mundas hold back the voters with stout sticks. When the results are announced it is seen that the young guy from the Youth League has won with a huge margin. By the order of the victor, Tirathnath sets off fireworks and gives a victory party and the cool guys from the Youth League invite themselves to Harbans's place. Harbans has to bring a lot of liquor, slaughter a whole sheep.

Before leaving the feast the honourable Member says to Harbans, There will be no tender call. All these British fashions. Now we'll work the Indian way. You'll get the contract not only for hollow brick but also for cement.

Your kindness.

But give us a cut.

Of course.

Twelve annas–four annas. Twelve annas are mine. Don't worry. You'll get such a rate that even with this you'll have a fat profit.

Harbans says 'bastard' to himself and says in words, Of course.

Here the tribals and the untouchables are too bold.

No no.

I know I know. I'll make everything all right.

They haven't done anything.

Don't cover up. I'm giving one area to each one of my boys. They're very good boys. They've put their lives on the line for me. These are the people who took care of that untouchable.

Harbans is shocked and the candidate is poked by one of his henchmen, gives a toothy smile and says, I'm joking.

Yes.

The candidate departs with his entourage. Harbans feels most unquiet. He wants contracts, to make money, collect profits. And with it he wants to build small and middle industry. Places like Bokharo and Chas are now thriving. This is the chance. But Harbans doesn't want any trouble. Neither he nor his father have ever touched a coolie or labourer. If they have asked for help in sickness or misfortune both father and son have come forward. Harbans has been living in their midst for a long time. Hardworking Harbans respects the tendency to work responsibly and honestly that he sees in Chotti and his people. Protecting his own interests to the full Harbans treats them more or less well. Some time ago Harbans made an unseemly amount of profit running hollow bricks and he gave his coolie-labourers thick Janta brand blankets from Dharwar. Chotti's blanket was rather more fancy compared to the others. They've murdered their way into local politics, and now they're saying they'll teach the tribals and untouchables a lesson. Who knows what they'll do if everything burns up? If there's a fire for Harbans's sake then suppose the Mundas fell Harbans with a poisoned arrow, pack up their homesteads and take off for unknown parts? Such things have happened. The manager at Narsingarh died by an arrow. Dukhia from Kurmi cut a manager's head off. Harbans is most worried and thinks to increase twelve annas to a rupee. Now he'll raise it to five quarters. He'll build goodwill. As a result no one will be vengeful toward Harbans. Thinking these thoughts inwardly Harbans discovers that he is scared to see the candidate and his disciples become little Hitlers with access to power. He can't think what to do.

He says nothing to Tirathnath. But Tirathnath notices his behaviour, perhaps he too is worried. For, at the time of buying maize he too gives the unbonded labourers five quarters wages and gives six annas food allowance to the bonded ones. He says, Such a boss you'll never find Chhagan.

By the grace of the Lord.

Chhagan utters these words with a depressed and sullen face. Whate'er ye do, he says, is good, very good. There's a lot of work all around now. Two and a half rupees for coolie-labour. And so in Kurmi and Narsingarh e'en field hands are gittin' two rupees, bonded labour one rupee for food. Now from town N.C.D.C. will come to Chotti. They'll get the coal cut. They give the Gormen rate, eight or nine rupees.

Then I too will stop hiring field hands.

The Chotti area graduates into modernity through the way in which the former Member was removed, the elections were won through fraud and armed robbery, and the post-election contracts were divvied up. The activities of the elected Member and the party in power also become professional and sophisticated. These are no longer the days when Tirath will take bonded labour and yet chat with a 'How do, Chhagan.'

Under this regime everyone's character is purged and made to adopt appropriate class-roles. Chotti says, Ye'll now see what ye've never before seen. Ye'll think how happy we were before. Dintcha see he murdered to win votes?

An' told a diffren story.

Yeah.

And why so?

Just think Chhagan.

Chhagan wrinkles his elderly nose, clears his throat and says, Saw it twice. Killed that boy in front of everyone an' told a diffren story. Killed this one in front of everyone, an' told a diffren story.

What do ye understan'?

Times 're very bad.

Ve-r-y bad.

What's happenin'?

What has to be. Motia s'd say nothin'. Might lose her life, yeah. There's nothin' they can't do.

Everyone's payin' more money. That's good at least.

Even at this age Chotti's eyes are dark and full of life. He lifts his eyes, smiles faintly and says, Lala and Chadha aint givin' more because they're good though.

We know. Everyone wants labour.

So they're givin'.

Ouf! Let N.C.D.C. come.

That's not in our lot. Gormen work goes at slow speed. First they'll spend a year to see where there's coal. Then they'll spend a year makin' up their minds if this place should have a Coal Board office. Another year to build a house. I think it's a three-four year business.

Mebbe.

T' sharp boys are spreadin' terror everywhere.

What's that to us? T' nekked beggar doesn't fear t' thief.

Chhagan's words are proved wrong. The policy that the ruling party follows after winning the 1972 elections with a huge majority is most fascinating. Within the five years of the plan, all the shoutings, proclamations, legislations et cetera launched by the Central Government help India 'take a high seat in the World Assembly' and the image of the liberating Sun is as delightful as the Egyptian god Amon Ra. But like the god he needs fresh blood. As a result, the hollers like 'eliminate poverty', 'bond labour's illegal', 'now moneylenders' loan for agriculture is illegal' become posters and get stuck on trees and stations and bus-bodies in the remotest parts of the country. But in reality people like Chotti and Chhagan continue to get ground down. These five reigning years are dedicated to the task of making the rich richer, keeping the lower castes and the adivasis crushed underfoot, and, above all, turning those designated hoodlums without portfolios into cannibal gods with police support. Objective, to renovate India as Baby's playroom. People like Chotti and Chhagan don't get to see this Baby, but they become his toys and receive his kicks. Soon it is clear that the time has come to rewrite old proverbs.

It is the naked who must most fear the thief and the armed robber.

Coming to this area to campaign for the elections it suddenly occurs to the candidate that the place is a trouble spot. He informs the Secretary and the party Secretary accordingly. The gist of what he reports is that, in spite of there being two bosses, Tirathnath and Harbans, the local adivasis and untouchables are not just bonded to them, they are allowed to earn other income.

The Secretary says, Sure, so what?

The candidate says that after talking to Tirathnath and Harbans he has the idea that, because of pre-existing personal relationships, they do not want to change the habitual patterns.

I know that I too have land, bonded labour, debtors. There's less chance of violence if there's personal connections.

Listen, you don't understand, these sonsabitches walk about free-free, their back's not broken.

I understand, sure. But remember one thing.

What?

Don't do anything with the adivasi folks and the untouchable folks that leads to violence. I am party and also Secretary. You've won with my support. So your name has been filed in the case of the murder of the Member in this revenue area.

Why?

Secretary laughs the shark's laugh of the tough politician and says, Has to be. Has to be kept in the proper place. If I become unpopular with you, if I'm . . . then it'll come in handy. I didn't think you'd kill him dead. I'd thought you'd understood my directions, you'd break up the meeting with a bomb.

Damn, a mistake.

It's not enough to get power. Must know how to hold on to it.

Awright, what's done is done. Now, I've told the boys, I'll divvy up the area. I'll give them a bitta area, and one or two contracts. These poor fellows have left home to do party work, they must be given a bitta support, no?

So give. Have I said no?

But . . .

What?

He was a lowcaste. And he helped lowcastes and adivasis. That's why these bastards are so fresh.

Hey, can't they be disciplined without violence? You must be smart. Let them find out what to do. There's a lot of work ahead of you now. If you're returned at the next elections you can even become a minister. You must show work if you want to be a minister. Public won't give support if you just do harm. We may not get votes every year by the rules applied this time around. You've got to do both good an' bad. You can play heavy with votes only where the public too supports you.

But will they?

Tirathnath and Harbans are in a minority. Railway staff's a floating population and also few in number. The majority's adivasi and untouchable. Chotti is a funny place. You'll have to walk carefully there. Otherwise—

What?

The Secretary's smile becomes even more poisonous. Bacchu! he says. You were born just yesterday. But everyone knows my name in southeast Bihar. And thank God I have connections in Delhi as well. If they don't listen to me I've nixed many a political career. So you too should know I was obliged to take your dad out in 1957. And poor soul, he passed away. And only because you're his son—

Yes, yes. I'd not have got it without your support.

One last thing. Chotti an' Dhai an' Kurmi an' Narsingarh. That area has its own history. I don't want too much poking around. If ye poke around too much in these village areas you draw blood, there's Naxal-pattern violence. Don't let any Naxal violence enter that area by your foolishness. Then you're gone. Don't forget there's been a Naxal death there.

I won't forget.

Don't make a row about adivasi feast days and fair days. One thing is very necessary. Adivasis and untouchables pull together in Chotti. It'll be good if you can strategically divide them. In Chotti there's an old man called Chotti Munda. He's highly respected in that area. The adivasi officer Dilip Tarwe gave him solid support at the time of his son's case. Tarwe is a good officer. Now he is Director, Tribal Welfare. If you can move with Chotti in your pocket, then you'll have a base in that area. Keep everything I said in mind as you go about your business. Don't you see the current role of our leader? Now he's become the leader of the eastern hemisphere. Brother! Your task is to support him in his work. I've seen his greatness with my very own eyes.

You have?

Don't you see the picture on the wall? That's me.

So it is. Then?

What?

I can't ask anyone. Yet I want to know.

What?

I keep the touch-restrictions, so do you.

Of course. Our birthright is the caste-system.

Is this true? That the Mahatma didn't keep the caste-rules?

Brother! He was a god. Do humans understand a god's affairs?

You're right.

The candidate leaves. Now the Secretary says to his secretary in turn, Do you see what stuff I've brought into play?

I saw. But why?

What 'but why'?

Deokinandan was such a good guy. Trained by you, a real village welfare boy. This motherfucker smuggled liquor in automobile tires in Dhanbad, ran a blackmarket on movie tickets, supplied hookers to Marwaris, was a suspect in a murder case, finally acquitted.

Why bring him?

Now Arjun Modi is on the rise. Now he's creating the Youth League in our country towns with loafers and hoodlums. And so I brought this asshole. Brother, I'm the cock on the weathervane, as you see in the movies. I know how to turn as the wind changes. Otherwise would I have survived? Don't you see all the killings in politics today?

Our time is over. Everything was working fine. What a profitable business politics was becoming. Everyone kept their profits. How many ways opened. Till I was sixty I hadn't even seen Bombay town. That me went off to Singapore-Hong Kong-Manila-Japan on a youth delegation. How many cameras, how many transistors I sold. Why? Did I kill anyone? Did I lose anything this way? What has happened in today's world?

Brother, you're saying what's in my heart as well. Do old patriots want violence? There he killed the Member. Don't I feel sorrow for him? Now the Adivasi Samachar newspaper is raising money for his wife and children. What a tried and true man he was, tell me? He remained a Member for ten years, and couldn't raise a pice? I pushed such a man away and brought this guy, can I be happy about this?

And why did he kill him?

The Secretary got excited and said, It's bad to kill, still I accept that you had to kill him. But kill in such a public spot? With a thousand witnesses? You didn't think of the party at all? Is our party a party of murderers? What did people think?

True true.

Nothing, nothing, you remember what happened in West Bengal in 1971 in Baranagar-Kashipur? Three hundred hoodlums went and killed two hundred, two hundred fifty Naxal boys 'n' police said nothing, Siddhartha Roy didn't do anything either, everything was hushed up, knowing that these people are alert now.

Is that correct?

Of course not. You are just a johnny-come-lately-hood. Are you Siddhartha Roy? D'ye know English like that? D'ye eat with the Prime Minister?

Hey, what a thought. Ye'll shit yer pants if you see the Premier-English! Does he know Hindi?

Let's see what he does.

The first thing the Member does is to go from the party Secretary to the State Secretary and tell the whole story. And the State Secretary says, What? He said all this to you?

So he did.

No, no, we must get rid of the oldsters. Their love for the tribals and the untouchables and their counsel to be cautious doesn't work in today's Indian politics. Go on fighting. Start some to-do in the Legislative Assembly right away. So that we make an impression.

Shall I raise a hullaballoo about cow-slaughter? A most popular issue.

No no. That can become highly sectarian.

Then?

Let me see. And listen. It wasn't correct to use Romeo to throw a bomb on the Member. He only knows money. If someone else pays him tomorrow he'll bomb you. Give him a little something.

I'm giving the three of 'em—Romeo, Pahlwan, and Dildar—a contract, money, and I'm giving them their own share of this area.

Good. Then think what you'll talk about.

Sir! I can't speak good Hindi.

Dildar will tell you.

The Member then goes drinking with his cohorts. Drinking he says, Forget it! I don't like wearin' clean clothes and eatin'

European. I belong to the masses. I'll drink country liquor, wear a lungi and dance in Dhanbad tishan with Miss Rumali, shoot a bullet into the tyre of a state bus for fun, now everything's over. I have to use soap, brush teeth. Even Rumali says, where's that stink I knew?

Dildar says, Listen man, forget all that.

How?

Think of the Legislative Assembly.

What s'll I think?

Read a coupla books.

You read an' tell me.

This reading is what ruins the case. The Member starts his education with a few fourth grade textbooks and he's furious when he reads the history books. He goes to town with his group and beats up Birij Tewari the author of the history book—the shaven-headed devotee of Kathiababa, an altogether good hearted guy—and says, So ye're showin' yer love for the untouchables?

How?

Why did you write the Buddha ate a pig at the house of an untouchable and died as a result? Won't the untouchables get a swelled head if they hear an untouchable killed a god?

Why?

Watch out, you! says the Member and tears up Birij Tewari's books and papers and says, Burn all the history books.

Birij Tewari immediately raises as much of an outcry as he can. The matter goes far. The news is highlighted in the papers. Adivasi Samachar prints the story of the Member's past and increases sales. Dildar had gone to Calcutta, he comes running. The matter is discussed at the Legislative Assembly. The Member gets a lot of flak right and left. Even the State Secretary chews him out. The party Secretary says, Fool! Ass! He wrote what is written. You've become a Member with this amount of intelligence?

The Member listens in silence and says, Okay. He says to his buddies, Buddha is a Hindu god. An incarnation of Krishna. Why did he do such a bad thing?

So it seems.

Whatever, I'm not opening my mouth at the Legislative Assembly any more. Let me straighten out my own area.

Everyone breathes a sigh of relief and now the tigers come out to play. The Member realizes that the advantage of this area is that news will not come out instantly in the papers. No one sweats for the tribal or the outcaste. Dildar says, With such a field at hand, Master, you lost yer head over Buddha.

Why did you go to Calcutta, you son of a whore? Would there have been such a scandal if you'd been here?

I'll not leave you alone again.

XIV

THIS IS HOW ROMEO, Pahlwan and Dildar enter the life of the Chotti area. The Member's hassle with the Buddha story hastened this infiltration. Thus did the compassionate sage of Shakya become an unwitting factor in the life of Chotti.

Chotti loses all contact with Tirathnath, his field and his field hands. Harbans becomes busy with a new job. He calls Chotti and says, Chotti! The rains are almost over. I never hit Lalaji's work before, and won't now. But a factry's running in Chama. Two hundred quarters planned. I don't know how many bricks they'll need. But I'll supply the lot.

Starving Chotti smiles at the future millionaire Harbans and says, This is a good thing, me lord. If another man had taken t' contract, he too woulda become king. Be king, me lord, let's watch.

No no Chotti, that comes later. Now I have to have a serious discussion with you.

Tell me sir.

I'll need labour.

We are here.

Now Harbans smiles. And says, We'll need many many people. Chotti, don't light that bidi. D'ye want a real cigarette? Light one, see how you like it.

Chotti takes the cigarette. Lights it squinting and says, What makes ye smoke this? Like grass?

Why're you putting it out?

I'll keep it. Harmu'll smoke. Koel brought from t' village market sometimes. He loved this stuff.

Now listen.

Tell me lord.

I need lots of labour-coolies. I know what I'll get from the village. But I like tribals better. Everyone respects you. If you get me folk from Kurmi, from Narsingarh, will you?

Folk'll come from Kurmi. For they've no work that side, them. So I go to Narsingarh, they come too. But sir—

Yeah? Go on.

They too get five bits?

Harbans has many times worked out how much is left over when this much is given. He knows that he'll make a profit even if he gives them five rupees. For his contract is for two hundred thousand rupees. I'll give two rupees wages, he says, and two hundred fifty of maize powder and a hundred of molasses for tiffin for sure. The only thing, you must get the work done in three months.

Chotti's eyes become calm and lovely like the sky before dawn. He says softly, Me lord! Ever'one'll be happy to hear this. I wish ye well.

I'm telling you frankly this is the rate for this work. I won't always get a contract. Then I won't be able to give this rate. That too I'm telling you.

I'll say that too.

I have more to discuss with you.

Say, me Lord.

You're getting on. You don't have to work as their equal. You just see that this labour works okay. I'll give you three rupees.

Lord, why that job? I aint a contractor. Me house'll fare a lot better if I tek a rupee more. But I ain't a contractor that I'll tek more, an' till now we've allus sweated all together. An' sir! Ye talk 'bout age and me heart's sore.. I'm still choppin' trees, still trackin' ten miles, still earnin' me own bit o' grub. Why not gie't yer pa? Let him do it.

Harbans says, You know best. Right, don't take money, but I won't let you work the same's them. You are our Chotti. We won't get another one when you go.

Who wants to go? Chotti smiled. A most incomprehensible smile. And said, How many times I saw Lord, let's see this as well? How was this Chotti, eh? Where you and I stand and talk, here sir, when I was a ten-year chit, here was a deep forest. I got in wit' cattle. The cow ran with t' tiger's scent. I climbed t' fig tree. It took a man and walked off by me. They were settin' down railway here an' there. When tiger got man's smell, t' line's work stopped with his terror.

Chotti, was this hill blasted off ?

No sir. It's t' same way forever. Half a mile gap in t' middle, two hills on two sides, we used to say two step-wives. Forever! Our elders had said, when t' world was made t' wives of t' demons went ta Haramdeo fightin'. Haramdeo threw 'em down, and so t' hills were made. But they didn' have to split t' hill here. They put t' rail in between. Many tales!

Then that's the deal Chotti? Shall I tell Chhagan? I didn't tell him yet.

I'll tell 'im.

Harbans feels an urgent call of something inside. He doesn't know what calls him. He wants to work by contract, wants to profit, to keep the big guys happy. The work of making hollow bricks will do well in this area. He used to think he had no love for tribals and untouchables. Now he thinks he does. It's a matter of long acquaintance. Moreover Harbans is himself graduate, reads papers. He wants to get his work done by giving his labour satisfactory wages. He doesn't like the Member's toadies' barbaric loutishness, their bestial drunkenness. Not just they, the Member himself is such an uncivilized brute, Harbans wouldn't have let him in the house if he hadn't been the Member. Harbans keeps thinking that he shouldn't enter the entire thing without consulting his father. Finally he goes to his dad. Partap Singh has now opened a motor service-repairing workshop in Chas and a truck service for long distance transport. Harbans's wife and children stay with him. His children go to school in Bokharo. Harbans's own mother is dead, his stepmother and stepbrothers have inherited the agricultural enterprise. The household is peaceful because of Partap's immense personality. His stepmother quite loves Harbans's wife and children. The brickfield and the Chadha Bus Service belong to Harbans alone.

Partap listens to his son carefully and becomes serious. You didn't do well, says he. How much of a cut will this Member take? Hearing the rate he says, I was always here. You didn't think to ask me? It's hard for people like us to work with people who have come into power now. We know everything that they're doing. Let me tell you what happened when the government took coal. The contractor gives labour, takes a cut from their wages. Whatever remains, the organization men take a cut from labour again. They are entering in every area of the relationship between labour and management. So there's a problem. All the cycle rickshaw drivers from town deposit something with the boss. And they even take from the few rupees that are left. And they beat up and chase off those who don't give. In a big place the rickshaw pullers union can talk to them and solve something. But in a small place there can be trouble. That Member of yours is very dirty. Do you know of the killings? That they removed the previous Member by killing him?

Harbans is quiet.

They're beating up on the untouchables everywhere.

Harbans is quiet.

Harbans's son comes and stands close to his grandfather's lap and says, Achhut means 'untouchable,' did you know that Baba? When Sister had chicken pox, I wouldn't touch her. Sister became an untouchable then, no Baba?

Partap says, Sure. Now go. We're talking. To hell with the untouchables, he says to his son. I am thinking of my son.

What to do?

You didn't ask me once? State Bank would've given you a loan to expand your brickfield. The cement company is building a new township. They would've given you a contract. I was talking to them. This sort of business is the best. They wouldn't have hit you in the back. If you run your factory with the bank's money, and sell your goods to the cement company, there will be such profit Harbans, that there's profit left even after paying your labour by the Wage Act. You build goodwill, and you get contracts with new government undertakings.

Father, a word.

Say.

You go on talking. I'll fight. If the factory works on a bank loan I'll be able to supply goods to the new township. If they raise a lot of trouble, I'll be able to get out of it, all won't be loss.

If you see fit come along here.

But the field is very good dear Father. And hollow brick is now a profitable thing and labour is also very good. They can learn casting-moulding-laying real well. This is not a job of much skill. Even my unskilled labour can learn. My factory is small. I can get the work done with the labour force I know.

Tribal labour is the greatest. They learn if you teach, don't slack off, use them with a little respect, work goes good.

Then that's the deal.

Yer trouble will be from those who raise a tithe from yer labour payment. My fear, that we don't get labour trouble then.

My worry too. If we betray Chotti it'll be hard to get tribal labour, and who likes trouble for nothing?

Hey! Chotti alive still?

Sure. Very tough still.

Shoots arrows?

His team shoots arrows.

What d'ye mean 'betray Chotti'?

Chotti is a kind of leader of the outcastes and tribals. How peaceful that is! I tell him, bring this much labour, do the job in so many days. Even my overseer likes him. No one works his labour so peacefully these days.

We'll see. I'll look out for the bank loan and township contract.

Harbans's spirit lifts. He eats cheese-spinach and cauliflower-peas cooked by his stepmother.

Then he goes to the cinema with his wife.

Chotti brings people in good time. To Harbans he says, Chhagan is responsible for whoever is comin' with Chhagan. I'm responsible for us. Bhagabat for t' Narsingarh Mundas, Mangal Oraon for th' Oraons. This Sugan's responsible for t' Kurmi Mundas. And sir! They'll tell me their stuff, ye'll tell me yer stuff. If one of 'em breaks word, I'll kick 'm out. Gimme a solderin' job.

Just men?

T' women come tomorra.

Harbans is blown away. Narsingarh's a far piece from Kurmi. How did you get ahold of everyone at yer age?

Did I go myself? I sent word, I called.

They came?

They've no brains, they're dumb. They listen to me.

Half-hour off for tiffin in the afternoon.

Harbans's overseers say: Send tiffin to t' field.

Chotti says, Why so? Now they'll speak their name and go off to work, t' snack is given them then. More convenient.

Harbans says, Right.

The work goes on in this way. Everyone goes to work with chick-pea flour and molasses tied up in paper bags. Even the overseer is surprised at the way they work. I don't have to watch, says he. The work gets done, I don't have to holler.

Because Chotti is there.

Amazing stuff.

Work progresses most peacefully, but still the worry lines don't disappear from Harbans's forehead, he keeps going again and again to his dad. The cement company satellite wants a new con-tract in the new tiny town, wants a state bank loan. He doesn't seem to remember that he has poured his entire savings into the brickfield in the hope of a contract. The reason for his distracted soul is the patriotic activities of Romeo and his brother in Kanata village, forty-one miles away.

Romeo is the hero of the event. He has earned the name Romeo. Their father had named them Shabankumar and Tulsidas. Two sons. Shabankumar extended his strident life in Patna Town and he was beyond compare in snatching girls' veils and cutting off the ends of their saris as he rode his bicycle. He developed a skill to harass all women from twelve to forty and he named himself 'Romeo'. At the same time he became a youthful soldier in the Youth League. It is when he goes to a picnic that he's put down. He asks one of the women of the group to dance in her birthday suit in blameless joy and innocence of mind after imbibing a lot of alcohol. She slaps him. As a result he takes her to the woods and rapes and kills her. As a result the matter has serious repercussions. The girl's father tries but cannot manage success in court. Next the girl's army officer older brother removes his parents from Patna, gives Romeo a serious beating and cuts off his ear lobes. Romeo cannot take any effective action against such a brother. He runs off in shame from Patna to the boonies. The group's youth leader assures him—wherever he may be, he'll get his due. Then Romeo discovers that, whether the girl's brother thrashed him everywhere, or for psychological rea-sons, he is not succeeding in the task of his manhood. His goods are not obeying him. He tries many cures. Burying rams alive and having their testicles fried in butter makes his belly heavy. He is not pleased. Romeo has to accept his impotence. Now he has an earthquake in his brain. After the final chapter he goes as his last effort to an old familiar prostitute. This prostitute had the reputation of raising an erection in a stone. Romeo promised to give her a gold chain. But when the prostitute fails, then in fierce frenzy Romeo presses on her throat soft as warm butter, presses on and on. This is so unexpected that the prostitute dies quickly. Her bleared eyes pop out, bloody foam on her lips and in her trachea. Lips, nails and skins are livid and swelling and cyanosis in the expected body parts—all are present. Now Romeo puts on his pants, his shirt. The elation of liberation in his heart. He realizes that he has found peace in killing. This is the killer's role. That is why fate or Sushma's brother had stolen his manhood. Romeo exits the prostitute's house in his proper role. Thereafter, he has committed many murders in the role of a youth guard. With a gun. Cause for much regret. There's more fun for him in killing by hand. Soon he wins fame. His brother Tulsidas's brother-in-law, the son of the former landlord of Kanata village, Daridranarayan Misir, gives him every kind of support.

A land battle was under way between this Daridranarayan Misir and the Rabidas untouchables. The Rabidases sharecrop the land. They have a written record. For a few generations, these twenty acres are the food source of these eighteen Rabidas families. Daridranarayan wants to take away this land without providing an alternative. The affair develops and now there is a police presence in the village. Police are guarding the place. The Rabidases are reaping paddy. Romeo thinks it is necessary to help Daridranarayan. Romeo enters Kanata in a Jeep convoy with a couple dozen soldiers from the Youth League. Keeping the flag flying he and his cohorts fire at random and kill four people, two women, three men. They set fire to the Rabidas area, they burn the paddy. Then they go to Daridranarayan's house to give the news. The police force remains detached spectators. Romeo threatens the precinct, Don't write a report today. He says to the Rabidases, I'll come again tomorrow and show you again where the low castes belong. To Daridranarayan he says, Now we can do anything. Tell every landlord-moneylender, we will teach these harijans—God's people—such a lesson in five years that it will take them five thousand years to raise their head again. Remove these harijans, these tribals. Let the poor high castes till the fields. If this programme is successful in Bihar, it will work everywhere in India.

Daridranarayan says, Bro', what'll the ministers say?

Romeo says, ministers? State ministers? Hey the Central Government in Delhi will support us, they're doing so now.

Daridranarayan wants to return the favour, he says, I've had rhinoceros killed in Assam and got their horn. Do you want to try and see?

No, no.

You are the mighty Arjun, and you've now become the hermaphrodite eunuch Brihannala!

Bro', all is different now. I've become Brihannala and I'm doing Arjun's brave work as well.

Sure you are.

I'll come again. If you take action like this from time to time the harijans will live in fear. If everyone took this advice the country would look different today. Look at the police, they'll be quiet for a while. Then if they catch anyone they'll catch the Rabidases.

The affair is not reported in any newspaper. Still the news spreads. Harbans is even more worried then. If Romeo comes to Chotti? Behind Romeo is the State Government, the party organization, Youth League, police, Delhi. What will Harbans do? How far is his power? Harbans cannnot tell anyone of his worry. He is afraid even at the thought of Romeo shooting to kill women.

One day he goes to see the work. Chotti sits on a stone and pulls on a bidi. He stands near Chotti.

Chotti says, How nice it looks.

What Chotti?

How all work together? All t' pain is ta git work, lord. Now they're all smiles at home.

Good, very good.

So much peace.

Yes Chotti.

But it won' remain like this.

Why? Harbans trembles.

Chotti looks at the people at work and says, Don' ye know what's happenin' in Kanata? Ye know. I know from yer face.

They know?

Ever'one. Life's spoilt Lord. Law-Courts-polis—all up for sale.

Suddenly Harbans seems to find strength inside and says in immediate felt sincerity, Don't worry as long as I'm here.

Me? Worry? I never worry. What's to gain in worry? What I see I try to solve as I can.

You are my one hope.

How can I ever be? Chotti calls out, Hey woman-folk! Why d'ye laugh? No work to do?

Chhagan's granddaughter calls out, We'll get t' job done buddy. Hurry up.

Chotti says again, Peace in a bitta work, peace in a bitta grub, even this bit they won' let us keep, lord! Times turnin' bad. Killin's so much on t' rise. There warn't so much killin'.

Harbans says, I'm here.

Ye've people, guns ev'n. Take care. They shoot right an' left, throw bombs.

Daroga came to see the brickfield one day and said the same thing, Mr. Chadha, what I say is between you and me. If anyone asks I'll deny this. But listen to me. D'you have a gun?

Yes.

How many?

One.

Buy another. I'll give you a license.

Why?

I'll speak plain. The police can't retain their own power. They have to do what the Youth League asks. You know I'm a Jana Sangh party man, and never have I hid this . . . And whether or not Jana Sangh, I've never done wrong in my work. I've given support to master-moneylender, and to trader. Now I begin to see that this Member's character is very bad. Romeo abuses me. Do I have to bear Youth League's abuse? But why am I asking you to get a gun? I'll be able to do nothing if there's trouble. You make your peace as it happens, I won't interfere. Mr. Chadha, if the harijans behave badly, of course I'll chastise them. When have I not? But shooting women? God no.

Harbans says desperately, What d'ye think will happen?

Who knows?

Harbans goes to his dad again. His dad's words are most consoling. His father has been networking. The Chadha family had been well known for patriotism in Lahore. Some uncle of Harbans had perished in the British massacre of Jalianwalabagh. Harbans's stepbrother is the hockey champion of the state of Bihar. Cashing in on these, Chadha senior has got hold of the Secretary of the Legislative Assembly. The Secretary has given hope. Therefore Harbans will get a bank loan and a new contract.

Harbans returns home with a happy heart and sees Romeo and Pahlwan playing cards on the porch of his house. Romeo says, Have a seat. We have to talk to you. How's work?

Going well.

Any labour trouble?

No. I never have labour trouble.

How's that?

It's a small area. If you know everyone there's never any trouble.

Amrican policy, eh?

Whad'ye say?

In Amrica they have policy like this. The big companies keep labour so happy that there's never any trouble.

Maybe. Some tea?

Sure, sure.

Chotti is not such a place that you can entertain an unexpected guest with store-bought food. Thank God Udham Singh lives there with his mother and wife. Harbans says to Udham, Romeo's here. Send some tea and papads. Don't let your wife come this way. This is a real dirty guy.

Now Romeo gets to business without tasting his tea. I hear you're giving the same wages to untouchable and tribal? he asks.

Yeah.

Why? Here you had a chance to break their unity, here one hears they are united.

Harbans saw and understood that he had no fear at the sight of Romeo. He said softly, My brickfield's not a thermal power plant or an A.C.C. factory, my friend. All in all a hundred and fifty workers. Seventy from my village, and people I know.

Others?

All Mundas. From the area.

What're you doing with that problem?

This is no problem. So what's there to do?

This is a strange thing. There's employer and the employees are labour, and no problem!

No, man. Have a look. Whate'er village they've come from has a village elder accountable. This arrangement is Chotti Munda's, and Chotti is respected not only in the village but in the area.

Chotti Munda! Do I know that name?

Everyone knows it. In the British days the lieutenant govern-
or's Secretary came to see him. Now the tribal director knows
him.

Ah, a fighter Munda?

No no. A good, wise old man.

I'm really surprised at your words. I think you yourself are a big
man. Mahatma. You're working with these bastards with a kind
heart.

I am a nobody. My life is lived with my father's blessing. Father's
friends are well known folk, sure. Rameswar Prasad—

Who, the Assembly Secretary?

Yes sir. And Bilas Sahay—

Who, the State Minister?

Yes, sir. The I.G. Police is also my father's friend.

Okay. You're saying there will be no trouble?

Why should there be unrest? Now the administration is going
well.

Going well, will go well.

That's what I said, no?

But I want to run the same system everywhere. When you give
them their weekly, a quarter per head will be Pahlwan's cut. For
contracting. Deduct that amount weekly.

But he's not the contractor?

That is not for you to see. And if they object I'll create a Kanata
here. Today we've spoken. Tomorrow we'll come to speak to Lala.
You say there's no problem here, that's because you're indulging
them. Tell 'em about taking a cut from their weekly wages. You'll
see problems.

How'll we work if you raise labour trouble?

Raise trouble?

Now Pahlwan shoots a toothy grin and says, There won't be
trouble. A couple of dead bodies, twenty-thirty huts burnt, they'll
crawl to work.

But they haven't done anything.

Romeo gives a smile Socratic in its wisdom and says, Look, in
the August of 1970 Mrs Modi said in Parliament about the Naxals,
The Naxals will be fought to finish! That's the green light. And
right after that they dragged the Naxals out and started killing
them. With that a great goal was achieved. The Naxals became
afraid. Action gradually decreased.

Are these people Naxals?

Romeo is now gradually plunging himself in a dream and feeling intense pleasure as he floats in dreams. He smiles sweetly and says, The Chief Advisor of the West Bengal government made an appeal in Delhi that very August. There are a thousand problems in making a case about Naxals in the law courts. Give all the power to the police.

These are not Naxals.

I know. With the Naxals the government blew off the law and blew off the Courts. Why? Finish off the Naxals, whoever can. Government wants it. Whether the harijan does anything Chadhaji, we have to go forward and teach them a lesson. Know that government wants it too. How do they make the law otherwise? The law doesn't work. You don't like it? Go to Court. At Court the untouchable always dies harassed and confused. Then? If government wanted harijan people to get official support, would they have made the law themselves, and then watched as their laws became a farce and a circus? Hey in Chhotanagpur thirty-four percent of them are sunk in debt, seventy percent of the village live below poverty line. Doesn't the government know this?

What're you saying?

Plain words. Keep the untouchable and the tribal under your shoes. They live well that way. Everyone gets cheap labour. Sowing and reaping go well. And the biggest thing. The glory of the castes remains high. You too will understand this in time. Whatever, Pahlwan will come to take the weekly cut.

Harbans says very softly, No. I'll give it month by month.

As you wish. But if you don't listen, you'll lose your contract. All this I said, keep in mind. We know well what government wants when.

Harbans says everything to Udham Singh. Udham is both his worker and his friend. Hearing each and everything Udham Singh says, What do you think?

What comes to your mind, tell me.

It's hard for me to say it. The money's yours.

Say it, say it.

If you cut four annas a week by their tally, he's asking for one hundred and fifty rupees a month. They'll work for three months. If you give four and a half hundred rupees in these three months there'll be peace on this side, and the work'll get done. It's not even that much money. I'd have given it myself.

I'm thinking the same, Udham.

We don't want labour trouble. We've had many tiffs because of Tirath. And Munda-folks know the worth of the given word. Chotti will tell 'em that the boss has taken a cut, did some treachery. And then if there's violence?

Harbans smiled faintly and said, If I had a big industry, and Pahlwan was the contractor, I'd not have cared if he took a cut. But I can't do it because I know them. This is my weakness. Still I can't do it. I'm not Tirathlala. If I let Pahlwan loose and he kills folks, will I get labour again? And why should I bear so much pressure? The Member will take the contract money. They too will get a cut. And we'll give a cut again!

Won't you give it now?

We must. Surface colliery's Chiranjilal let Pahlwan loose upon labour. Fires burnt, bodies rolled, but the colliery's shut.

You'll be rid of them if you give them some stuff.

I don't want violence.

Pahlwan and Romeo laugh when they get the money. They said, So you gave us a packit, but you couldn't tell them?

I did what I thought.

There's no use with people like you. Now I'll give you labour. I'll get rid of 'em. If you take our contract you must take our labour too. If not, your contract's gone.

Romeo says, Hey, I'll go to your labour. So their boss has given they must give too. If there's any bother we'll take action.

Harbans doesn't want to give up either. He wanted to show his father that he could stand on his two feet with a brick kiln. The brickfield is his entire life. He sees in his mind's eye that all is about to be destroyed.

So he has to tell Chotti everything. Chotti says in an altogether calm voice, If you take bullyin' once, t' bullyin' gets bigger. Do whatever you think is t' right way for you. We won' give cuts. If you wish, let us go. We'll know our starvin' days're comin' agin. But we'll die fightin'! They want truly to kill us.

I don't want violence Chotti. That's why I'm giving a cut.

We too won' take a handout. We'll work an extra hour. We don' want wages. Ye'll get some of yer money back that way. But let t' thana know.

Thana will not take reports on them.

No one? That you can tell?

Who's there?

There's t' tribal offsir I know. Here t' polis will not notice if harijans are killed or burnt. But if you make Mundas or Oraons mad, fires will burn, and that they don' want. Now Gormen is a big bastard, but they don' want to tease t' tribal.

If they kill you?

Hey my lord! Your affair is a million rupees. Our affair is two rupees, and we aint scared to die either. Good if they kill me. T' Munda people will light a fire. They'll kill fo' sure, and then they'll die.

I'll go myself.

Harbans runs to his father. From there to the county seat. The current I.G. Police has just started to fall from the government's grace. There are efforts to put together a portfolio without responsibility for him. To his name is added many a deed such as subduing numerous armed robbers, consequently receiving the Paramvir Chakra award, rescuing harijan infants stolen for human sacrifices, organizing the Prime Minister's visit to a drought area, et cetera et cetera. So he has stakes in various places. It's not easy to lay off such a person fast. Tom says Yes, Harry says No. Dick says, Why? Jack says, Definitely not. The I.G. might not have had to move. He will have to because of the bee in his bonnet. Everyone has some bee or other in the bonnet. The I.G. is a man of the colonial period. He calls his breakfast 'elevenses'. He thinks the police should be responsible to the I.G. He cannot bear political pressure on police activities. He does not like the goings-on of the Youth League party. He's especially incensed with the police because of the Kanata affair. Even more irritated with Romeo and Pahlwan. He is not particularly sympathetic to harijan or tribal. His stand is correct on a point of law. But he is immensely displeased that Romeo and Pahlwan are taking police support for illegal work and is absolutely persuaded to give them the greatest possible trouble.

He listens attentively to Harbans's account and lets it be understood by saying 'by Jove'—'audacious'—'bugger' and so on from time to time that he is at one with Harbans, that Romeo and his ilk are to be removed with pesticide spray.

Good-bye, he says. Let me see.

He goes to the Home Minister. Describes the entire situation. Arjun Modi's cohorts, says the Home Minister, are now all in all. Still one shouldn't allow such depredations in the name of the Youth League.

He speaks to the Secretary of the Youth League. The Secretary says, That Member is a fool. And his toadies are bastards. I'll look into it, don't worry.

After all this, the result is that Romeo says no more about the Harbans affair but smoulders with resentful hostility. Harbans survives by delivering material according to contract. He says to Chotti, God willing, brick will be made again, we'll take labour again, and we'll not let them get in.

The state is theirs, me lord.

We'll see.

Danger will arrive from t' Lala's end.

What to say. The Lala does as he pleases.

No one knows what Lala Tirathnath thinks. But his work starts. On payday the Lala gives five quarters, a rupee and a quarter.

But you'd said two rupees.

You got two rupees. The party boys took a three quarters cut.

Why?

Ask them.

Chhagan says, Okay. From tomorra no one will come without bond, lord. Now ye caint get rice fer five bits a seer.

By the power of some unseen force Tirathnath says, in a self-contained voice, Whatever you do, think carefully.

I've thought.

Chhagan! Accept whatever they say. The times are bad, Chhagan. The state belongs to these guys. We'll have to take what they say.

We've taken it, no?

The work will be bonded? And yet you don't all show up?

Who doesn't show? Ajan Dhobi, Shib Dusad and Mohar Dusad ain't here. They went to show their fever and the doctor kept them in hospital. He said it's a catching fever. They'll need the needle.

Mohar's wife?

Her babe's no more than a month.

Then what's the head count?

Take it a score, lord.

And the work's okay with so few?

What to say?

You're their head.

So what do I tell them, lord? You'll give five quarters, if they go to the man who gives two rupees, what do I tell them?

What a botheration!

Chhagan puts some baccy in his mouth. Then says, They wanted to cut from Chadha, but he didn' cut from our wages, he gave.

What? He himself?

Sure.

Romeo gave a frigid smile and said Lalaji! I know what Chadha did. Is that what you'll do?

No no, but the cut percentage is over now.

Why?

No one will come without bond.

So that's it?

Yes sir.

Where will they go?

Naxals are in Calcutta. A good few merchant types have bought the surface colliery. Could go there.

Wages?

Two rupees. And tiffin.

Let 'em go.

Romeo gets active and the unbonded folks of Chotti village start work at the colliery. On payday the boss says, Wages when party man comes.

Why?

He'll take per head.

The persons from Chotti look this way and that. In due time Romeo and Pahlwan and Dildar arrive. They lay their guns on the table, make their reckoning, and take their cut. They laugh and say, Next time we'll cut five quarters.

They all know that Romeo himself killed the former Member, so they remain terrified and quiet. Returning to the village they say, We go seven miles each way, and get just a rupee. Then Lala is better. Five quarters and we stay in t' village—These are Gormen folk? They ne'er took cuts before? What's the big need now?

Tirathnath's face is quite shrunken now. He likes to keep Chhagan's group under his feet. But he doesn't like the way things are going. He just wants to suck them dry, to control them, to keep them down. But if you keep them under ceaseless control the personal angle goes to hell, this he doesn't want. If you keep them under ceaseless control you have to keep some baton and gun people, this he doesn't want. Mathura Singh killed police. Tirathnath wants people to have faith in the old order. That they'd like small wages without protest, that they'd give bonded labour. If it's like that then Tirathnath wants to give them temple food from time to time, to give them something from the new harvest. At present the situation is most complicated.

Tirathnath says in a melancholy voice, Will you work, my children? So work. Why did you split? Now the state's coming to break your back.

An' ye're keepin' our back whole?

What good's smart words, Sana? Those partymen say, now we must give them buck for buck. Not me fault, Sana. Their words.

Sana and Chhagan say. Let's go to Chotti.

Why? Why go to him? Does he work for me?

Take his counsel.

Don' make him my enemy, boys.

Let's go to him.

Chotti hears everything and says, Go tell 'im one sole thing. Say, don' give money. Give us last year's maize for t' same amount of money.

Tirathnath is happy with that. The paddy in the field is gravid. The ears are sprouting. Autumn's at an end. It's not useful to halt work now. To lose labour is not a good idea. Many types of work elsewhere. Labour's scant, it's not just that. Outside people don't want to come instantly to a village where Chotti Munda lives. Tirathnath says, Do that then, my son.

Chhagan says at work, Hey these days the sun comes up in t' west. How many times did Lala say 'son' these last days?

Sana says, Now he says 'son', who knows when he makes us say 'Help, help'. Can't trust him.

Tirathnath tells Harbans everything, as usual. Harbans hears all and says, Don't think for a moment your trouble's over. They'll ask for a cut.

They'll take maize?

They'll want money.

Then?

I did give.

You know how much that costs?

I do. I didn't give happily. But I avoided violence.

There'll be no violence.

Lalaji! Know the times. They won' let you go half way. Either this way or that, can one walk two ways at once?

Brother, you are agin those men?

Why? I supplied my contract.

Received payment?

Yes. Some.

Let's see what the Almighty does?

The Almighty worked in a mighty crooked way. Romeo and Pahlwan and Dildar scream, Don't give the dogs maize. Give 'em money, take a cut. We'll settle with those who don't take cash.

They leave quickly. The 'dogs' run off to their homes. Romeo returns with three Jeeps and about thirty young combatants. The group's flag flies at the Jeep's head, on the body of the Jeep the group leader's motherly face, dripping grace and compassion from her eyes. The villagers run into the jungle when they see them come.

Pahan and his wife come out to see what's happening. They see that the Dusad-Ganju-Dhobi dwellings are burning. The fire spreads and Tirathnath's shop burns as well. Not getting anyone else, Romeo shoots Pahan, his wife and an escaping porter. Then he pours petrol on the maize stacked as payment for Chhagan and the workers. Then he disappears, shouting slogans for the Queen and the Crown Prince. They do not hear Tirathnath's screams and fire from the stack of maize flies into Tirathnath's office. Seals fly off stacked cans of kerosene in the heat. Fire.

Chotti says, Let t' bodies of t' pahan an' his wife remain here. I'll go ta town. Let Motia's body lie here. Th' old lady couldn' run.

Harmu says, First t' thana.

The station porters force the station master to come with them. Because railway staff had died, they took Harbans's bus. The station master takes it. Chotti says, We'll take four bodies. All died t' same way.

The Daroga notes this down almost in a fainting fit. He too comes. If he wants to save his own skin he has to go to town. Chotti lies flat in front of the tribal director Dilip Tarwe. He says, Pahan or Pahani ne'er worked on Lala's land. They were comin' out ta look at t' fire. They killed 'em lord, they killed 'em.

The matter gets complicated. The reason is the youth brigade's imprudence. The current regime beats many a drumroll about harijans in the outside world, but everyone knows the real order—no one cares if all the harijans and untouchables die. Just in 1969 the police, to save a landed farmer's face, arrested four hundred people in Surmahi and other villages of Singhbhum, committed every bestiality upon women's bodies in public view, burned a few villages, killed people.

The police are experts in such conduct in this regime. The I.G. understands that his day of departure is imminent and for the excellent purpose of giving the Youth League the greatest possible trouble at this time he says, Mr. Tarwe is absolutely correct. I agree that untouchables understand nothing. They cannot keep their relationship good with the moneylenders. But what has now happened? It's a rail worker that died. Their labour union is up in arms. A sick old woman died. I saw in the morgue that even her bones are charred. The Munda community leader priest and his wife died. They neither worked these fields, nor were they involved in these quarrels. If law and order falls in the hands of sons of bitches this is bound to happen. The former I.G. was in the Surmahi operation. Did any questions arise?

Dilip Tarwe blows his own horn as much as he can and says, A great injustice has been done to the tribals. We need an investigation. I know that Chotti Munda and the deceased pahan built up a good relationship among different classes and groups in that area.

The administration understands that this is not a piece of nonsense made up by mischievous journalists. S.D.O and I.G. go to Chotti. They promise compensation and the one's whose quarters are burnt down get twenty-five rupees per head. The nephew who claims the pahan's body gets one hundred rupees. Everyone says in surprise, Would we have gotten anything if Chotti hadn't gone to town? Whatever Chotti does is fabulous.

The family of the railway porter also gets some compensation. A tight order is issued in the Chotti area, that nothing of this can be told to journalists.

After the departure of the forces of law one evening, with his head and ears covered, and nursing a hollow cough, Ananda Mahato appears in Chotti's hut. He says, Your name won't appear, no one will know anything. Tell me what happened.

I don' care for meself. Pahan's face and t' hole in Pahani's bare chest has made me forget me sorrow fo' Koel. But if me name comes out Chotti village'll burn.

Your name won't come out.

If it does? Huts'll burn agin, bodies fall, will ye look after it? That Member of yers is dead could he do anything?

Ananda Mahato smiles palely and says, Do you think my situation is any better? My day is also over.

Why sir?

I know. I feel it.

They'll perhaps kill yer? That what you say?

That's all they know. Don't you see, I've come under cover at nightfall?

So! Chotti realizes that Ananda Mahato is also in distress and he may have to die as a result of his visit. When the powerful want to kill someone, they have to die. The former Member, Motia's charred bones, the split chests of the Pahan and the Pahani. He feels a solidarity with the man. He says, There's a tain right away. Go now.

Won't you tell me anything?

Not now. Now each 'n' ever'one has an eye on Chotti.

Ananda Mahato said, This place got a bit of rescue on your account. Everywhere it is evident that they return to the places of their misdeeds.

Chotti scowls and is silent. Then he says, They killed t' railway porter, that was their mistake, Pahan-Pahani! Me lord, what's this world come to? What do they want? What happened in Surmahi happened in Dhamura. If ye kill Dusad-Ganju-untouchable not a single Gormen man blinks an eye. If Gormen want untouchable–tribals to die, kill 'em. Let's die fightin'. If we die fightin', we'll know we did somethin'.

They don't want it. Who will work their land without you?

Go off. Someone'll see.

You won't say anythin'?

I'll cross t' Dhai and go to Baramu to fell trees. Come there? Right.

Now go. Be careful. Me lord, dyin's nothin'. All t' pain's in livin' on.

I'm off.

Wait, not from t' tishan.

No, no. I've come with the railway labour union boys.

Where are they?

Outside.

Chotti called them. Said, A bitta molasses, a bit o' salt for all of ye. T' sweet's to keep our deal sweet, and t' salt to keep off betrayal.

Ananda says, Chotti, when're you going?

In a week ten days. Now we've set t' mournin' fire for Pahan–Pahani's funeral. They're settin' up t' pahan's nephew as Pahan. This pahan had book-learnin'. If t' nephew's not thus, more work'll come me way.

Ananda Mahato leaves. By Chotti's request the dead pahan's nephew becomes Pahan. The burnt huts have to be built again. Chotti speaks of their misfortune to the jungle contractor and gets some wood for doors and windows. Tirathnath waits for Chhagan, for all the others to come begging for thatching straw, for loans to buy foodgrains. No one comes near him. The autumn crop lies in the field. Even at his summons, bonded labour doesn't come. After all's said and done, their behaviour hurts Tirathnath, angers him.

Tirathnath is terribly unhappy. His office is burnt, his records incinerated. Books that are required for official submission—no loss if they're burnt. They can be instantly prepared. The Assistant can do it. But the books where Lakshmi, the goddess of Tirathnath's wealth, resides, the books where the interests for the creditors' cash and crop loans are recorded, the books on the basis of which Tirathnath takes interest and bond on labour, these books have to be prepared again.

Only Aminchand of Dhanbad can do that work. He can manufacture two-hundred-year old records, documents, ledgers, mercantile records et cetera. Tirathnath decides to fetch him and prepare a double set of books. Aminchand tells Tirathnath's Assistant, five thousand rupees.

Tirath has to agree.

And he goes to the washerwoman Rakhni in the hope of consolation. That beloved delivers the greatest blow. Many years ago Motia did pimp-service for Tirathnath. Tirathnath was delighted. The woman was twenty-two at the time. There was an arrangement through Motia that the girl will get monthly wages, she will get her own hut. Then she had a son too. He stayed with Motia as a child. This girl's hut also went up by Romeo's hand. For his office Tirathnath gets out twenty-five thousand rupees from Gormen and brings in some skilled workmen. The only thing left is to talk to Aminchand. Then he thinks, after this comes the autumn harvest and its relays, its threshing and preparing the field for the spring crop. For this he needs workmen. He feels incensed with the party boys. Is this Surmahi or Dhamura? You'll subdue the low castes by creating a catastrophe? Everyone from the rail-labour-union now knows that Tirathnath is a son of a bitch. So much trouble over his land!

Perhaps to make him lose face Anwar wants to transform his long-idle arable land into a flower garden. He says to Chhagan and Chotti openly, Prepare me the ground in yer off time. Work a couple hours. It'll get done. I'll give five quarters. I don't want that there's work everyday.

Then it'll catch their eye, says Chotti.

Just ten people will do.

Good.

I'm giving you a fifty-rupee advance. For ten people. Five rupees per head. I'll take off quarters when I pay.

Very fine sir.

Chotti says, Put th' ash from their burnt huts on yer land. Fallow land. Land never rests without owners me lord. Land has a soul too. Who knows if t' soul's good or bad. If ye put a bitta ash, whate'er rage it has'll go. Too, t' soil'll be happy.

Do what you like.

Ye haveta do it.

You won't spread these words, will you?

Chotti scowled as if to think of something. Then said, Me mind's not content. T' tishan was t' Gormen prop. T' porter staff is boilin' at t' porter's death. T' Lala will say nothin' right now. He too has a worry about his fields. Chadha won' say.

Then that's the plan.

Tirathnath is depressed by this. He even thinks he's defeated. He says to his wife, I'm losing face. I want to control my bonded labour, my field hands, why did outsiders butt in?

His wife makes a face. You know best. This kind of stuff brings a curse on the house. That's why I've reared the boys in Patna. They don't know land. Service is much better.

Hey, they'll sit in my office when I'm dead.

God's will. The milk cow died in the cold weather of snakebite, the fruitful guava tree dried up.

What to do!

With this Tirathnath goes to his washerwoman lover. She says, Where will you come? Is there a room left?

What's your worry? I'll send straw, I'll send bamboo.

No, no, everyone will give me the eye.

Then cash?

I've lost pots and pans, bed and bedding, all.

The washerwoman cries a lot. Weeping she squeezes out four hundred rupees. Then Tirathnath goes to see Aminchand in Dhanbad. He has to stay there for a day. When he returns his wife laughs with hostile glee and says, What happens when you prize another more than your wedded wife? Your washerwoman took the cash and ran.

Lies!

Go find out.

I'll bring her back. Bitch!

She's run off to Patna. She'll open a laundry there.

She went? She left me and went?

Apart from land and interest Tirathnath had never laid his love upon any human being. This washerwoman is the only exception. His wife thought Tirathnath would explode in rage. But Tirathnath breaks down seriously and asks his sons to look out for the washerwoman. They do not keep such a request from an old decrepit man and he takes to his bed with blood pressure related problems. He remains under herbal medical care for the longest period and is finally cured. Romeo asks him, Shall I get news and drag her here kicking and screaming?

No no.

Tirathnath nurses his complaint, if Romeo and his crew had not created terror the washerwoman would not have left. He wants to know, why did the washerwoman leave? Just to know that bit he is dying in his mind. Romeo says in parting, You expect gratitude from low castes?

He sends Harbans's driver to Patna in secret. The driver knew everything. He brings news. Says, What can I say Lalaji.

What did they say?

I can't tell you.

Tell me, please.

She said, You burnt their area. Then if she had raised a place with yer money people wud've stoned her.

No, they wouldn't've.

And she was mourning for Motia.

Why?

Motia was her granny Lalaji.

What d'ye mean?

We all knew.

Tirathnath has to accept everything. Even the pain of this separation. Then his field of grain makes him forget the sorrow of separation. No one but the few bonded labourers are showing up. He can get help if he informs Romeo. But Tirathnath's mind can't agree to this. Again trouble may arise from whatever little thing. Now he looks for workers outside and finds out that, as a result of Romeo's activities, outsiders are afraid to come here. His heart bursts when he looks at his drooping paddy fields. Forgetting self-respect he sends for Chhagan.

Chhagan says, Let me ask Chotti.

Why? Why him?

We'll be in trouble if we don' let him know.

When he comes back from Chotti Chhagan says, Okay, we'll get the job done. But ye'll give daily wages.

Take it that way.

We'll not give anyone a cut.

All right.

Our bonded workers will go. All others will be Mundas.

Why?

Chotti said.

Right. I've fallen in the ditch, now the frogs kick me.

Romeo is pissed off for this obeisance but Tirthnath says, What would you know about land? And if we don't accept now, what's going to happen to the harvest? Low caste, bad types, but still they'll do the work after all.

Hey! You have the government behind you and you still can't stop worrying about your harvest.

No sir!

The country is not getting ahead because of buffalo-brains like you. Let the harvest rot. Keep the trash in control, and get the job done by outside help. Giv' em two quarters—half a rupee. Your villagers will then croak hungry and fall at yer feet, man. One harvest to rot? Not a thing to worry about, man. Take a loan from the state bank, get the cultivation done by tractor, you'll even get a concession on your income tax with field labour.

That's what I want too, yeah.

But you don't do it in yer acts. Brought in Mundas, what a piece a' shit. Don't let there be tribal bother.

Chotti Munda did everything.

Which sonofabitch? I know that guy.

No no, Chotti aint an ordinary Munda.

Fuck off then. Grease their feet with yer own hands.

Sir, I don't want any bother.

I'll see how they get by without a cut. Chadha'll take out a contract again, yeah? Y'think the ant lets it go once it's tasted sugar's sweet?

That I can't say.

And you'll see, Vijaya Modi wants the same. Otherwise, why's there never a solution for any harijan-torture?

You'll know better.

Look here then, if they bother you again don' fergit to ask fer support. We are soldiers. Our work is to settle bother.

We'll inform.

Don't let ev'n Chotti Munda go.

Suddenly at this time, the Secretary of the Youth League speaks up. Chotti! Chotti Munda! Don't mess with him, Romeo. He gave back my uncle his life. Uncle was a Daroga, and a wild boar had done him in.

Tirath says, Yes, in my field.

The tale is told yet once again. Tirath says, I keep them quiet with bond labour, loan, interest. I don' let 'em raise their heads. This is much more useful. Guns and hut burnings make too much noise.

Romeo says, That's needed too.

Thus Chotti and Chhagan win a partial victory over Tirath. A momentary peace settles over the Chotti area.

Ananda Mahato and Chotti meet in secret, Ananda Mahato sits on a cut sal-tree trunk and writes everything down quickly. Chotti says, Now I've said all. If for yer sake we're done in ye know ye won' stay alive.

Ananda smiles briefly and says, Kill me?

Sure. Chotti smiles too. If it'd been for Harmu's sake, he would've had to die. That's all I say now, lord, we'll finish t' man who brings us harm. An' I'm tellin' yer, I'm not scared to die.

No, no, no one will know.

But Ananda Mahato does not realize how efficient the Administration is these days, how ruthless in the suppression of fact. It is a missionary father who urges him to collect this information. Ananda reads his own reportage, the priest tapes it and stores the tape carefully in the pocket of his cassock. Ananda gives him the written report and asks, Why did you keep it this way?

It always pays to be careful.

He destroys the written report and flies with the cassette to Delhi. There he gives the cassette to a foreign journalist in disfavour with the Administration who is about to leave India. By this journalist's efforts a dubbed cassette reaches a Mumbai newspaper and a fortnight later the news appears in an English weekly published from Italy and in a Mumbai weekly, with the names changed to letters of the alphabet. The Central Government is alerted first. A notorious Member of the opposition and a notorious troublemaker asks for a Justice Department investigation in parliament and creates a furore. Now the State Government picks it up. The I.G. is suddenly transferred to a post for the moral instruction of the police into non-violence. Dilip Tarwe is brought to Delhi for disseminating further enlightenment on tribal handicrafts. Two trucks smash Ananda Mahato's moving bicycle from both sides. 'Few Words, Much Work' is written all over the truck's body and on the back is written 'Ta ta. God is Good.' The office and warehouse of the *Adivasi Samachar* newspaper are burnt down. Under the leadership of Romeo's gang the Youth League asks for a judicial inquiry in the Legislative Assembly and calls for a 'shutdown' of the state capital. A commission sits. A court case is started. After the two truck drivers are turned into truck owners they serve a prison sentence for careless driving and manslaughter, without squealing.

The trouble at home is managed this way but the trouble abroad? Then some material appears in the Indian press, that just as the Naxals are hitting at the very root of Indian democracy at this end, so at that end the enemies of India are spreading evil misinformation. Then some other material appears with much photographic evidence, whose main subject is that the Prime Minister is a friend of the tribals. The photos show many black-faced adults surrounding the Prime Minister and Toda-Maria-Baiga-Ho-Munda etc. children in arms and lap. In some pictures the Crown Prince's bald pate can be seen. Thus everyone is happy and the affair is brought to a close.

Romeo's every wish is not fulfilled. For Harbans Chadha enlarges his brickfield with aid from the state bank, inaugurates it by inviting two ministers—Community Development, and Arts and Crafts. He gets the brick contract for the cement township and he brings the modern age into Chotti. According to Tirathnath. Because now he buys a motorcar.

The cousin who'd been the forest contractor is now transformed by Harbans into a labour contractor. The forest contract descends upon the shoulders of the more youthful cousin. Romeo thinks, now Chadha has to be taught a lesson by hook or by crook. He comes one day with Pahlwan and says, I hear you're cheating labour, is that correct?

What d'ye mean?

Poor tribals and untouchables don't know reckoning, you built a brickfield with state support, are you giving the approved wage?

I'm giving the rate fixed by the Labour Commissioner.

How do I know that?

Why should I care if you believe me or not? Harbans smiles benignly. The government auditor will audit.

Well, remember me if you need me.

Sure.

Whose quarters are those?

Don't I need sentries?

Good, good. So are you getting labour?

I will.

So what percentage are you giving on this contract?

Friend, there's no percentage in this. What there is, is in the beginning. For labour payment there's a designated person.

Who?

Outsider. By government regulation.

Very good, very good. Now Chotti will be a town.

By your good wishes.

Romeo leaves with his cohorts. Hearing all from his mouth the Youth League Secretary says, The work went to hell because of you people. If you hadn't gone on a rampage, who could have dared cut us out of this five hundred thousand rupees project? Okay, no more mischief now. We'll get in when we sense a good time.

Will the day not come?

It will, it will.

Time passes and passes. Chotti, Chhagan and the group get unskilled wages at Chadha's brick kiln. What used to be a link between Chadha and Chotti now becomes a distance. Now the work is by hour. Someone else pays wages. Chotti says, This is better. Today as we're gettin' three rupees a day, things are so dear ever'day that t' three rupees're worth eight annas, a half rupee. Let it be. Times change, rites change. Keep ahold on Chadha and ye won't starve.

What did Chadha call ya for?

Advice to outside Munda labour. Tells them, Tell Chotti what ya need. Tells me, Ye're here, I'm happy. Tells me that I have s-o-o-o much power. After that I tek three rupees like them and come home. Even wants to raise me wages.

Why not tek?

Tell me, at day's end I come home with four, you with three, we'd've lost trust.

Ye're right.

Chadha's better'n Lala, but who doesn't want to set up quarrels and disputes? They can't bear us comin' together. T' way of t' boss tribe.

Why is yer wife choppin' turmeric?

Me grandson, Harmu's lad, is gettin' wed.

Harmu's son gets married. A daughter is born to the new pahan. Koel's wife Mungri dies of dropsy. A shiny new teashop opens under the old sisu tree at the station. Surprising everyone, Tirathnath's son marries a Madrasi nurse by the rules of the Arya Samaj Hindu reform movement in Patna. For some reason archery gets going again at the Chotti fair. Chotti laughs and tells Harmu, Now t' Mundas live and sweat year round with other tribes. On fair day a Munda wants to be a Munda for once with a bow in his hand.

Me son has no mind for 't.

Let him not.

But he's yer grandson?

Why think that way Harmu? Times are changin'.

The times change. Chotti's kind doesn't wait at all for the times to change. They are mere spectators and their active role is kept on the same minor level. But Romeo, Pahlwan and Dildar wait. Must have more power, more power. The times are theirs.

The waited for time arrives. Emergency.

In villages and towns the Emergency comes in two ways. The jail gates open and swallow prisoners. The voice of the newspapers is strangled. But since city folk are good boys and pleased with a little, they're quite pleased. For load-shedding or power-cuts decrease; trains run on time, all vehicles run efficiently at the behest of the slogan 'work-talk-more-less', in fact one can even get to see clerks at government offices.

Therefore does darkness descend upon the villages. Since India means village, it is the villages that know the real appearance of the Emergency.

In the Chotti area the first blow is taken by Harbans's cousin Rajbans: Romeo appears one day at his log-splitting works in Tohri. Every enterprise in life does not follow arguments of the 'A-therefore-B' type. There's always a split between fact and theory. This can be demonstrated by two examples from the two completely separate incidents involving Dr Amlesh Khurana and Basmati Oraon. However, the log-splitting works at Tohri are as beautiful as Kashmir the earthly paradise, but Romeo doesn't go there for that reason. He goes for the sake of Pahlwan. The Member whose sidekicks Romeo, Pahlwan and Dildar are does not keep track of them at the moment. He has told them short and sweet, he'll get his work done with others. In Chotti and the surrounding areas, industries, although not quite of the number one category, but of at least the number two-three-four-five-six-seven varieties, have grown up; and native and foreign money is flowing in like floodwater along the channels of those industries, so let Romeo and his gang feed themselves by beating the area. The Member will remain happy if they receive four 'cuts' from each project. And the aluminium works are more or less anonymously the Member's property. Therefore the Member cannot think of anything else.

He says, And yes, a doctor will visit us to assess what is necessary for the economic development of our area.

Doctor?

Yes, yes.

Here it is necessary to mention that the Member understands that the doctor is coming to assess the region's problems and needs and at the same time, because of his innate simplicity, he assumes that this man's a doctor. In consequence many complications arise. This Amlesh Khurana is thirty-six. Since he's very intelligent, and since he's the foster child of a person in the confidence of Vijaya Modi, some foundation or other is racing to get hold of him and give him financial aid as soon as he receives his M.A. 'Racing to get hold of him' is correct, because his days pass in flying from town to town, from university to university, and from seminar to seminar on the globe. It is India he hasn't seen. This is precisely why he is well known as an Indianist expert in social economics. He believes in theory and statistics, not in the reality of the situation. Recently, sitting in France, he has released a napalm about Indian small handicrafts. Very attractive napalm.

He says that the root cause of the entire problem of poverty in India is dependence on agriculture and industry. India does not need agriculture or large-scale industry. If one can bring a revolutionary change in peoples' mindsets people will work very fast. Therefore peasants should manufacture paper by hand, fisherfolk should weave mats, potters should run handlooms, weavers make Bengal lights and carpenters wool from animal hair. Objects of unusual quality will be produced as a result. India will be able to buy from outside whatever is needed in the line of industry and food. Amlesh has done research with a number of working people such as farmer-potters and blacksmiths to prove that these people are tired, tired of their own line of work. How will they demonstrate excellence in work for which they feel no enthusiasm?

This napalm has raised a furore in the most advanced academic-theoretical circles all around the world, quite like Daniken's unearthly predictions. The Government of India always loves these statistics-based paper theories, on the basis of which it is possible to construct completely unrealistic projects—in the implementation of which millions of rupees can be given to unsuitable persons—which are never implemented or come to no use even if they are. Therefore, Amlesh has been brought to India with an incredibly large sum of money. Here it is necessary to say that there is no evil intent behind the theory-construction of an academician such as Amlesh and the support given by the Government of India to such a theory. Behind both is present a desire to transform India into something as beautiful as the gardens of the Lutyens model Teen Murti House in New Delhi.

The local Member understands nothing but his 'cut', his whore and his debauchery. These are not faults that can be ignored. For it is on their basis that most members of the Legislative Assembly receive their nomination. Even today. In backward areas. The local Member also does not understand that behind Amlesh is the Government of India and some other foreign government.

He receives an order to rent the best house in Tohri for Doctor Khurana. There is no spectacular bungalow in Tohri. He asks the S.D.O to empty a hospital ward.

Why?

This is for a dug-thar.

Everything can be done under the rules of the Emergency. But releasing patients from hospitals to provide living quarters for the doctor has not happened yet. So the S.D.O has no clue what to do and by his infinite good fortune directives from the Magistrate arrive instantly. Relieved, the S.D.O. calls Rajbans Chadha. He says, the Government of India is sending a scientist. There will be some people with him. There is no suitable accommodation in Tohri. But your residence remains locked.

Yes sir. I'm not there all the time. I've now struck tent in Lahara Forest. So how long do you want it for?

About three months. You'll get rent.

No sir. I won't rent it out.

Why?

My brother forbids it.

You think the government won't let the house go if they take it?

No sir. Do I have the power to think that? You're requisitioning houses and setting up police posts right and left. We are savage jungle folk, what is our crime that so many police have descended upon our area? So sir, if you say that the state wants the house, who am I to say no?

The S.D.O. is an efficient youth, not a bad type. The mainstay of the ruling machine in the jungle-belt is the jungle-contractor. Rajbans Chadha is not a first-level contractor, but he's not altogether negligible. The S.D.O. likes the Chadhas. They are civilized people of refined tastes, and do not create difficulties with labour. Perhaps if they reach the top they will become little Hitlers. But they're not yet. Rajbans behaves well with the tribals.

Take the rent for three months? says the S.D.O.

No, no. But inspect the bungalow sir. The hospital on one side, and my saw-mill on the other. There'll be noise.

Let's see.

The S.D.O. takes a look and says, Furniture as well. You won't take rent. Let's do this. Let me give paint and polish, let's fix the gate, they'll park their car. And let's put in a bathroom.

There's arrangements for a bathroom. You just have to put in fittings. And a tank.

Everything's done in a week. Then Khurana arrives in a station wagon. His wife and secretary is a young Khasi woman. His typist is a young man from Kerala. His driver's Marathi, cook-cum-bearer Goanese.

Amlesh sets himself up as soon as he arrives. When the S.D.O. says, Let me know if you need anything, he says, Of course. I need privacy for my work. Otherwise I won't be able to function on schedule, which he pronounces 'skejul'. S.D.O. says to himself, Showing off your U.S. connections. He says aloud, Let me know. Now lunch?

We have everything. Where is the water?

In the well.

We'll boil the water. And I want a few Munda villages, a few Oraon villages, some villages with mixed Munda-Oraon popula-tion, some Dusad villages, some Dhobi and Ganju villages, some Rajput villages, some villages with mixed Rajput and Brahman population, and some leper-majority villages.

Meaning?

Is the meaning not clear?

There are no villages with such populations.

Then you're not well-informed. Mr. Shukul prepared me a report. I need twenty-five villages.

I've been here for three years. I've visited nearly every village because of the drought. I've never seen such villages.

Then?

Villages with only Oraons or only Mundas would be difficult to find, but can still perhaps be found way in the interior. Pure Dusad, Ganju, Dhobi villages? None. Pure Rajput villages? If only Rajputs live in a village who will wash and shave them? Whoever prepared the report did not take this area as his base.

Amlesh's Khasi wife, wearing jeans and a kurta top, says in pure Hindi, This problem can be solved easily. In each village we'll count each caste or group neighbourhood as a village. That's it.

But leper villages?

Not even that? Amlesh Khurana, whose home is the universities of the entire universe, becomes altogether pained and hopeless about India.

No. But you can go to the leper village at Tomaru mission.

But that won't do at all.

I don't know what your work is. But I can take you around actually existing villages. Amlesh says, How can that be? My work is to survey the projected economic necessity.

Please forgive me. But what good will that do?

Amlesh bears infinite contempt for administrative officers. So he says in a voice for explaining things to an infant, This is the work of surveying by scientific methodology. The government will build projects on this basis for the development of the area.

The S.D.O. is altogether depressed. He has seen such surveys and such projects about seven times during his period of service.

Amlesh takes pity on him and says, You have actual experience. But Shukul is a theoretic-academician. This report is much more reliable. Because it's made by a scientific method.

As an S.D.O. of such an area he generally encounters ordinary people. Landed farmer–moneylender–gang youth–Brahman priest–poor adivasi–field hand–outcaste-fighters of the Jharkhand armed struggle–sly contractor. The S.D.O. is amused to see this intellectually arrogant project theorist who will cast aside reality and solve national problems on the basis of theory. He laughs uproariously and says, Fight on sir. If you can find even one village that fits your report, I'll be delighted. Let me just ask you to let me know whenever you need anything.

Yes, yes, I will. I'll go only to you to find out if there's any political unrest.

But I must know if you go to visit a village.

Why?

I'm responsible for your life. I'll give you a guard.

Police? I despise the Indian police. From behind Mrs Amlesh speaks up in a voice of strong support, Do you know that they beat up harijans and support moneylenders? They also abuse women, old people, children.

How strange! But I'll still provide a guard.

If we don't accept it?

My job will be in trouble.

What's wrong with that, says Mrs. Amlesh. Will you be able to build a new India as a hardcore bureaucrat of the British legacy? Leave your job and get into actual cultivation, hold the ploughshare in your hand.

The S.D.O. leaves precipitately. Amlesh is pleased with the house. He points at the saw-mill and asks, What's that?

Factory for splitting timber. Saw-mill.

On this side?

Hospital.

Okay.

S.D.O. goes to his superior. He tells the Magistrate everything. And asks, What to do?

Give 'em a guard.

And?

Do what they say.

All my other work's going to hell.

These are Delhi's adoptive sons. They want pure caste-villages, leper villages. One sits in Delhi and writes a report on the Chotti area, the other comes from France. And Delhi will make area-development projects on the basis of what he writes.

Pour money.

The Magistrate smiles and says, Don't you understand the real thing? The government doesn't want development to stop. But the government depends on theorists, and modern education prepares the theorists by removing them from the country. And I don't know who this Khurana is. But in the eyes of Delhi he's the legendary roq bird's egg.

The S.D.O. thinks that perhaps it was not necessary to preserve all the ancient problems of this area and deposit a roq egg upon this laterite soil. But he does not say so. When the Bishop of Daltonganj prepared his report on bonded labour, the S.D.O. had helped him. In 1973 there had been an uproar in the two Houses of Parliament as a result of the Bishop's report. In consequence a study team came to the area and ran an investigation of five villages. S.D.O. helped with that as well. He's therefore not well-liked at all by the state administration. Now he does not add to the trouble by commenting on Khurana.

In fact, Khurana quite unwittingly raises a tempest in these troubled waters and helps Chotti Munda to become a legend yet once again.

The reason is Basmati Oraon.

Basmati Oraon is the daughter of Dhaotal Oraon of Chotti village, the wife of Birju Oraon of Dhai village. Basmati and Birju cut timber in the forest for Rajbans. Basmati carries construction materials and tree trunks. They both come and go at the Tohri saw-mill. Birju is learning how to split timber at the mill.

After the Emergency, Romeo's gang realizes that Chadha has slipped their grasp. But Romeo says to Pahlwan, it is our right to take a cut from the work of labour. That way little drops of water make an ocean for us. Another thing. After the troubles at Chotti village the people of Chotti may think we've forgotten them.

We haven't, guru.

They also sweat labour for Rajbans Chadha.

Wherefore? No brick-kiln?

Everything's there. They are doing piecework.

Then shall I go there?

Yes, go.

That's where Pahlwan goes, and says to Rajbans, the rules have changed with the times. I'll take a rupee cut from everyone's wages. I'll collect from you. I want to vomit when I smell these bastards. He can't finish his words. He falls to the ground with a blow from a block of wood. And instantly hears an irritated female voice, Who're you? Blind or what?

Pahlwan gets up and is dumbfounded at the sight of the speaker even as he thinks to retort. He looks, keeps on looking. Basmati puts down the cut bit of tree on the ground from her head and turns around. Pahlwan is perhaps seeing her for the first time. Basmati knows him well and starts to say something and stops. Rajbans says in a dry voice, Get outa here, Basmati.

Stop, says Pahlwan.

Rajbans says in a low voice, Don't do this.

Pahlwan says, I'm a Punjabi boy with a load of balls. I'll do what I damn please. Do you have the power to stop it?

Basmati leaves fast, moves out of sight. Pahlwan says, I'll come in the afternoon and pick up your Basmati. He leaves. It's quite natural that Pahlwan should be so crazed. For the voluptuousness of Basmati's body is out of control ineffable. Rajbans goes immediately to where the timber is being carried. There he sees Chotti. The sight of him seems reassuring. He says, Chotti? You?

Yes Lord, so see only five years're left for me to get to four score. Can't sweat every day sir. Harmu's gonna buy a buffalo from Birju. I came to give word. So they say sit f'r a bit.

I'm glad you came.

Why? What's up?

Rajbans tells briefly. Then Chotti says, Let the girls go right away Lord. Let 'em go on home.

Basmati says, For fear of 'im?

Only a fool don' fear a snake.

Now they look for Birju and it's discovered that he's two miles away. It'll be late afternoon before he gets back. Chotti talks little, ponders. Then says, Lord! Will ye let me sleep at yer works this night?

Why not Chotti?

Tomorra I go wit' ye to their sektari. Ye know who their sektari is? T' nephew of t' Daroga who was chased by a boar, who I saved. Yer big brother was a lad then. And ye a kid.

Come, we'll go. These people will cause a work stoppage.

We won' let them dishonour our womenfolk.

The women move off each to her hut. Chotti says, Basmati, if ye're feared, then come to t' woodshed. That Romeo knows yer neighbourhood. And bring Birju's bow.

Basmati is now afraid. She says softly, I'll bring chickpea flour and molasses for ya.

Jagir Singh is the watchman for Rajbans's timber-works. He's furiously angry. He says, I'll finish these three gang leaders tonight.

No. They'll set fire to the works.

In the late afternoon Pahlwan, Romeo and Dildar come by. They go to the Munda quarter. They don't find Basmati. Then Romeo starts beating Basmati's mother-in-law. And gets word out of her. And then, before going to the timber-works, the three sit in the jeep and open a bottle.

Darkness falls. Jagir Singh whispers that he'll gladly bust his guts to neutralize such wretches. Pahlwan has taken to coming by and snatching his cash at will and Romeo kicked him one day when no one was about.

Chotti says, Nothin' in this here place. Our boss'll die.

Why here? In the jungle.

Ye must listen to me before ye act.

Will ye shoot yer arrow?

We'll see. Chotti now whispers directions and waits. At the expected time the Jeep enters and halts.

Basmati, hey Basmati!

They push open the door. All three enter swaying. Dildar shines his flashlight. Birju, Jagir Singh and the other men laugh as the light falls on their faces. And then they leap. Romeo shoots. Jagir Singh throws him down and starts gagging them with swift fingers and binding them with rope. Truss them like pigs, says Chotti.

Trussed they are left in a corner. Suddenly the words 'what's happening here' are heard.

Amlesh Khurana and his Keralan Assistant.

What's this? Who are these?

Altogether unbelievable. But Amlesh recognizes Romeo's bunch. Says, Hey, aren't these the leaders of the Youth League?

An old, emaciated, self possessed Munda says, Yes lord. Who are ye? Why have ye come here?

I am a research officer for the central government. I came hearing the ruckus. Why have you bound up these men?

Chotti tells him everything. Says Amlesh, How strange! Such misdeeds from Youth League leaders.

Yes Lord.

Who are you?

Chotti Munda.

Your name . . . your name . . . the doctor spoke of you. You shoot arrows, no? I heard.

Yes lord.

What are you going to do with these people?

What powers do we have? This guy brought a gun. One of us ud've died if it hit 'im. So we've trussed um. We'll show 'm to sektari.

This is terribly wrong on the part of the Youth League . . . Amlesh and his Assistant depart.

Day breaks. Keeping Basmati, Birju and the others waiting Rajbans and Chotti take Rajbans's Jeep to a spot six miles distant. They tell the Youth League Secretary and the Secretary of the party everything. The Youth League Secretary comes to the timber mill. Receiving the news from somewhere the S.D.O. and the

Daroga arrive. Chotti says, We kill our girls if they are dishonoured. I'm in death, I'm not afeared to die. I had me arrer, so know ye, I coulda killed 'm if I'd wanted. I didn' cos you'd raise hell with Chadha.

At this point Amlesh Khurana walks on stage and gives his account. S.D.O. is happy in his heart. The Youth League's face is pale. He knows who's behind Khurana. Chotti seizes the moment and says to Khurana, Lord, they'll take revenge in no time. I hear ye know Gormen. So why don't ye write up t' true story?

I will if need be.

S.D.O. tells the Youth League Society, Do what you have to. I'll submit a report.

The Secretary says in a dry voice, The matter needs to be settled now, here. He says apart to the S.D.O., Now Khurana knows, everything's screwed up. What information he'll give, what the reaction will be, will I be screwed as well for trying to save Pahlwan?

S.D.O. says, Let 'em go.

And Chotti adds, First ye give yer word, lords, that ye won' make trouble by reason of this?

The Youth League Secretary says, No. Not to worry.

Amlesh says, But I won't let it go. I've come to survey the needs of the area. And I see that the greatest need is to save the honour of tribal women from Youth League leaders. This I'll write in my report. Amlesh leaves suddenly.

S.D.O. wipes his face and says, Who's going to say no to Khurana? Youth League is also depressed. Now Chotti's group leaves as well. Jagir Singh smiles and sits quietly.

Youth League undoes the bindings of the three. Jagir Singh says, God be praised, send the hospital janitor sir. Everything is soiled. They shit and pissed their pants.

The three climb into the Jeep. The Youth League Secretary looks at all three and shakes his head in disbelief. He opens his mouth only when he gets to the Youth League office and says, To advertise ourselves in this way in front of Khurana. Do you know who Khurana is? Do you know what'll happen if he submits a report?

Pahlwan says, I've understood everything.

Romeo says no more than, I too will get mine back.

From whom?

Everyone.

The Youth League Secretary says, That's enough. Don't make me laugh. Romeo does not attach much importance to his words. He asks, Who's Khurana? What does he know? Suppose I do nothing more than bring case against these dogs in the city courts? He's a foreign egghead, he'll scram if he has to give evidence in court.

The Secretary of the party does not remain silent. He too runs around as needed. As a result, the three goons are summoned to town, to a small well-appointed bungalow. Three Keralan officers are sitting at the table. And Khurana's Keralan secretary relaxes in an easy-chair. One of the young officers at the table asks, Is this report correct? He reads the report aloud. He stops the protesting Romeo and says, Is the report correct?

Let me talk. The officer holds the smile on his face. Then he says, Have you heard of IAD? Investigate-Apprehend-Destroy? You have? Good. I don't want any bother in that area while Khurana is here. IAD will descend if there's trouble.

Understood sir.

Hope you remember this. You may go.

Amlesh's Keralan secretary says, Can one not just make a Maintenance of Internal Security Act issue out of these guys? Why keep them outside?

The Officer says, Khurana will be here only a few months. I will remain here now. For no reason, note it, for no reason at all, he says, pointing his ruler at the map, do I want any breach of peace here. People like you are a burden on the country's shoulders.

After the abovementioned dressing down the others understand, but Pahlwan doesn't, and, in a few days, meeting Khurana's secretary drinking tea by the roadside he says, Hey! Why didn't ya tell me that you were an IAD-ist? The secretary comes forward smiling and presses down on some spot on Pahlwan's neck which renders him numb with pain and lifts him into the Jeep. Takes him to town to the beforementioned bungalow. After a couple of days an enlightened Pahlwan's released from the city hospital after treatment for various sorts of internal injuries and is established in the bungalow of the aluminium factory to heal his body. And now he understands the true meaning of the proverb, one shouldn't scratch one's ear with a cobra's tail.

For reasons such as this a certain peace reigns in the area. But it is an electric peace. There is tension inside. It is as if no one believes anyone. Chotti and Chhagan's lot begin to get a relatively good wage from Harbans and Rajbans. Romeo's gang doesn't come to get their cut. Tirathnath is quiet. Eating chickpea flour with yogurt and molasses at the tribal Sohrai feast Chhagan says, Everything is going well right now. The seedling's are out on Anwar's land. I got a lotta maize outa mine. This time. The party bosses're foiled cos Chotti was there. So everything is quiet.

Chotti sat with his back to the tree, watching the feast. He says, So much quiet is not good, me lad.

Why?

See what they do agin.

Chhagan's young nephew is new to the area. He says, They made trouble twice in three years. Our homes burnt, four heads died. And what a thing around Basmati!

There'll be more.

More?

I know from t' wind.

What's that?

Hey, that Gormen.

Wife's wearin' a cloth today. Wears pants mosta the time.

Amlesh, his wife and Secretary. The station master's with them. What's going on? Amlesh asks.

Our feast, Chhagan says. They bring out a charpoy, they sit down, Amlesh says, Great, great! Railway trains running on the other side, the soil rich in uranium and monazite—and at the same time a tribal festival.

This is not a tribal festival, says the Secretary.

Then?

They are different lower-caste Hindus.

But I see a few Mundas?

Invited.

Strange, strange! Why don't the lower-castes live separately, why do the Mundas respond to their invitation! It's painful even to think about this. India Bharat is too complex for me.

The wife says, We're going abroad in 1976, my darling.

And I see Chotti. Chotti!

Me lord?

We need a fair.

What me lord?

Need a fair.

Can one find a mela like that, lord? Chotti smiles.

The Keralan secretary now says in the regional country Hindi, He wants to film a fair. It'll have an archery match, witch doctors will chase spooks, sacrifice a pig to the sun.

Chotti says, Thas all!

What's the matter? Fix everything up for us. We'll pay.

Me lord! Yer talk like babes. I hear ye git ever'thin' in town. But lord we're bare-assed beggars, what do we have that we can bring t' boar of wintertime and t' ripe mango of summer? Ye pay that mango tree and tell it ta git ya fruit outa season? Will it do?

The secretary laughs at this. Says, What did I say wrong Chotti? No doubt what I said was wrong?

Lord! On Dasera day there'll be a fair here. Oh that fair is our eye's delight. How many Mundas from how many villages, how many dances danced, drums beat, and then all'll come to shoot arrers. Thas a fair. And then, on yer light-feast Diwali day, we'll all go to top o' Kurmi hill, there Deora-Pahan'll chase off spirits, and then we call God Sun and tie t' pig and throw it down from w-a-a-y up t' hilltop. That's a diffren job. And ye say, fix it all up, we'll pay. Can that be?

The secretary says everything to Amlesh and says to Chotti, Then we'll take pictures at the fair. Do you still shoot arrows?

Pahan says, No, he judge.

Amlesh says, You can't any more?

A faint smile plays on Chotti's lips. He says, Who knows? I haven' raised a bow so long.

Show a bit.

Everyone begs Chotti. Finally Chotti satisfies everyone by blowing off Amlesh's straw hat from his head and dropping on the ground a fruit hanging from the tree. Amlesh brings out two ten-rupee notes from his pocket. He says, Have a drink everyone, have fun.

They leave. Chotti says, Go git some booze. Guy's like a kid.

This is one day. Many others come and go. Then one day there is a summons. Right after Chotti fair. Hearing the summons they all come to the station. Daroga licks dry lips and says, To let y'all know is the order.

What's up? Sana's worried.

Me children, what's goin' on makes me head whirl. I never thought, never knew, this could happen.

What happened?

Wait, let's read ye the nootish first.

Daroga spits and says, Let me drink a bitta water first. Gormen made kings outa y'all?

Now he reads that by the Ordinance of 24th October, 1975, the bonded labour system is at an end, illegal. All of you bonded labourers are now released, you no longer have to give labour. Now in no way can anyone make anyone give bonded labour, no one can force bonded labour. Apart from that there are a thousand little details of the law which I'm not reading. The main point is, whichever boss or moneylender has a bond, or an old debt, all that is cancelled. No debts to be repaid, no boss to be bonded to. If your home and land are in hock with the moneylender for an old debt, the moneylender will return it.

Lord! Chotti lifts his hand.

Say Chotti.

If t' boss take bond labour, don' return home an' land, raise trouble o'er debt, what s'd debtor labourer do?

Complain at the Courts.

An' what punishment?

Three years je-hell, and fine.

Chotti laughs, keeps laughing.

Why do ye laugh, Chotti?

Lord. They've made t' law, t' law's made, but they put a stone in t' law, an' t' law tumbles. T' debtor, t' labourer, will charge that boss? By what strength lord?

Chotti shakes and shakes his head. Daroga leaves. Now Chhagan's lot and the other Mundas run forward. He says, What's this that Daroga said? This I don' get Chotti.

Who'll mek us get it? They've made t' law fer our good, but they nev'r let it be known.

Come let's go ta Tohri. That Gormen is true. He'll explain. Les go there tomorra.

Les go ta Chadha first.

Harbans got his paper by the evening train. He says to Chotti, The news is good of course, Chotti, but . . .

So good that ya caint believe't.

Just so. Look, I go to town constantly, let me find out. There's a new officer, let me find out.

Th' old un was good.

This one's not bad either. Daroga came and told ye because he asked or pulled strings, otherwise d'ye think this Daroga would have moved?

He too knows that nothin'll happ'n wit' this law. So he joked an' said, ye're now kings.

The law is not bad, Chotti, but nothing works by the law. For the law is never applied.

We know ever'thin', lord.

I'll find out an' tell ya. I would've been most pleased if it had been applied. Can this go on in a civilized country?

It can lord. It'll go on fore'er. Tell me why not? Who's there for us? If we want our rights t' party boys'll kill us, and polis'll follow their orders.

Yes.

Harbans's face hardens. His and Rajbans's experiences are recent and bitter.

The next day Chotti and a few others go to Tohri. Amlesh says, This is a clear message Chotti. There is no bonded labour. You won't have to pay back old debts. For the first time . . . wait, wait. Shankar!

Yes?

Ah! Ah! What an opportunity!

For what?

Is the Bonded Labour Act in the papers?

Yes.

Just the other day these people were slaves. Today we can see some free human beings. Let them be seated. Let me make a movie. Listen to their reactions on the tape recorder, I mean tape them.

Shankar says, Good idea Khurana. We can syndicate it. Mary, Mary! Look after them, give them tea.

Chotti lifts his hand. Says, First make 't clear lord. If boss takes interest from creditor by force, takes labour, what'll 'e do? Any word o' that in t' law?

Bring charges at the S.D.O.'s court.

Then?

There'll be punishment according to the law.

Chotti remained silent.

What's the matter? You're quiet suddenly?

What'll I say, tell me? Chotti's voice holds the lament of the ages, and Shankar turns the tape recorder on. Chotti says, What'll I say, tell me, lord! Upon what day, how many years back someone took five kilos of paddy, ten kilos of maize, three rupee coins. And t' price, hoo lord! More'n gold. To repay that debt ye gie labour from father to son on and on, belly-debt stays unrepaid. Gie's int'rest, goes on givin', t' principal's not repaid. Debt upon debt, to keep food in yer belly.

Tell, tell!

Ta get justice in a court case! Who's gointa press charges? Ye're Gormen, lemme ask ya, who'll press charges? If boss-moneylender takes yer life t' polis see no fault. If t' debtor-labourer says a word they catch 'im. Me dad he went crazy with that Lala's father's terror and put a noose ta his neck. And this Lala sends me son Harmu to je-hellhouse with land pressure. Who'll bring charges agin t' Lala lord? There's allus drought, there's famine. We've to go to t' Lala to borrow for food. A court case! Chotti's voice grows long and high with misery, Munda lives in village, and so does th' untouchable, does he know to read and write? So he grasps law, grasps rights? Is there anyone beside him, behind him? Will t' court take him? Doesn't t' lawyer and t' clerk skin alive Munda, Oraon, t' Not-to-touch? Who makes this law?

Government.

Where does this Gormen live?

In Delhi.

It's far away, nah?

Yes.

Makes t' law, does good, stays afar. But if adivasi or untouchable dies in t' forest, they don' know.

No, that's not it.

If they wanted to know, they could know.

Be quiet.

Chotti is startled and falls silent. Now Shankar plays the recorder and Chotti's voice is heard. Everyone is amazed, they laugh, they listen. Amlesh says, Beautiful. Now hear their statements.

Everyone's voice is recorded and everyone listens. Shankar says, We'll film another day.

In time the cassette is broadcast in India and abroad. There Chotti's words are erased but Chhagan's elated deposition is kept.

The entire experience amazes the people of Chotti consider-ably, and brings joy as well. Chhagan says, What a day today, eh Chotti?

Sana says, Chotti is no' happy.

Chhagan says, He's not a bonded labourer after all. Can he be as happy as we are? Not true, eh Chotti?

Chotti says, I'll eat t' mango and know how it tastes.

Meaning?

If boss-moneylender accepts t' law, no problem. But will they so? Me brain says, from this law there'll be fire.

Everyone goes home, but Chotti's experience doesn't end there. Harbans calls him the next day. Says, Chotti, adivasi officers and others don' yet know much. New law, after all. They said, they'll make arrangements to spread the news as soon as they have it . . . one word though.

What, lord?

Chotti, you're not a bonded labourer, yes?

No lord.

Then why are you so busy with this law?

Chotti says right away, I'm not lord, but Sana, Budha, Mitua are bond labourers. And Mundas, Chhagan, so many of 'em! So I'm busy lord. Someone's home's on fire, why d'ye put it out? Yer home might burn too. Not me, but there are many, and Harmu's son might become un.

The law will stand by them.

T' law's already there, lord! And yet Motia and Pahan died! Did anyone go to je-hell, was anyone punished? Harmu did nothin' and went to je-hell. No lord! As long as Diku has t' power to make t' law work, so long will Diku watch Diku's rights.

Suddenly Harbans thinks he too is Diku in Chotti's eyes and perhaps Chotti cannot trust him either. He feels uneasy. Then he says, As I was saying.

Tell me lord!

A friend of mine, Bhunya by name and caste—went to College with me. Now he does some kind of work for adivasi welfare in Gomo-Dhanbad, 'Adivasi Welfare Service' or some such. I met up with him suddenly. Came to Father's house. He wants to see you once.

Why?

I don't know. Don't tell anyone.

Is he too Laxalite?

No, no, but times are not good. There's not much trouble here, it is here they'll come. I'll let you know.

Lord, no troubles will arise from this visit? Those who do harm'll go on doing so. Ever'one has t' right to harm adivasis and untouchables. E'en well-wishers don' grasp this. And so polis raises terror. Homes burnin', bodies fallin', don' like this any more, lord.

No, no, I too move around carefully Chotti. No one's pleased with me either.

From Harbans's words it seems that he regrets having said yes to his friend.

When Harbans's friend comes, it can be seen that he's wearing saffron pajamas and top, but his soul is not as pure as that holy saffron colour. Speaking to Chotti he goes to the farthest edge of the deserted brick kiln. Then says, I don't know you, but I've been hearing of you since my childhood. When Puran Munda died in Dhanbad, it's me who looked after him.

Puran? Puran's dead?

Uh, five years ago.

What'd he have?

TB.

So Puran died?

I heard from him, and much more. Mahato told me everything after he left you.

Are ye his man, lord?

No. He managed a newspaper. He was my friend.

What do ye do.

My name's Swarup. I . . . what to say?

Laxali?

I do some things like them, but I'm not a Naxalite. Of course the police call us Naxal. But our goal is to watch for and preserve adivasi rights as far as possible. Our aim, to build a separate state for aboriginals.

Lord, Ye're dreamin'.

One must dream, Chotti.

Birsa dreamt. He became god. At one time I sat at his stachew's feet at City Hall. Me boy was in je-hell. He turned god, and his Mundas die as before.

But one must dream.

Don' take offence, lord. If ye gie th' adivasis a state, where do th' untouchables go? They die our deaths too.

Are their problems and yours the same?

Where there are Munda-villages and Oraon-villages and Ho-villages yer words are right. But all adivasis don' live in such villages lord. In our Chotti village untouchable-adivasi live together. In work-sweat, in joy-pain, we're one. Look lord! Only adivasi-untouchable leave their own earth and set forth, and they go adrift. So dream on about that state. No Diku-Hindus in that state, then?

No. No Diku, no moneylender, no boss-farmer, no police. No one terrorizes there.

Lord! Ye say t' state, I see in me mind. I see endless land there. Yes Chotti.

So gie them too that land. Ye can't gie by hand, give in dream. No expense there.

I understand. But this is not a dream.

T' people who buy humans from generation to generation for a bushel of wheat, will they let a handful of land go lord?

Chotti's words disturb the man repeatedly. Why so, Chotti doesn't understand. He is a Munda, patience and calm are in his blood. The man says, Well, the reason I came to talk to you.

Tell me lord!

The law abolishing bonded labour has been passed. Now, far from implementing the law, boss-moneylender will give battle simply because the law is in place.

I too know that.

Here you have real forest from Chotti to Komandi. We have posts there. If there's trouble here, we'll come and fight.

Then?

We'll see.

Why d'ye hide?

The government has a law, MISA. MISA is catching everyone. We have a hospital and a nursing home as well. First we start work with that kind of stuff. Yet, they're catching even us now.

Ye called to tell me this?

Chotti! There's less likelihood of trouble in Chotti village after the Basmati Oraon incident. We begin the movement to get the bonded labour law moving from right here.

With whom lord?

With you people.

Lord! Suppose everyone raised arms at yer word. Then? T' party bosses'll kill, t' polis will make t' girls nekked, put us in je-hell chop-chop, then? Then who'll guard, give lawyers, save t' homes from t' bosses' hard hand?

Your words are not wrong. Yet . . .

Ye're Dikus and still think of us folks, this is sure good. But ye wish ta work fer us then live with us. Teach us. So we know our own right.

There was a chance here Chotti!

And lord! Think also of t' good of Dusad-Ganju? I'm a stupid Munda, not a bond-worker but still think, I'm still thinking of 'em, of bond labourers, an' ye in yer new kingdom caint give them bitta land e'en in dream? Chotti smiles.

I'm thinking.

Ye'll give backin'. Won' t' polis catch ye?

Police? IAD's on the scene.

What's tha' lord?

Special police to capture groups like ours.

See that. If Diku's good, their brains caint ripen. T' polis and his dad is on yer case, and ye'll gie us support?

Is it any use being afraid?

But there's no point in dyin' like dumb sheep either. Forgive me.

Thus conversation and discussion remain indecisive. Swarup leaves on his bicycle. Chotti returns more depressed and serious. Harmu says, That crazy Gormen from Tohri has sent message. He'll come to have a powwow wit ya tomorra.

Oh more palaver! Diku knows how to talk. Wife! Heat up a bitta oil, me feet hurt.

The next day he goes to Tohri. Amlesh says, Magistrate and SDO—whatever, they will make committees.

They might—Shankar corrects him.

They might. There's talk of setting up a committee. Taking their members from the untouchables and the adivasis. You will be there.

What'll come of it lord?

You'll look out who's obstructing the implementation of the bonded labour law, who is trying to make trouble.

Lord! What's this talk?

Why?

Is this a joke sir?

Joke? What's this you're saying?

If all bosses take bonded labour, Gormen will support them with polis an' party boys, don' ye know that? What happen t'other day at t' saw-mill, if ye hadna been there our carcasses woulda bin transported. An' still ye say Chotti, watch out that t' law is kep' up? Is a joke?

Shankar says, He's right.

But how can that be? I've given a report. . . .

Khurana, no state wants even to acknowledge that there is bonded labour. And as for what the law is . . . you'll understand if you go to the meeting.

Amlesh Khurana discovers matters unknown to him at high-powered state level meetings. He knew nothing of all this. He may be very famous in Delhi and the outside world, the government of India can send him to make a survey to put together a project, but on the state level not much importance is given to this.

Amlesh is asked to speak first and Amlesh plays the tape recorder with Chotti's words. Hearing this, among the assembled power-figures, A says, What a bastard! And the Bonded Labour Act is to give them relief? They should be kept bonded for gener-ations. A lot of activity in my state of Andhra Pradesh, Telengana–Girijan–Naxal—could they get anything done? In my Andhra, there will always be caste-Hindu rule and bonded labour.

Amlesh says, This is a completely wrong and unjust attitude you have. It is through you that the law will become strong.

Why?

Read on.

I've read. You're a very good man. Scholar. I too joined the Indian Administrative Service after a First Class degree in Economics. I know how thoughts arise in the head of a scholar. But why should I strengthen the law? Here's the Minister. Tell him. He belongs to the State Government.

The Minister says, Doctor Khurana, administration is a compli-cated business. It's not the scholar's affair.

Amlesh realizes that the Minister, who is supposed to give the orders to the Head Officer of the district to make the law strong, does not want a learned man to infiltrate administrative work. And the district-in-charge thinks of adivasis and low castes as pests to be destroyed. The thought comes to his mind that this law cannot be enforced and strengthened by way of these ignorant, blind and violent people and he will deliver this news to the right place at the right time.

The Minister says, One must judge everything initially in a calm way. I couldn't even understand why we needed to call such an urgent meeting. The meeting was called simply because Doctor Khurana is here? Is this 'law' being implemented in any other state?

Shankar raises his finger at this time and says in a dry voice, There isn't a Doctor Khurana in every state. There is a greater reason for implementing the Bonded Labour Act in the state, because there is much greater oppression of the lower castes in the states of Andhra and Bihar and Uttar Pradesh. Your state is close to West Bengal. There is a much greater likelihood of armed struggle here.

The Minister laughs now and says, Who wants the law to work? Does anyone? Look how many loop-holes the wording offers me: the State Government 'may confer' powers and tasks as needed to make all sections of this ordinance active. Why 'may confer'? Why not 'will confer'? I'm getting the space to save myself in that word-ing. Now tell me?

A points at B and says, Let the honourable Minister give me spe-cific responsibilities, and I will delegate it to this colleague.

Amlesh says, Will you implement the Act if the language of the Act or ordinance is corrected?

The Minister says, No, Doctor Khurana. The Central Government understands nothing. Just passes Acts. Look, the Central Government knows full well that if an Act is passed for the welfare of adivasi or untouchable, it should never be imple-mented. Why not? Because that will light a fire. Are untouchables and adivasis a factor? And landlord, moneylender, landed farmer. These are the pillars of the government. Who gives campaign funds? Who controls the vote?

I have all the details. The landed rich and the moneylender, if they give ten thousand rupees to the government, they cheat on taxes and take the opportunity to clear a million rupees.

Oh Sir Doctor! Of course this happens. This is happening since India became independent. Did the leaders not know this? Or did Vijaja Modi not know this? Look at the Minimum Wage Act for farm workers. No State Labour Department in

India has implemented it. And is it just the government?
The ones who wave the red flag and make peasant movements
have also said not a word about the minimum wage. Though
they're Comnis they are true Indians, and they know that if you
give minimum wage the big farmers will be enraged. And you
cannot do a peasant movement if you anger the rich farmers.

But this is atrocious talk!

Be calm Doctor Khurana. Those who don't emphasize the
implementation of Acts for the welfare of the poor, whether they
are Congressites or Comnis, they love the poor, the untouchable,
and the adivasis more than you learned men. They know that if
the Act is implemented these poor souls will die at the hands of
the boss and the moneylender.

You will keep India in the Middle Ages?

Hey, why do you think no one does anything for the untouchable and the adivasi? Because they love 'em. And even so, as Mr
Shankar said, in Bihar, Andhra and Uttar Pradesh the harijan is
tortured. Be practical.

Then you're not going to implement this Act?

Doctor Khurana, we need realism, not idealism. I love the
outcastes and tribals of Bihar more than my life. But I am a
realist. It is Emergency time now. The police have a lot of power,
the Youth League have guns, the press is muzzled. Trying to
implement the law at this time, shall I throw the untouchables and adivasis of my Bihar into the tiger's jaws? How can that
be?

Bullshit! says Amlesh and leaves. And says, Shankar, I'll give a
report that they all need psychological treatment. Very interesting, you understand? Medieval and feudal ideas feed their psych-
osis. They are like the White racists of the U.S.

Yes, write a report.

Shankar, what they said, is it correct?

Some of it is.

Why isn't any Act for the welfare of the outcaste or the adivasi
implemented?

You heard.

I received no answer from their words.

You could say that.

Why did the PM pass the Act during Emergency, knowing that
the Act will not be implemented?

Why not?

Why?

Nice Act. Nice to hear. Her credit rose outside India. Now it will be understood that she is the liberator of the poor.

Are you joking?

Not at all. After all, the real objective behind this law is good. That cannot be denied.

Can the 'mays' in the Act not be changed to 'wills'?

Look, when an Act is put together, experts are consulted about its language.

It would have been good to have taken Chotti on the committee.

No. Some bloody Youth Leaguer would have killed him. Moreover, Chotti is a dissident man.

Hey, that's the reason why! Give a dissident person a little power, a little importance, they chill out.

Chotti is not a person of that type.

No. A true-blue guy.

Yes. But that true-blue guy can be more dangerous than ten idiot ministers in the area of national security.

Why?

They are the ones who do violent acts.

Shankar, shall we kill him?

No no. He has to stay alive. If he's around we'll be able to catch other violence-breeders at some time.

What shall we do with them?

We'll kill 'em.

Chotti?

We'll see then. Listen, you stay with your theory and survey. On the level of action and operation people like you create hurdles.

Amlesh says with childlike simplicity, But I like to see action-operation. Violence is so necessary.

When the gunbutt is in my hand, then it's necessary. Not the other way around.

Shankar, how many have you killed?

Stop! Even little kids don't ask so many questions. Go home, take your pills, sleep. Send your report tomorrow.

You know what? It wasn't right to silence the press. One can't get any news. The thing seems really weird.

Go and tell her.

Okay, I'll be quiet. But don't you think the same?

You're chattering too much.

Amlesh shuts up. Shankar says, Don't let Chotti go. Hold on to him. Some people are known at a glance. Whatever happens here, Chotti is somehow in it. That's the fact.

What does that prove?

Either he's extremely clever, or his luck's like this.

I like him.

Me too. I too like him.

Why are we opposing Youth League?

Otherwise, why will Chotti's crowd believe in us? And these Youth League boys are scoundrels. They have to learn a lesson. They just increase problems.

They get to Tohri.

XV

CHOTTI'S GROUP HAS A MEETING, as does Amlesh's group. Bonded labour is now illegal, this excitement has slowly abated. But people are still quite confused. One should be happy, but happiness doesn't seem possible. They are Tirathnath's bond slaves. Not a word from Tirathnath. Chhagan says to Chotti, Maybe we go sit in front of yer pahan's place?

A'right.

What a state we're in! There's a pain, but no bairn, not at all like a woman with child, eh?

I know.

What will you understand, Chotti? Weren't you in bonded labour?

I don' know.

You're a clever bastard, I'll say.

Migh-ty clever. Don' ye see me mansion? Chhagan! I'm tired of living mate.

Why?

Who knows what terror'll come aft'r this law. I can' see this any more Chhagan, me heart sinks.

Chotti, these words don' fit you'n me.

Where'd ye want to go, I'll come.

What's this Chotti? A straw rope? Hey how fancy! Bound up in red thread, how lovely it looks.

Harmu's mother's work. Now the kitchen work is done by me grandson's bride. But me wife, she can't sit idle. Here she fetches kindling, there she sweeps the yard. What else she does y' know well.

I know too well.

Chotti's wife went to Etwa's house a few months back. There she had a real quarrel with Etwa and his wife. It may be that Koel is dead today. But what about Etwa's father? Or his uncle? Maybe Etwa's daughter is seven years old now. Shouldn't she be brought to Chotti from time to time? What a pair! Etwa and his wife—having said all this with great heat Chotti's wife brings Etwa's daughter home. The girl is full of life, a real charmer. Her days pass well in this house, in everyone's affection. But she had a terrible belly-ache that twisted her body. Chotti's wife took her to hospital. The doctor gave her some medicine that made a huge worm fall out of her belly.

The very next day Chotti's wife takes Sana's sister's granddaughter to hospital. How strange, a couple of worms fall out of her belly as well. Gradually Chotti's wife comes to have profound faith in hospitals. At this advanced age. Now she is an enthusiastic organizer for taking children to hospital, getting them admitted, having them looked at, getting their medicine. If there's any illness in the homes of Chhagan, Chotti or the Oraons they now come to Chotti's wife. Chotti's wife takes them instantly to hospital.

Chotti says, Thas good work, love.

Why not? Ye do good work. I'm doin' too.

A trip also.

Yes dear. I like it. Goin' comin', so many diffren people at hospital. I have a few words with 'em. And then on t' way back I sit in t' tishan, drink a bitta tea, I like it dear!

Ye drink tea?

They offer?

Who?

T' people I take?

Ye're doin' work an' gettin' paid.

Sure. Drink tea, smoke bidi, see t' tain come, I like it.

The trip to hospital is not every day. So the rest of the time Chotti's wife gathers wood. She makes quilts, she looks after hens and goats and grows peppers and brinjal in the yard. Twists straw to make rope. Splits logs, ties rope and makes seats. She never rests.

Chhagan and Chotti sit in Pahan's house. Chotti says, Today we hev only one thing to say to ye mate. Bond labour. Y'all know there's now a law. Y'all know too that I'm not a bond-slave, nor me son, nor me grandson. Still I had to come, for I'm scared.

Of what?

Whatever happened with Basmati Oraon, then she became ever'thin' before t' Gormen. That Gormen has a lot of power-respect. That's why t' League boys raised no terror. That's why today they've so much power, such pull, and guns in their hands. They've killed the Member of before. They've killed Ananda Mahato. No one's forgotten what they've done in Chotti village!

Then?

Who said this word? Ah, Upa! Whatcha say?

Upa said, Why talk o' old things?

Seeds of new words're sown in old words.

Now there's a law, no?

There is.

Then why s'd we gie bonded work? Ye'll tell us to.

This ye don' say true. Chotti never gies an order to anyone.

Hey Upa! Upa's father Dukha roars, When he raises word, we don' talk, and ye, a brat born yestiddy—

Chotti says, Dukha boy! This isn't an official Village Council—a Panchayat—but it is too a Panchayat, all will say for sure. Speak Upa.

I'm at fault. Ye say.

Then let me say now. When Motia and t' pahan-pair, and t' railway porter died, then t' tribal offsir, t' polis boss, thought on us some. That's why they didn't make any more trouble. Otherwise in t' villages of Barh, Dhutra, Sarahi—such trouble, huts burnin', bodies cut down, and our daughters—lock an' key on me tongue ta say it—our daughters made mothers, and t' polis standing by watchin' t' fun. No judgement, no trial. Ye build yer burnt hut agin, they come agin. Ya. Moneylender's grace! Boys of t' party! Raisin' trouble agin.

Say, say it Chotti!

What happened 'n Chotti, then we went. Offsir, polis, heard our grief, so then no more terror, an f'r porter t' Railway Unine gave some help. An' fer Basmati t' Gormen took a stand. That's why they raised no more trouble. Howsomever, Upa! An' young an' old think upon it, those who made such terror, were they je-helled, or fined?

Nothin' happened.

Raisin' terror upon terror, cuttin' down t' bodies of t' poor, they aint punished, an' when cos of someone else's force, someone else to obey, they caint terrorize t' folks of Chotti village, they don' fergit it, they keep their rage saved inside. Their rage rises by percentage like Lala's interest. They'll remain mum while that Gormen is in Tohri.

An' after?

Trouble.

Yeah, trouble.

Now say what's to do.

Two things we can do.

What and what?

Chotti gives an innocent smile and says, One's like this. If we say 'no bonded labour' they'll cut us down, burn us down. Now is t' time of t' black law, polis have more power. Polis'll do nothin' and help them along. Askin' for judgement, we'll have to go to Court. I've asked one after another, and told t' Tohri Gormen, there're blind alleys in this law. Gormen is makin' fun o' us. I asked, if a boss still asks for bonded labour, what s'll we do? Which way'll we go? What's t' law say? T' Gormen says, Why? Ye'll go to Court? Now see this! To Co-o-ourt will go Mundas, and Oraons, and Dusad, and Ganju—who caint live without bellyloans fr'm moneylender, they'll go complain agin boss. So, gie bonded labour like other years. Then there are no plaints and charges against bosses an' goons, an' they won' mek trouble.

An' we'll live better that way? says Chhagan. Did anyone say 'We don' listen to Bonded Labour law' in Barh, in Dhutra, in Sarahi? Why terror there?

Chhagan! Why say this when ye know everythin'! Why did this happen? Why does this happen? Happens, happens every year. Happens allus. T' word of t' boss—bonded labour and violence on t' field hands—is kept, t' word of trader-chief-Brahman's violence upon ye's kept. Polis an' boss wear same hat, that word is kept, word of Gormen gang givin' support ta Hindu bosses's kept, an' when all words come together fire burns. These thin's that I say, tell me which one's not there? All this is there, and so t' fire burnt in Barh and Dhutra and Sarahi.

Chotti! I don' understan' as much as ye do. Ye say one thing, we can go on givin' bonded work for fear o' force. This too ye said that even if we go on givin' bonded work, since we are low, even if we obey the high castes there is violence. Why because boss-polis-party are one hat.

Wrong or right?

Right!

And how's the work? Chotti, I don' understan' all that. Tell me, Chhagan, do this job with yer own kind, and I'll do.

No Chhagan. I am not a bonded worker, so I can't say who'll do bonded work. I can say, this is a way. Ye think on't. Think about 't and do 't.

And what's t' job, let's hear?

That's like this. I'll drink some water Pahan, I'm much thirsty.

Pahan says, All drink. Lot o' things to talk about.

Pahani brings wet gram seeds and dry molasses on a brass plate, water in a clay pitcher, aluminium tumblers. They all chew gram and molasses, pour water into their mouths from the tumblers. Yer well-water's so sweet? Chotti asks. Or is this water dug out of me breast, Pahani dear?

Ye've caught it! It's t' water from t' dugout canal of Chotti river.

We had th' idea of diggin' that canal. Or else Lala'd have killed us with th' excuse of water. So see, ye're all here now, I'll say it. T' sky looks like bad weather. Relented a few years, but drought's around t' corner. Me mind says we s'd keep t' river bed dug good. Chhagan says, don' die Chotti, we'll be swept off if ye go. E'en what we all know don' come to mind.

How Chhagan takes me in wit' sweet words, see ya'll. Where there's no Chotti, ever'one's bein' swept off, they don' understan' t' ways of wind and water.

Say t'other thing?

I'll say Upa. That thing is easy.

What?

No one'll gie bonded labour.

Will not? Ye say how much violence comes down if we don' give.

Of course violence. No mistake there. Still, that mischief is whirlin' in me head. Daroga came and tol' us that bonded labour's illegal. Wham! No one gives bonded labour? Now there're some jobs, at Chadha's, or fellin' timber? Chiranjilal comes from Gomo. On Kurmi hill there's work breakin' stones. We go there too?

Tell us, tell us more, we like ta hear this.

If Lala asks ye say, What's this? Daroga came to tell's that bonded labour is now illegal. So we won' do it.

An' if he brings force?

I'm tellin' ya. See that's all we hav to say, since we never know t' law. T' two brothers Chadha gie good treatment, wages, and others gie what they gie. But even those wages cheat us. Doesn' give by Gormen law. We don' know that law. But this we know very good that Gormen has rules not for bonded labour but for field workers. Ta gie us six seers o' paddy and three-quarters o' a seer ground chickpea, or two an' a quarter seer rice and three quarter seer ground chickpea. Ta all men an' women. And fo' t' kiddies t' rule is ta give four and a half seer paddy and three quarter seer groun' chickpea, or one and three quarter seer rice and three quarter groun' chickpea. T' boss who doesn' gie, will reckon out t' price and gie that. Now see, they all know that this law was made. But they ne'er let us know. And no boss or moneylender gave us wages by t' law.

When did this law pass?

Same age as Chhagan's littlest grankid. Two years.

We know nothin'.

They don' wan' us ta know, we don' know.

We've known nothin'. Whate'er t' Lala's given, whenever, it's as if it's by great kindness.

It's cos we don' hav booklarnin'! When Harmu went to je-hell, ask 'im how many Munda, Oraon, Dusad-Dhobi he saw in je-hell. They're in je-hell fer land rights cases, but they don' know what they did wrong. Two were field hands, t' man for whom they worked t' fields, sold his field land. They didn' know. They went to plough and t' new boss put force on 'em, send 'em to je-hell.

Harmu says, In je-hell they grow old.

That's it! We don' know t' rules. I've ev'n seen Diku boys put t' polis in court cos polis has beaten illegally. How is it they can do't? They know t' law, thas why.

Now tell us.

We didn' know t' law of field labour. But this law t' Daroga has made it known. So I say, let no one gie bonded labour. If Lala makes us work, 'twill be with wages, like everyone gives. If Lala is unwillin', we don' give work.

If he brings force? Upa asks.

That too ye think through.

Will they beat us up? Will there be party boys, polis?

Sure. This is fun fer em.

Then?

Think it through.

We'll beat 'em up too.

Will ya stay together, or break rank?

Together.

Not by yer words alone. See what Chhagan's bunch says?

If we stay all together, says Chhagan, What'll ye do?

Chotti says, If ye tek t' first way, I've no work there.

Ye old mule! Ye're on another way?

Yeah I am. Kin ye get work out o' an old man?

Ye don' know th' answer?

I know. But ye go and think fer yerselves, me dearest boys. If there's force then women and old folks, kids and tots'll all die.

Hey, he first off speaks of dyin'. First talk it out wit' Lala? Let him bring force? And then ye think.

Hey Chhagan it's good to think of harm afore. I'm off.

Where to?

Go on home. Ye think on this, lemme know. Ye bonded workers have a talk, ye've gotta think it through.

An' if we say we won' gie bonded work?

First put in mind that e'en then I hev work.

On'y two or three families aint bonded. All t' rest is bound fo' sure. T' ledger book burnt up, but he made up another.

That book's his life, so he had it made up.

Two hours later Harmu comes by and says, They're comin'. They won' gie bonded work, an' they'll tell us how they've made up their minds. But . . .

What's up?

Who's gonna make ye understan'? But, we aint bonded, Aba? But we'll hae t' same fate . . .

They'll go, an' how many Mundas are there that we'll save our bodies? Can we save ourselves like that?

No, we caint save ourselves.

Now bring me a little kerosene, go.

Why?

Me feet hurt. Heat it up and massage.

Harmu's mother comes by with salt and a bowl of kerosene set on top of a lantern. Lemme do this job of honour, said she. Father will go to fight, so lemme massage t' fighter, it's me honour.

Where's t' fight Ma?

He'll start it.

No way.

I know yer dad better'n ye.

Ye're dreamin'.

Harmu! Were ye in me belly, or I in yers?

Chotti's wife sent her son off with a scolding, and said to Chotti, Where ye went, what ye did, will ya return alive and well, I go crazy with thinkin' on this. Then I had Koel, and next Mungri. Now think a bit on me?

Who s'll I think o', tell me this?

Do I know?

Wife.

What now?

Somchari?

Chotti's wife was so startled that she'd have fallen if she'd been standing. She was embarrassed when her surprise ended. She took a quick look around. No, there's no one nearby. Then she said, Aren't ye ashamed? I'm a mum, a grandma, when me grandson has a son I'll be great-grandma, does anyone call such an old woman by her name?

I do.

No, I feel shy.

No, ye're lyin'. Ye're glad as glad.

Shush. What an old man is this!

Old? S'll I lift ye, hold ye, an' dance?

Hush.

Now I don' know what'll happen, I don' know what I'll do. But Wife, all think Chotti Munda is an honest man.

Honest fo' sure.

Wife it's not what others say. To stay true ta oneself one must do right from time to time.

Why d'ye do it? When have I said no? Dintcha go fer Puran? Dintcha bring t' Laxal boy home? Dintcha go ta save t' pahan,

Kurmi pahan? Didn' say no, won' say no, but me heart breaks. No Koel, no Mungri, all near an' dear ones gone. Me chest feels dried up. Lemme go now, they're all here. Daughter-in-law! Where are ye all? Harmu? Bring a mat.

Harmu throws down a huge grass mat. He says, Ma, everyone weaves mats out of grass. But nary a one weaves such large ones. When there's no more farm work, I'll go to market and sell t' mats ye weave.

Do that.

Why're ye tyin' it with fancy coloured thread?

Don' ya tech it ever.

Why?

T' Gormen in Tohri has asked for it.

Everybody came and sat on the mat. Sana and Chhagan told the two sides decision.

No, they won't go to give bonded service. It was clear that young folks like Upa Munda and Jugal Ganjee were thinkin' ahead.

Upa says, We won' let 'em bring farm workers from outside. They'll hafta get t' job done with us folks.

Chotti says, Good. Now there's more ta do.

What!

T' words we talk here, if it gets out, I'll catch traitor and tear out his tongue.

Say what ye were sayin'.

We'll let t' Tohri Gormen know what we're doin'.

That's all!

There's more.

Chotti also talks about his discussion with Swarup and says, I'll go to t' forest meself. They're sayin' they'll gie us help.

Ye'll go to find that out?

And more. If it gits to that two or three may hafta hide. And then they can stay with 'em.

The next day Chotti stays at home, If anyone asks say I've gone ta Dhai.

Swarup had said that his outpost was in the woods between Chotti and Komandi. That's unbroken forest, a bit lighter on hilltop, dense below. Near Chotti, the entire forest is known to Chotti. He enters with his machete. Doesn't move around to get lost, rather goes where the springs are. Self-concealing folk will stay close to bodies of water.

The first day he can't find them. Returning home at evening he says, Me legs hurt. I don' have t' strength I once had.

His wife says, Tomorra Harmu'll go with ye. I won' let ye go alone.

It's better with Harmu along. Harmu says, Come let's cut across? Hey behind those hills there're deep springs on t' down climb Aba. Even now elephants bathe there.

Yeah elephants! In th' old days, ye get into t' forest, there's tigers, there's deer, so many animals. Now not a one can be seen.

Come, I'll show ya.

The jungle gets deeper and deeper. Deer do actually run in front of Chotti. Ah, let it be! Chotti won't tell anyone this news. Here the forest doesn't even have winding trails. Feet sink in rotting leaves, the forest floor is cold clay. The tank is huge and shallow toward the edges. Chotti says, I didn' know before.

Elephants still come Aba.

They see Swarup after they pass the water-hole. He is wearing a green shirt, green pants. Their hideout is in the cave in the hills. Swarup takes them in, asks them to sit down. Chotti sees at least thirty people and not all Dikus. About ten adivasis. Swarup says, Have a drink of water first.

Chotti drinks water. Says everything openly. Swarup says, When ye realize that there will be a clash, send yer son. These fifteen adivasis will go to the village with yer son and hide with different families. When we fight they should see these people only. Then people won' easily understand them to be the outsiders. Everyone is not present here. I will send word.

You'll let t' boys stay if needed?

Sure. And in this area this is our hideout, with another one in the forest on the slopes of Kurmi hill.

These ones'll fight?

Taught by yer, why s'dn't we fight?

Hey! Ye're that Bisai from Narsingarh, no?

Yes yes. Really took us through target practice.

Who else is here?

Many known people, yes, all yer students.

Chotti's mind is strangely turbulent. Swarup says, It's good that I was here yesterday. Tomorrow ye wouldn't have got me.

Bisai says, Let t' messenger bring some ground pepper, some salt. We're short.

Ye just eat chickpea powder?

Swarup says, We don't cook, there'll be smoke.

Ye're still on t' run—

Now I'm a pricey guy Chotti. There's a price on my head.

Swarup shows them the way to the shortcut. Asks, Do you have news of Sarahi? Have you heard anything?

Lakhan Sahu called the Youth League and burnt up villages twice.

Two Youth Leaguers are badly hurt, also Lakhan's son.

Y'all did that thing?

There were also some villagers. It would've been better if we'd got a place near Sarahi. We should give up our old hideouts now.

After Sarahi t' way north takes half a day. There's a forest too in Damoho, an' many Munda burial places. Once twas a Munda village.

That's good. Then that's the deal.

Now I'm old, so I worry.

Still ye came.

I asked 'em to think, they made up their mind, so I came.

They decided themselves?

Yes Lord. We'll talk about that later.

Chotti rests a couple of days. Then, with a mat woven by Harmu's mother on his back, he starts off towards Tohri.

Amlesh thinks the mat woven of grass is exquisite. He and his wife decide that next to the woven blankets of the Navajo Indians of America, they have never seen such amazing aboriginal artwork, and they press Chotti to accept money. They want to know the price.

Chotti says, This don' have a price.

Why?

First, lookit caref'lly?

Chotti's wife has woven the mat piece by piece. Then put the pieces together with red and yellow thread. The design in red and yellow thread is lovely.

We are saying again and again, it's lovely.

It don' have a price, Lord.

Amlesh gives an incredibly superior smile, and you realize from his smile that, whatever comradeship he may overtly express, he actually thinks Chotti and others like Chotti are as negligible as insects. Amlesh says, compassionate towards a human being inferior in intelligence and inclination, There is nothing that hasn't a price, Chotti. Whatever is made of human labour must have a price.

Chotti smiles with sweet forgiveness and says, Lord! Me wife wove this mat with wild grass. Me brother's granddaughter, brother's gone, that granbaby gave t' thread. I carried it on me shoulder. Now tell me, how will its price be repaid? Wild grass costs nothin'. And you can' measure t' price of Harmu's mother's weavin'. th' old lady weaves fer ever'one, fer love.

Shankar says, Ye're right Chotti. There's a design quilt that my mother sewed. Wonderful designs of elephants and horses and leafy creepers I can't measure its value. But we could have spread 'em out on the floor if we had a few mats.

Buy it at market, lord. T' girls will get a bitta cash.

Tell us, what other news?

Chotti doesn't speak of everyone. He does not say that Upa and his friends will not let Tirathnath take farm hands from outside. He only says, Now you mus' give support lord. No one ever tol' us so we didn' know that there was t' minimum wage act for farm labour. But let that go. This act t' Daroga informed us, so we know. Now t' bonded labourers of Chotti say, t' Daroga is also Gormen, when he came and tol' us, we won' give labour no more. And we won' repay our debts from before.

Amlesh and Shankar say—

Right?

Right.

But I say, we'll let y'know.

You think there'll be some trouble?

Lord! Why make Chotti say it?

Shankar says, Say it.

There's trouble e'en if ye say nothin'. Innocent bodies are cut down, that's a big crime, we won' gie bonded labour no more.

Understood.

We let ya know.

So we see. The Daroga must be informed.

T' party boys and t' polis wear t' same hat.

But we are here.

Chotti leaves. Amlesh says, What'll ye do Shankar?

Tell the thana to support the bonded workers, that is to say to beat and catch those who kill 'em. It comes to mean the three louts from the Youth League.

Amlesh says, in the voice of a little boy, Why?

If there is such a confrontation, naturally the other activists will want to join. My work will be easier.

Who are they? C.P.M.L.—Communist Party Marxist Leninist?

They don't work under that banner. But the goal is more or less the same. The land will be in the hands of the peasants, landlord and moneylender will be removed, and peasants will form an armed struggle collective to protect their own rights.

These are good things.

Of course.

What will you do if the activists are caught?

Eliminate them.

But they are much better people than Romeo's group.

No doubt.

Then?

To each game its rules, Khurana.

Sometimes I'm afraid of you.

That should prove that you are intelligent.

Shankar lets the S.D.O. know, and the thana. Daroga shilly shallies and receives a phone call from the I.G. towards afternoon: Idiot! Don't you know the limits of your rights? Do what Shankar says.

Yes sir, we will.

Helpless, the Daroga hangs up. He says, Crazy stuff! All my life I turned the gun-barrel towards the untouchables and the adivasis. Now I'll have to turn the barrel around?

Shankar comes again and says, When we need you, don't let us hear 'I went on another case elsewhere'.

No sir.

Daroga assumes that Shankar and Khurana are great men. He says, I'll give service sir, but then you must give me a certificate.

If the Youth League hears all this . . .

They won't sir.

Shankar is delighted and goes home after buying at market a number of fish strung on the sharp end of long grass. Says to Mary, Ask them to fry these. Very fresh and delicious fish.

Amlesh says, Did you get everything said?

Yes.

Will it work?

You know well that we are not obliged to answer anyone but Delhi?

Thus they discuss everything. Meanwhile Tirathnath says to Romeo, I understand nothing. Everyone is quiet.

Call the bonded labourers, talk to them, tell us what they say. Then we'll do what there's to do.

Tirathnath's manager calls Chhagan's group and Sana's group. Chhagan and Sana say to Tirath, What's up Lord?

Harvest time is coming, you know.

What s'll we do?

What do you do each year?

Year after year we give bonded labour.

So what's new this year?

What d'ye mean, Lord? That Daroga, he's Gormen, tol' us that bonded labour's illegal from this year. So why s'd we give it?

Won't give?

No lord.

The paddy will just lie there?

No, we'll cut it. We'll take wages.

I see.

Yes Lord.

If you don' give bonded labour we'll take outside workers.

No Lord. We won' let that be.

Won't let?

No Lord, that we won' let. There's a law for field workers' dues as well. We wouldna known if Chotti hadna tol' us. Don' want that rate, but gie what ye gie.

Good, I hear ya.

We'll come as soon as ya let us know.

Why did ya take Chotti's name? He's not a bonded worker, and since Harmu went ta je-hell he doesn' ev'n work in me field.

Can our work move wi' out'm?

Chhagan and the others come away. Tirath goes to Romeo. Romeo advises Tirath appropriately. Tirath makes it known that he's ready and willing. But he'll give wages week by week. Hearing this Chotti says, There'll be trouble on that pay day. He goes to Tohri again and Harmu goes to the forest with ground pepper and salt and pickles of the red karamcha berry. The harvesting goes on. The weekly pay day approaches.

Chhagan, Sana and the rest go to the office. The Mundas and Oraons sent by Swarup wait in every home. They are very calm and collected. They don't have to wait long. A tremendous altercation is heard. Harmu's son is known as 'Red' because of his reddish coppery hair. Red comes screaming, Twenny of 'em have raised guns. Won' let a penny be paid. Les go to thana.

Before Daroga can arrive from the police station or Shankar on his Jeep, Upa's father Dukha falls by Romeo's bullet, and now Chhagan and his crowd begin to throw stones, and the Mundas shoot arrows. Tirathnath tries to escape but hears, Where'ye goin', Lord? Tirath sees bow and arrow in Chotti's hands.

An ancient fear grasps him and he says 'Don't kill me Chotti' and falls. At the other end Romeo's group seems to be caught in the office room and fire-tipped arrows fall into the paddy heap, inside the room. Pahlwan, Romeo and Dildar say to the other youths, Exit shooting. They exit and stop arrows. The others shoot arrows and throw stones and immediately sit down behind the heaps of grain and one guy feels an arrow in his ribs and shouts, The arrows are poisoned, poisoned arrows! Chotti shoots with steady aim from behind the column and says to Sana, Lemme hurt their gun-shootin' arms first. His arrows pierce the shoulders of the gun-shooting arms of Romeo, Dildar and Pahlwan, all three, and their guns drop. The other young men get nervous to see their leaders fall to their knees, and they stop arrows right and left. From the top of the tree Upa's brother shouts, Polis! and the adivasis of Swarup's group run off instantly. With the police arriving the young men want again to burn with pious resolutions and scream in unison with terrific force. Opening Tirathnath's silo Chhagan's crowd throw fistfuls of ground pepper.

Daroga. Police. S.D.O. Shankar. Now the arrows gradually stop and Chotti comes forward and says in a completely other voice to the S.D.O., Because the Daroga spoke to 'em, they didn' gie bonded labour. They spoke of wages with Lala. On his word they came to get weekly wages. Lala kep' these others hidden in t' room. Raising his gun this'n—pointing at Romeo—killed Dukha and soon's Dukha cried 'Water!' that'n—pointing at Dildar—he pissed on's face. Then we brought bows, we brought stones, and Dukha he's no more. See if Jugal Dusad's dead with his ribs hurt.

So much havoc with arrows.

I held the bow lord. Their good fortune that I hurt their gun arms. Ye lord! Ye saw t' harm done by arrers but not t' harm of guns?

Seen, Chotti, says Shankar.

Now?

S.D.O. says, The wounded must be taken to hospital. What's this? This person is dead? Were the arrows poisoned?

It's possible. Don't guns have gunpowder?

Where's Tirathnath?

Do I know?

Shankar says, Chotti, let it go. We're here.

Chotti seems to have become a new man in the last hour and a half. He says, Why s'd I let go? Find out now, field worker comes to take his weeklies from t' boss, why does t' boss set up these devils? Who broke t'law first? Then Lord! Weeklies? No one leaves without it. First divvy up t' weeklies.

Two policemen pick up twenty guns, bullets. Shankar says, record everything. Take up the wounded.

The S.D.O. is enraged because he has to engage in such unprecedented activities under pressure from IAD. He says to Tirathnath, I'll take you as well. You stirred up clear water and raised a storm, now who bears the consequences?

Shankar says, We'll talk about it later.

Romeo says to Shankar, IAD or no, I'll get mine back, you son of a whore.

Ah! That nice guy! Shankar shakes the arrows stuck to the shoulders of the three louts, and they yell. Shankar says, Terrific, terrific aim Chotti! Perhaps all three will have to have their right arms removed.

The wounded are transported, two bodies. It's clear that Jugal too will become a body soon. Now the women and children, and the infants arrive. Such a crowd of black faces is most uncomfortable. Chotti's wife comes and pulls Chotti by the hand. Says, in a low voice, They've left. Chotti inclines his head. Chotti's group don't give up. Tirathnath pays them their weekly wages surrounded by burnt grain, destroyed office, the screaming of the wounded and the desperate weeping of Dukha's wife. Then he goes to thana to make his report. Chotti accompanies him. He says, I am not a bonded labourer, nor a field hand, but when they killed Dukha with a gun, I saw red.

The wounded go to hospital, and Chotti, Chhagan and Tirathnath go to thana. Because Shankar is there it's not possible to play around with the report. Shankar says to the Youth League Secretary and the Party Secretary, The entire district is in your power. Don't poke your head into this belt.

When the Youth League Secretary hears that Shankar and Khurana's regional presence is as temporary as everything else in life such as the season for guava and wood-apple, the film 'Dream Merchant', the fashion for girls to put their hair up in a ponytail, then he says to the three musclemen, Don't worry, bro'. Let 'em go, we'll burn Chotti village. But you're lucky. If Chotti'd wanted, he could have pierced your necks and killed you.

Romeo roars out, My right arm will go. The iron is rusty on the arrowhead, I can get tetanus.

A bow and arrow in Chotti's hand. Not a simple matter, eh?

Brother, he shot these arrrows at greater speed and frequency than bullets. You can't believe yer eyes as ye see it happenin'.

I won't let Tirathnath off. He s'dn't have called ye with IAD on his neck.

The sonofabitch.

Chotti-operation bears a most poisonous fruit. Dildar dies of tetanus. Romeo's right arm has to be cut off from the shoulder, Pahlwan's right arm is cut off from the elbow. The families of Dildar and the youth killed by an arrow receive a hundred thousand rupees and a petrol pump. Romeo and his group want posthumous Paramvir Chakras for them, but they don't succeed.

By some chance no one goes to jail and Tirathnath, chastised, gives his manager orders to have the paddy harvested at the proper rate. Lala goes off on pilgrimage with his whole family. Amlesh gives fifty rupees aid apiece to the families of Dukha and Jugal and earns a reputation for 'magnanimity'. And a hitherto completely unknown Shankar comes to Chotti's house and says, Which outsiders were present on the day of that disturbance, Chotti?

Outsider? Who was there? No one was there.

Your arrows also carry poison?

They can.

Do whatever you like yourselves, Chotti, but don't be taken in by other people's words. They come disguised as friends. That's fake!

How cin we accept that? For me ye are th' only outsiders. And ye gave a hand.

Well, just to let you know.

Where are you goin'?

Towards Dhai.

Right.

If we're not here they might make trouble. But so what, eh? You too can fight, you'll get support from police and judge.

Chotti smiles slightly. Says, Ye'll have yer fun, lord?

No no.

Shankar and Khurana go to Dhai and thus give the green light to the Youth League. Now Chotti village is an open battlefield.

XVI

H EARING THIS SWARUP SMILES slightly and says, The hideout was good, but must go. We can still be in the forest beyond Kurmi Hill.

Can ye walk that far?

I am coming and going on foot.

Then listen carefully. Goin' South, t' river Chotti goes around Kurmi an' enters t' forest around a mansion. I don' know to whom that mansion belonged, when. For about two miles t' forest is very dense. Ground's flat, t' river spreads out. Herds of elephants walk that way to t' Palamau Reserve forest. No one goes in there.

No hills?

No. Stay in trees. Set up hangin' platforms! Not too many people go into that forest. For why, t' forest is right on t' river, t' soil is soft mud, plenty of snakes too.

Let me move these men there.

And where'll ye go?

To other dens. Words of caution are needed. I don't like the way things look. This is after all true, that IAD has entered to demolish organizations such as ours.

Go there.

How will ye let us know in case of need?

If we get t' time, we'll send someone. Or else where river enters forest there's a sisu tree to t' west that goes through sky an' heavens. Under it is a big stone. T' boys'll break tree branches on t' stone?

Keep your eye out daily? And, Bisai knows my place. He'll come?

That's best.

Hey why're y'all runnin' away?

They've pressed many charges against everyone.

Don't delay sir. Tis an ill wind blowin'.

An ill wind is blowing, the time goes out of joint. The day after Swarup and his group move out, the police force enter the abandoned forest as if receiving information on the wind. They search the forest in minute detail and leave.

Report: There was a group hiding in the Chotti-Komandi forest belt that day as well. Burnt bidi-leaf cigarettes, empty matchboxes, bits of candles and paper bags have been found in the caves. Here one remembers that, in the incident at Chotti village, at least thirty-five adivasis shot arrows. Were they all inhabitants of said village? The slain Youth League youngster had the extremely potent poison of the kuchila seed in his body. Here we are reminded that small thin arrows with kuchila at their tips have been seen in the action-operations of organizations such as Adivasi Forest India Association, Birsa Group, Adivasi Service Committee and the like. The second and the third have been destroyed almost to the root. It's the organization of the first that is strong, the group is nourished by the support of adivasis and Swarup Prasad is still active . . .

Soon 1976 comes. July. Precipitation delayed, still it rains. The wet streams of rain zigzag, gurgle and leap into the open breast of Chotti river. The ground is covered in grass blades. The trees in forest and village are relieved to bathe at last and the elephant belonging to the priest at the Siva temple in Tahar goes into the pond and doesn't want to come out at all. For some reason a sisu tree falls in the station. Tirathnath returns to the village. Now is the time to sow seeds into the rainwet sappy soil. Tirathnath descends from the train with a few sacks of government seed. At this time Udham tries to take the shortcut through the brickfield and gets bitten by a striped snake. The snake can't sink its teeth properly into the thick sock, but Udham is faint with terror. Hearing of this Chotti runs up as well and goes with him to the hospital in Tohri. He goes saying to Udham, Ye'll live lord, no fear lord, couldn' bite good, lord. The doctor also repeats Chotti's words in doctor language. Then they return home with Udham. Harbans says uncomfortably, Don't tell anyone that it was I who put you in touch with Swarup Prasad.

No lord.

They are really looking for him.

Is't so?

When he returns, Chotti's youngest son Somchar says, That Bisai's come an' waits fer ya, Aba. Say summat to ye.

Bisai says, D'ye know where Swarup's gone?

I'll know?

T' forest has as much water as snakes. That Swarup brings med'cin. We're fastin' three days, so we bring chickpea powder and pepper and ask where'd he go? Dja hear anything? Dja hear if anyone from our group got caught?

Where all are yer hideouts?

Narsingarh, Dhai.

There they've drummed it that no one's to sell ground chick-pea and pepper to unknown folks. Chotti reflects and says, Now it's dark. Wait a bit—he looks at their own stocks, and says—How many of yer there?

Thirty head.

All Mundas?

One Diku. Swarup's brother.

Wait.

Chotti exits and calls Upa. Hearing everything Upa brings ground chickpea-salt-cayenne from each family. Chotti gives as well. Then Somchar and Upa walk along the river-bank on this dark rainy night with Bisai. They come back at midnight.

Unquiet vigilant waiting. Then the Mundas and untouchables of Chotti village are called to Tohri, to the bungalow adjoining Rajbans's saw-mill—where a good deal of Chotti's life has been spent in gossip, laughter, drinking tea or coffee. In the company of Amlesh and Shankar. An unknown Shankar sits at the head of Swarup's corpse and says in a quite unknown voice, Take a good look one by one, see if you know him.

No nails on Swarup's hands and feet, many black holes on his naked body, genitals like mincemeat. Chotti takes the lead. Says in a clear voice, No, never saw 'im, I don' know 'im.

Everyone says the same and in disgust the flies rise from Swarup's body and then sit down again.

They return to the village and see that there's police presence at the station. There's a green polythene tent by Chotti river. Chotti says in a low voice, Go each to yer place. Times are real bad, real bad. Upa, come to me room after dark.

When Upa comes he says, That time ye and Somchar stayed in front and raised yer arrers again and again. Go quick and tell 'em at home, and run off into t' forest with Somchar. Go tell 'em, this is me word, Swarup is dead. It's no use all of us dyin'. Ask 'em to go to t' forest on t' slope of Kurmi hill. No one will go there. Ye leave too. Hide out with 'em. Ratan Munda of Kurmi will give ye chickpea and salt. Let 'im gie to t' ones who're there too.

We'll leave?

Yer dad died, ye were in front, so was Somchar.

They leave. How timely this departure was becomes clear the next day, when the police look for Somchar in every household in the village. Hearing they've gone to Dhanbad, the police ask, To visit whom?

Chotti says with irritation, Do I know? These two are t' biggest loudmouths. They get their wages, they have to buy yaller vest. These guys even wear rubber sandals on their feet. They'll cut coal in Dhanbad, take more money, watch moving pictures, look lord! Some contractor tempted them at market. Can't ye catch these contractors? T' Munda boys leave at their behest.

Send word if you find out.

Sure will. But why lord?

Send word.

After the police left, Chotti says to his wife, Weren't ye bawlin' sayin' 'Why send t' boys to t' forest?' Now d'ye see?

They'd've killed 'em if they caught 'em.

Fo' sure. Swarup was a Diku boy, booklarned, fam'ly had a house in Pareshnath. I heard dad's a lawyer. How they killed him?

Tirathnath's summons come now. Time for sowing goes by, come give bonded labour.

No one goes. Chhagan says to Tirathnath, bonded labour is illegal, so we didn' give it last time. Such terror. Why would we give now?

Ye would if ye had brains.

Seeing Shankar in this new role the ancient mistrust of government and administration return redoubled to Chotti's mind and he says, This time t' terror will be greater.

Chotti understands a lot, but doesn't understand everything. Shankar says in a dry wooden voice, No obstruction in the first stages. I want to see if people from Swarup's gang come to their aid. It's not to catch their gang. We must catch those who do politics by violent means, whatever group or doctrine they adhere to. I know they contacted Swarup's gang at least once. It's natural that it'll happen this time as well. So, let there be Youth League action in the first stages. If no one from Swarup's gang comes to help them during this action then, we'll get rid of the Youth League so these people note it. Then they'll feel safe, they'll be careless. Swarup's gang will definitely come for the next action.

Is there any need to let the Youth League know?

Definitely not. I have no contact with ruffians. They are necessary for me, as long as it takes to catch Swarup's associates. They are uneducated, uncivilized, barbaric.

Chhagan's group do not respond to Tirathnath. Then armless Romeo and Pahlwan come to Chotti village with fifty musclemen, flying the flag of the group. The police officer says in a dry voice, What's this? What do you want?

Putting his head out of the polythene tent Shankar says, What's going on? Is this a picnic? Why no guns?

Romeo goes blind with rage and says, Today is the day for an act of purification. We'll break the pride of every whore's son and revenge ourselves by destroying IAD.

They pull out Tirath's manager, giving useful slogans such as Ha-ra-ra-ra, Victory to Mother India, Long live Vijaya Modi, Long Live Youth League. They say, Show us which motherfuckers won't give bonded labour. Tirath comes running. And says, Brothers don't kill any more this time around. Talk first. Stuff gets done through talk. Oh Lord! I'm scared. I ran off last time? But how many times shall I run off?

Romeo says with great elation, Run away you son of a whore. You cowardly sonofabitch, you have the heart of a pigeon.

The manager shows him Chhagan's hut and runs away. The bullet hits the fleeing Chhagan in the back and at the same time Chhagan's hut blazes up. The women cut a window and escape. Bullets again. Then arrows pierce the smoke and keep coming. Tirath screams and falls as he catches an arrow in his foot. The scene becomes interesting in a minute. The Youth League, dazed by smoke and fire, shoot guns at random, and when the smoke clears one can see on the fallow ground behind Chhagan's hut a few unhitched carts, heaped with straw. Behind it only fifteen Mundas, arrows in their hand. Shankar looks through binoculars and says, No, they aren't there. At this time it starts to rain. The Youth League is a bit uncoordinated. The arrows keep coming, however. One Youth Leaguer shouts, then another. They try to shoot their guns again. Shankar's voice is heard on the mike, Both sides, stop. The police are coming.

Now Romeo kicks a Youth Leaguer in the back and says, Coming. Put a bullet in that IAD.

Shankar arrives and bends Romeo's left arm behind his back and hits the Youth Leaguer's head with the butt of the gun. The police quickly disarm the Youth Leaguers and push and shove them into the camp in the heavy downpour. Shankar curses the Youth League silently and says to the police, Take up the dead, the living, the wounded.

Chhagan and one of the Youth Leaguers is alive still, badly wounded. One Youth Leaguer's dead with an arrow in his heart, and also dead are Chhagan's niece Putli and Ram-Kumari Dhobin. Chotti and his people are also deprived of their bows and arrows. Chotti does not respond to any questions put by Shankar and continues to call Chhagan with uncontrollable passion. Tirathnath cries at a distance with his back to the wall, saying, Dad never beat you, and you broke my leg? Such treachery?

Chotti looks away and says, How many years has it been that I saved Lala from being cut in half by t' train. When? When he had put my boy in je-hell. Today he's makin' these animals kill our women and calls my grandson a traitor!

Didn' call you.

If I'd hit ya I wouldna hev hit you in t' foot.

Shankar stands by the two women's corpses and shakes his head repeatedly at the Youth League's idiocy. He looks undone with grief. Chotti doesn't look at him either. Shankar is pleased. He wants exactly this kind of immaculate and white, enraged reaction. Chotti, remain Chotti. Then I'll be able to catch Swarup's gang.

The wounded and the dead are put in one part of the train, the others in another. Shankar builds a proper case and it is the Youth League that's proved to have provoked the incident. For some reason the case does not reach the courts and the wounded Chhagan and the Youth Leaguer recover slowly, very slowly, in the same hospital, in the same town. Hearing that Chhagan would recover Chotti says, Now let 'em put him in je-hell, let 'em hang him 'n a noose, no pain. For some reason all of Chotti's crowd return with no more than reprimands and rebukes.

Again the police comb the forest, go searching.

Now it is as if Chotti understands everything. The police presence remains. In the rains the brick kiln is waterlogged. There some person or persons wrap Tirath's manager in a blanket and beat him senseless in the dusky dark of evening. Tirath comes back from hospital and sends the manager to hospital. The manager is unable to tell anyone's names. Tirath calls Chhagan's brother. He says, We won't go, and we won't let anyone else go.

It is Chotti who goes to Kurmi in these heavy rains. Says to Ratan Munda, Th' other day Gormen looked at us with a glass raised to his eye. Bullets fly, bodies drop, but that motherfucker don' move t' glass. Now I know he was lookin' for Bisai and those others. Go to Narsingarh, find out where their hideout is in t' north. They keep their eye on me. One of ye s'd tell 'em to move. Why did they let us go? When they skin ye alive for much less reason? I killed a boy after all.

I hear t' Gormen gave a lot of support?

Stupid? Idjitfool? When you're Gormen, you kill Munda Dusad without guilt. Why is he givin' support? Known snake givin' kisses, not bites. I'd've credited him if he'd given me je-hellbars and the noose.

Whatcha say. We know you, yeah.

I can' hear that no more.

Chhagan will live.

This time no money business. We'll put up Chhagan's hut. Chadha and Anwar've given a bitta money. I've gotten some cracked brick fro' Chadha. Chhagan'll come back to a brick house this time.

Three months after this particular incident, in the holy fortnight of the feast of Durga, the police camp becomes strong again. Shankar appears on stage again. Mentally somewhat disturbed. He censors himself on his own IAD training. If mistakes and weakness appear, the IAD officer will remove himself from the field of action. According to the other IAD analyst, Shankar's failure is proven on these grounds: a) he should have realized at the time of the first action in Chotti village, that Swarup's people were involved with the action; b) the police should have entered earlier in the Chotti-Komandi jungle belt; c) it was utterly stupid to kill Swarup. Swarup alive should have been driven with torture first, then care, torture next, care again, and so on. If the living Swarup had been kept as bait, his entire crew could have been captured.

Shankar is given a chance. Of course he'll get a chance. Now there will be an action, and Swarup's group will come. If they don't, Shankar will offer up Chotti with Chotti Munda to the hands of Romeo and his group and, after the hassle of the action is over, depart.

The officer of IAD informs the Secretary of the Youth League, Romeo must not trump Shankar in any way shape or form. IAD is not sitting in Palamau forest for nothing.

Romeo swallows this reprimand and since his mind is a dense forest, he says to his faithful companion, if he is IAD, I too am Youth League. Who can restrain the forward march of Youth League in India. He has insulted me twice in his own place. Now I'll take revenge. In this forest, because I am the sidekick of an idiot candidate, I lost my right arm. And the person who made me lose it remained alive.

Who? Chotti?

Chotti is the number two enemy. Where did he get the courage to shoot me? From that Shankar. Shankar gives him support. Shankar and Chotti! Tirath is a coward. Motherfucker keeps neither a gang nor a gun. I'll finish off both this time. Then I'll go to Dhanbad. What's here for me? There you can kick around some cash, kill off some labour, some union workers, no one will ask a thing.

Guru! I'll do whatever you say. But nothing bad will happen I hope?

Hey, in these parts my carcass has more power than Shankar alive.

Okay chief.

Shankar knows nothing of this. For some reason a different IAD officer also comes this time. Shankar realizes that he too is now under surveillance. Perhaps IAD thinks that, living under the influence of the exploited adivasis, Shankar himself is now demoralized. Please God! Let Shankar get the chance to prove that it's not true.

As soon as they see the police camp, Chottis's crowd sends the women, the elderly and the children across the river, to Chotti's land. Whate'er happens, he says, I won' let 'em die by t' bullet.

When they leave Chotti sighs and says, Some terrible thing is bound to happen this time. This time they won' keep me alive.

He sends Chhagan away. Chhagan has just returned to the village. He shakes his head and says, This time bodies will fall afore Gormen polis, all our huts will burn.

The possibilities seem terrible, and the railway coolies leave for Chadha's brick kiln.

Romeo comes with his cohorts. This time they are more than a hundred. Shankar is all ears, focused in waiting. Why don't the adivasis of Swarup's group come? Why don't they let themselves be captured, be killed? They are bound to be captured. They have no right to any violence. Every right belongs to the government.

The village of Chotti is silent. Dangerous silence.

Shankar realizes that Romeo's group is now spread out. Moving toward the village. He leaves the tent, puts up his binoculars. Ah! Chotti and the others must be behind those oxcarts, in a minute there'll be gunfire, arrows will fly. Expectation brings a serene smile to his face. An IAD officer feels completely normal only in the urgency of great violence.

And right then is heard a surprised utterance, Hey? Whore's cub? And the surprise of the utterance is instantly transformed into an animal glee, Who's gonna save ya today motherfucker? Before anything can be grasped a Youth Leaguer runs toward Shankar and empties all six bullets from his revolver into Shankar's cardiac space, all around his heart's desire to eliminate every trace of Swarup's group. Instantly a whistle blows, a piercing whistle. The Youth Leaguer turns his head to give Romeo the news and drops from a IAD officer's bullet. From all around police, police, special police stream out, and, what is most astonishing, now the police chase the Youth League boys themselves. They are used to terrorizing, to giving chase and beating up, not to being chased and beaten. And consequently, discovering that for the great sin of killing IAD they too can be chased by the police, they too drop here and there. And then it is they who are tied up by the police and who climb into the wagon. The police leap on them inside the closed wagon. Trembling, Daroga tells the IAD officer who is kicking Romeo and Pahlwan, sir. These are Youth Leaguers.

And I belong to IAD.

Everyone is put in the wagon, the wagon alone is hitched to the engine, and they take off. Chotti's group stands at a safe distance from the tracks and ululates with glee. Jeep after Jeep takes off from Tohri to the IAD headquarters. Khurana is told, Pack off. After that there is continuous torture in the IAD way, with no loss of life. As a result there is great tension between the four groups: Youth League, Congress, police, IAD. The first three groups fight for three months, fight in secret. To no avail. Khurana lets the Lady know in Delhi, in the next elections Palamau will vote in her support. In the aforementioned secret conflict IAD remains unmoving. On the state level no one has the right to demand an explanation from IAD. In January 1977 the Emergency ends. The adivasis of Swarup's group come out of Kurmi forest and disperse in ones and twos in Munda-Oraon majority villages. Black mingles with black. Then come the elections. The dice fall the other way. Now Upa and Somchar return to the village.

Have t' days of fear gone? Chotti asks. Who knows?

Gone Aba.

Nah Harmu, I've no faith no more.

But t' Congressi boys are gone?

Les see what these boys do.

Harbans lets Chotti know in secret, Romeo and Pahlwan are in jail.

So what?

There's no trial. Just rotting in jail.

They'll let 'em go.

No no. It's a different regime.

S'll I then see that t' new reign does justice? You tell me. I don' think so.

You'll see.

Lemme see.

Romeo and Pahlwan come out of jail in mid-1978. Knowing that they won't be able to operate in Dhanbad with their bodies broken, they quickly start keeping company with the Janata Party. Because the Youth League had not been able to save them from

IAD's rage, they call Youth League an 'asshole organization', they say 'politics is a bad thing,' and, bringing Chadha's contractor business under control with disproportionate bribes, they establish themselves in Tohri. Hearing this Chotti smiles a bleak smile. Upa! he says. Somchar! Harmu! See now. Chadha did sich a thing. Put us in their hands, didn' let us know. Diku diku wear the same hat.

And that's what happens.

Ancient apprehensions thicken in the tribal and outcaste quarters of Chotti village.

XVII

THE REPRESENTATIVE ELECTED from this area in 1977 held a meeting and went to Chotti immediately. The train stops, the Member descends. The station staff arranges for chairs, dhurrie, wreaths, tea and sweets. The Member is small and thinnish. He speaks on the significance of Indira Gandhi's fall and the coming of the Janata Government. Then he says that like past regimes, the Janata Government is also based on the principle of non-violence. It is true that some lamentable event transpired in Chotti village during the previous regime. But one responds to violence with non-violence, not with violence again. Since the Janata Government wants the advancement of the entire nation, it wants Chotti to advance as well. Advancement will indeed come to this poor area, inhabited by adivasis and outcastes, but one must wait for it. He will look at all the complaints relating to this area with care and do whatever he can. But the people must not lose patience because the solution to some problem is delayed, must not take the law in their own hands. Socialism will succeed in democratic India. Having said all this he looks at his watch and says, Brothers! Do not be unhappy that you are poor. Your Prime Minister also has two or three shirts. As soon as he stops talking he picks up a rail porter's half-naked runty cub and smiles with his dentures. A hapless looking local youth snaps a photo. Instantly he puts down the child and suddenly roars, We must deliver a beautiful India into the hands of these infants. Come, let us put our hands to that work. Hearing his roar a few of the half-naked runts sitting on the decrepit dhurrie begin to wail. The meeting ends.

Chotti shakes and shakes his head. Come Chhagan, he says. You 'n' me are old mates. When my Harmu was a four-year slip he wanted to wed yer ma and how she laughed. Come, let's sit by t' river and drink a gulp or two, let's have a talk.

They sit in the sand of Chotti river. All's changed, says Chhagan, But t' river's t' same.

Nothing's changed. Just t' pressure's on t' rise.

Ya know who this Member is?

Nah.

T' contractors are big in Dhanbad. His brother's a contractor there. Contractors' pressure's worse than polis trouble. His brother's given a heap of money. And so he's a Member now. Contractor's his brother.

I see.

What d'ye see?

If it's a contractor they'll take coal labour from here. T' contractors are t'big farmers o' t' coal mines, y'know. And country Mundas like us are their bond slaves. Swarup'd worked at t' coal mines. He knew.

That's it. But will it be good luck for us?

T' contractor fellas are Congress. T' way he talks, I think he's Congress with a name change.

That's it then.

Now it's a worry. Will they catch us and harass us?

Who knows?

Chotti smiles and says, We'll get to know Chhagan. Second and third months are comin'—t' rains—Lala won't keep t' land barren. Then we'll know. Then Lala'l gie's trouble.

Tirathnath lets them know it's enough in June 1977. A lot of unwanted harm has happened to his land and his sowers and reapers. He too is welcoming the new administration. The new times. Now one must talk to folks and start work. The talk should be between him and his field hands. Chotti Munda hasn't worked Tirath's fields for a long time. He is no longer young, he is a respectable man. He should not be brought into these talks.

Chhagan says, I'll let you know later.

Tell's now, Chhagan.

Sir! No one will give bonded work. Give us a day's pay, some tiffin food, then you may get work.

Tirath brought a terrible urgency in his voice and said, Don't say that Chhagan. With that there'll be trouble again, and believe or not, I'm a Jain. I'm old, was born here. I don't want trouble.

You'll bring the Congressi boys again sir?

Congressi? Who's Congressi. Everyone's Janta.

Everyone?

Everyone.

Sir, you don' want trouble, we don' want trouble, and yet there's trouble. Do you want trouble or not?

Bonded labour's not ended, son.

Isn't there a law?

The law's there and bonded labour's there.

Then we say also, no one will give labour.

You don't know your own good. The boys will come.

Why talk more, sir?

The news must have travelled by the proper channels, for the S.D.O. suddenly comes to Chotti. For an hour or so. He puts deep compassion on his face and says to Chhagan, I understand everything. We are trying to give financial compensation to the families of those who died in the unpleasant events at the time of Emergency. There's no Emergency, but one must obey the law. I hear you had words with Tirathbabu?

I had words.

What words?

The boss will take bonded labour, not give wages. I said we won't give bonded labour. Then he says, Congressi boys are now Janta boys. They'll come and make trouble.

This stuff! S.D.O is pensive. No Emergency, still such words.

What's not there, sir?

Emergency.

What's that?

Those were bad times. There were new elections. When the Emergency ended, and you all voted. So see, there's been a lot of stuff with Chotti. As it's true that there's no bonded labour, so it's true that you must talk as much as possible and come to an understanding.

Sir! Don't blame us. I got bullet in back, didn't think to live. So what're you saying, I must say yes to the Lala?

No, that's not what I said.

Lala won't listen to a word we say, we'll listen to all he says, then why d'ye say bad times are gone?

SDO notes internally that Chhagan's tone is insurgent and says aloud, Don't do anything yourselves. Let me know if you need anything. And yes, the people of Swarup Prasad's Adivasi Welfare Bharati are involved in murder and criminal cases and they're underground. Let the police know if you get wind of them, we'll give rewards.

Okay, sir.

Chotti hears all and says, Now think how t' bad times'll pass.

Why should we think in our minds, we see in front of our eyes.

Chhagan is quiet for a bit. Then says, So what job's left. Now all'll sweat at Chadha's kilns.

Yeah.

They can' do forest work. The Congressi boys do contractin' there.

But the area's labour's touched. The Member wasn't elected Member for nothing. His brother's now an immensely influential contractor in Dhanbad. And Big Brother's son is his best protector. He runs the Trade Union. The miners of Dhanbad are his empire. His brother sends Arkathi and some tribals and outcastes, especially tribals, start going to Dhanbad. Chotti smiles drily and says, T' miners'll go down mine—and come up as Puran Munda.

Suddenly, Tirath too understands, just force is not enough to get labour. For one, the place is sparsely populated. If labour leaves by the indirect support of the Member himself, who then will till the fields? So he has to say, I'll pay wages, work.

Give in our hands day by day.

I'll give weekly.

Yeah, ye'll give weekly with thugs.

That's past history.

Chhagan says in uncharacteristic anger, Past? History? That's past history? You'll give back the lives of Jugal and Dukha, of my girls? My back'll straighten? What's past history?

Tirath says, Ten days for the thief, one for the saint. Do what you will. But my day will come.

Hearing this, Disha Munda of Swarup's group, from across-river says, No, no, can't bear no more.

Chotti says, Go again to Kurmi forest, there's price on your heads. Lala's just goin' to those boys, t' polis are just comin' to village.

It's his words that are proved true. Tirathnath goes to Tohri. Romeo hears everything and says, I now need labour. Now who's going to think of you?—Romeo does not use the 'you' of high respect but goes on in the familiar way—helping you I'm in this state. So why d'ye have problems? They speak loud, and you say yes?

Tirath says sadly, You got compensated, made a bit o' money.

Listen mate, the way the IAD. took us to the cleaners, it can't be compensated with money.

Tirath is obliged to return home. Now he thinks what his boys say is right. Why should you remain here with the bits and pieces of bother of your landed property. You're getting old. Sell everything and come to Patna. Perhaps their view is right. Someone has poured salt on the joy of landed property. Tirathnath wants to weep at his own plight. How it was in the old days! Men like Chotti and Chhagan would take minimal wages, they gave bonded labour, personal relations were never harmed. Why have the villagers changed? Hasn't Tirathnath remained the same? Bonded labour is a system, why should it be oppression? Why have they changed? How long it's been since Tirath has been to their feast days. He used to go before, to see. Even today, Tirath feels at ease with the companionship of the ones with whom there's this friction. He doesn't have the fads of reading books or going to movies or listening to the radio. As amusement he used to hear gossip from the washerwoman Motia. This brings his beloved to his mind and Tirath says to himself, You've put this stake in my heart, this is a great sin for yourselves. And immediately he feels cheerful. Then he thinks, Must sow pigeon-pea in the next spring sowing. His dad used to discuss what to sow when with Chotti's father Bisra as equals. He heaves a sigh. Romeo too gave no support.

Romeo and Pahlwan come to Chotti. To Harbans Chadha's brickfield. Four persons from the Youth Wing of Janata are with them. Their faces are known to Chotti and Chhagan. They had guns then, as they do now. Always.

Romeo says to Harbans, This is my labour-force.

How?

When you sell your house you also sell its front door.

What does that mean?

Romeo is used to lying easily. My brother he said a lot, forest contracting is a profitable business. That's a bluff. It's a losing trade. That's as it may be, I took the business with all its assets after all.

So what?

So doesn't asset mean labour?

Labour talk we'll have with labour.

Send them tomorrow.

Never. They are working here after talks with me.

Hey, Punjabi businessman! You don't understand.

I've understood well that Bihari contractors are thugs.

A certain Janata Youth says, No Chadha you haven't understood. You will, later.

They leave. Harbans goes to the S.D.O. who says, those labour fellows are jerks. I know they've taken money from Romeo and Pahlwan and still come to work for you. Romeo has already reported. Now let 'em go and take other labour.

What are you saying? They haven't worked a day.

They'll let you know? You don't know the pigheadedness of tribals and low castes? Don't speak for them at all. Have you ever heard of Swarup Prasad?

Yes.

Your labour is hand in glove with his gang. Shankar died trying to catch that very gang.

These guys killed him.

But hey, they've paid the price, Chadhaji. Don't forget that. So see, think on what I said.

Harbans understands very late that when Romeo makes trouble S.D.O of this regime won't support him either. He sighs and says, What to do! How do I get labour in an instant?

Take time, take time, I'll make it mutual.

Mutual?

Finish the work you've started? They too haven't entered the forest since they've taken the contract. Let 'em have a look-see.

He tells all to Romeo. Romeo says, Fine. All I want is to get at them once. I want to create a situation where there's no Chadha, no Lala, only me. Then I'll show you how to break 'em in. I'll skin 'em for shoe-leather.

Romeo waits for such a chance. The rains come. You can't cut timber in the rainy season, so the work stops at the brickfield. Romeo goes for a site inspection, what sort of support he'll get if he brings off such an action/operation, and gets a good contract to supply wood by a government project. They vanish for a long time, and everyone is relieved to think that everything is at an end. But they return at the beginning of October. It is the holy fortnight of the worship of Durga. The station-staff at Chotti places an order in Calcutta for the image of the goddess, looking forward to the festival. For this occasion, there is a plan to bring two films—'Saviour Goddess Durga' and 'Rustum in Hiding'. And forgetting all previous agreements, Romeo lets it be known that he wants labour in the forest right after the festival. He wants everyone whose name is in Chadha's book. S.D.O starts to say, The arrangement was for after Chadha's and Lala's work is over.

No, no, I have a government contract.

These words are announced in Chotti village. Everyone is stunned for a while. Then Disha says, Me, Upa, and Somchar must leave. Polis will come from this trouble. They'll turn us into Swarup. It's best that th' able men leave.

Where to? Chotti asks.

We'll see.

No one knows when they leave, at what late hour of night. Chotti assumes that he'll never see Somchar again, that he won't see Harmu's son Lal. They will not be able to return, ever. Romeo, Pahlwan and the four young men go to survey the forest. It's Chadha's man who takes them. Romeo says, Scram. We won't get lost in such a forest.

Laughing they enter the forest, infiltrate. The four young men come back. They take a Jeep to bring liquor from the bungalow in Tohri.

They were the last to see Romeo and Pahlwan alive. They drank themselves silly, got more liquor from the shops, and returned. They yelled 'Boss!' and crashed on the green grass. When they awoke they sensed that it was night. They hear groans, and being cowards they cry 'Bear!' climb into their Jeep and drive back. Then they finish off the rest of the liquor. At the height of intoxication they remember that if indeed Romeo and Pahlwan have been taken by bears in the forest, they may die, but may also not die. If they return alive, the two bosses will take terrible revenge upon them. Only recently has Pahlwan, trying to secure a contract, kicked a former Youth Leaguer so hard in the lower belly, that he died pissing blood in hospital. It didn't touch Pahlwan. They won't be touched if they kill these four. So go to Dhanbad to save your back. On the way from Tohri to Dhanbad, with their drunken heads they crash their Jeep in a deep ravine. They are rescued the next afternoon. The driver's dead, and one of them is comatose in hospital with a concussed brain. The other two are hospitalized with diverse injuries.

And therefore there is no news of Romeo and Pahlwan. The boys of Chotti village return home on the night of the accident. Don' let anyone know we'd left, say Somchar and Lal. Disha's gone.

Where?

Kurmi.

Why?

He'll go underground again.

After the accident, Romeo and Pahlwan are not seen at the rescue. No one can recount the subsequent events. In the end an Oraon boy hears the shrill screams of hyenas as he herds cattle. He goes forward curious and sees the corpses of Romeo and Pahlwan. Both bodies are shot through the heart with arrows.

An incredible uproar is the result. After postmortems their bodies are burnt. Wreaths are placed on the bodies from the offices of both Congress and Janata parties. And the police from the county seat enter the forest with hunting dogs. Everyone deplores these reprehensible murders. The police say, Since arrows, the killers are adivasis.

Village after village is combed. At last the police give up. They cannot reach a confession even after beating the hell out of people. Harbans and Tirath say to the S.D.O., Look for the killer? How can this be? Be our turn next to swallow arrows?

S.D.O. is stone cold in a chaste resolve, Such a great crime can't be tolerated.

What will you do?

I'll bring all the adivasi archers to the Chotti fair. I will surround them with police. Then we'll see.

Hey, first arrange for our security. Lalaji and I are scared.

Okay.

Let's go Lalaji.

They go home together. Thus are the deaths of Romeo and Pahlwan successful. Lala and Harbans belonged to two different eras. They are united by these noble deaths. Harbans says, There

are only servants at your place. Why not stay at my place for now?
I'll not be at peace thinking of you all by yourself.

Whatever you say bro!

S.D.O. calls all the tax collectors and asks them to beat drums
in all the villages. It is obligatory this time to come to Chotti fair.
Any absentee will be taken to be the assassin of the two great
heroes.

The drum beats and beats in Chotti village as well. The big festival drum beats at the railway station. There are no crowds there.
The presence of Mundas and outcastes is unwelcome. It is clear
that everyone's shocked. If Romeo and Pahlwan had killed every
adivasi in the area, no one would have found it 'unexpected'.
There are adivasis, there are subcastes, the Romeos kill them, it
happens like this. But if one or a few adivasis kill the Romeos it is
an unexpected event. The Romeos kill, they're not killed. This is
the rule. Under all regimes.

The sound of drums floats into Chotti's hut. Adivasi and outcaste women and children look at the railway station with thirsty
eyes from a distance. Chotti's thinking of something, he thinks
and thinks. Then says, Somchar, let's go and put flowers on t'
Sonshan-Buru shrine?

Chotti places flowers on the tombstones of Koel, Mungri and of
his parents. Then he stoops to avoid the wind and lights a bidi.
And then says in the softest voice, Somchar? Y'all killed 'em?

Yes, Aba.

How many of you?

Me, Disha, Upa, Lal.

No one else.

T' Mundas of Narsingarh kept watch.

How d'ye kill?

Somchar explained at length. The plan for the kill was Disha's.
He'd said in advance, if they remain alive there'll be trouble
again. The aim will be to capture Swarup's party. If they die
there'll be trouble as well. Since trouble can't be avoided, then it's
best to kill them.

Disha said everything alone?

At first alone. Then it seems everyone put their heads together.
First they leave and talk with the Mundas of Narsmigarh. They
hide their bows and arrows in the branches of a dense banyan.
They themselves hide there. They had guessed which forest the

former retainer of Rajbans Chadha could show. Romeo and Pahlwan made it easy for them by plunging so deep in the forest. Somchar and the other three had surrounded them from all sides. Pahlwan had begged for his life. Romeo was abusing them.

Who killed?

Whoever's right. Disha killed one for Swarup, Upa another for Dukha.

Chotti keeps quiet. Then he says, Come, let's go. Don' you tell anyone else.

No.

Disha's not here, you, Upa, and Lal must touch my knee an' swear not to tell.

They swear. Chotti remains thoughtful, withdrawn. He is quite altered, for, sitting down to eat he suddenly tells Harmu in a voice of great concern, Etwa is a brother of yers. Never fergit it Harmu.

No Aba.

Suddenly, he says to Harmu's mother, Ye don' know it, but t' box's inside t' wall at t' top o' t' high step. There's money in't. A lot. By day, I'm puttin' in. Three score and one rupee.

In the daytime he says to Harmu's mother, Don' work no more Wife. Come sit a bit near me.

Harmu is worried. What does yer body say, Aba? He asks. What's all this, why Aba?

I'm growin' old, boy. Me father went, me ma went, Koel, Mungri, all t' dead that I seen die, I think on 'em.

No, Aba, I cannot bear. You're not there, t' sun and moon are gone. Thought of such a day can' get in my head.

Harmu! Lord Birsa died, Dhani died, Swarup died, sun and moon still rise son, they'll rise when I die too. One thing!

What?

Chhagan's git'n old too. Tell 'im to take that drum on fair day. It's his long time wish.

Right.

And ask that Lal to tell everyone, let even th' old uns come to t' fair.

They're all scared Aba.

Chotti becomes god Haram, lights up his countenance with a transcendental smile and says, What's to fear son? I'm here, no?

They're scared.

Listening to the drums Chotti says, Of course they're scared. They didn' let us see t' Durga puja, they're drummin' to scare us, why're they callin' to t' fair this time? To catch and kill t' ones who shot th' arrers that killed 'em.

Yes Aba.

It's no use gettin scared now.

Everyone comes to Chotti's place at his call. Know why they're callin to t' fair this time? Chotti says.

We know.

When they catch t' killers they'll show us terror like we've never seen.

We know.

But ever'one'll go.

Ever'one?

Yes. There'll be no one in t' village but crows and dogs. Everyone'll go from th' oldest to t' baby. Womenfolk too. I'm Chotti Munda, you've gie'n me a lotta respect fo' a long time. Then this is me word. Ever'one must go t' fair.

We will, we will!

Another order.

Say it, our Chotti!

There's singin' and dancin' before th' arrer play. Then you let ever'one know, and know yerselves, that no one must hit t' target with an arrer at t' games.

Then that'll be so.

Come all no fear.

Everyone came. The young carried the very old on their back. Never had so many adivasis come to any fair as they did to the fair on the last day of the Goddess Feast—Bijoya Dashami 1978. Everyone brought bow and arrow. And two hundred and fifty armed police came to keep an eye over a thousand adivasis S.D.O., Daroga, Tirathnath, Harbans, they were all there. There was tremendous tension in the air.

The singing and dancing lasted only a very short time. Then starts the archery competition. The different Oraons and Mundas of the different villages and clans keep hitting their ancient drum—their nagara—dim-dim-dim-dim. But no adivasi steps forth. S.D.O. watches and watches with the sharpest eye, and rage gathers in his mind.

He holds the megaphone to his mouth and shouts, Why is there no one? You think you'll get out of it by standing off? I'll beat up every old man, thrash every young man, grab the child in arms and put him in thana. If you want your child back, help us catch the murderers.

No one responds. Seventy-two nagaras sound dim-dim-dim. There's people from seventy-two villages.

Don't think anyone will return from the fair. Why aren't you coming up to join the game? Why aren't you coming?

Chotti looks at his wife. Harmu's Ma's eyes widen. Looks at Chhagan. Then he casts his glance on everyone. Everyone looks at him.

Why aren't you coming?

Chotti rises from the judge's seat. There's winter in the air. In the coldstruck air one sees that Chotti is a seventy-eight year old man. There are a million lines on his whole face and body. White hair folded back near the nape and held in a brass ring. White pith in his pierced ears, short white dhoti around his waist. A bow and an arrow, his arrow, he brings it every year, by ritual law, at the time of his judging, and he takes it back. An arrow ritually blessed. His rising is such that all the nagaras stop. Only Chhagan's face lights up. His head lowers and he continues to play the nagara in deep compassion, in an indivisible, mild, stern sorrow. Chotti looks at him and turns his head away.

And says, Lord, no one'll come, give it me. S.D.O. is most startled. He gives him the megaphone and says, You, you, tell them.

It's not to tell 'em, Lord, it's to tell ye. Who's dead, Lord? Why will ye beat up all t' men to catch their killers, and grab all t' mites from their mother's breasts and fill t' thana?

Chotti!

Shush lord! Standin' here today, ever'thin' comes to mind. Me father died by reason of that Lala's dad. I ne'er did a betrayal, and still he sent me son to je-hell, and I saved him from t' wheels of a movin' train! Munda–Oraon–Dusad–Dhobi have never broken trust! And what did we get for that Lord? What did you give to us? You'll raise terror over us ta try their murder, but did they not raise terror? They went to take t' honour of our daughters, all t' daughters of t' families of t' pahan, his wife, of Motia, of t' railway porter, of Dukha, Jugal, Chhagan—they died, and then there were no polis lord? Did you not work this way?

Chotti stops a bit. Clears his throat. Each black face is now alive.

How'll you catch, anyone? Chotti asks. What do they know? Now hear, I killed 'em.

No—say a thousand voices.

You!

Yes Lord! Now all t' shopkeepers of t' fair, all of you, Munda-Oraon-Dusad-Dhobi—all of you are my witness. I did that job. I crept up hidin' in t' forest an' kep' sayin' t' meself, no Munda or outcaste will die at their hand. I won' keep their life. They've raised much terror, thrown a lotta bodies. Gormen has given them much help. As he talks Chotti's voice rises and cracks. D'ye know how I killed? T' night before when they all slept, I went an' hid t' bow. T' next day I said 'I'm off to Kurmi' and went there. It was real easy when t' boys left. Instantly those two, no! I didn't let 'em say 'Mother,' Lord—Chotti gives up the mega-phone. He strikes his chest and said, I've killed, yes, I am that Chotti Munda. And if you raise terror for this—then Lala an' Chadha in Chotti village, and you at th' Office, none of you'll stay alive. Polis? If Swarup's group shoots arrers after dark and pickles your blood with poison of t' kuchila berry, whom'll you save? No terror.

Chotti's wife swoons beside him. Chhagan goes on playing the nagara, an inscrutable smile on his lips.

With a pale face the S.D.O. says, You! You shot the arrow? Can you see the target?

Chotti gives an innocent smile and says, I'll show ya. Then says fast in the language of the Mundas, Dhani Munda! I'm raisin' yer name an' shootin' yer arrer today. To stay true, meself to meself.

Chotti comes before the target with light and fast footsteps. And tells everyone, No fear y'all. Then he shoots, into the target.

Then he waits, unarmed. As he waits he mingles with all time and becomes river, folklore, eternal. What only the human can be. Brings all adivasi struggle into the present, today into the united struggle of the adivasi and the outcaste.

Time still passes. Chotti throws the bow to Harmu. Harmu catches it. Says, Why go on? Catch me? I had but that one arrer.

S.D.O. seems to break some spell and stands up, goes forward.

But instantly a thousand adivasis raise their bows in space and cry, No! The non-adivasis raise restraining hands.

Chotti on one side, S.D.O. on the other, and in between a thousand bows upraised in space. And a warning announced in many upraised hands.

Translator's Afterword

THERE IS AN AIR OF FESTIVITY around the last stages of the production of this book. Mahasweta Devi herself, the book's editor Anjum Katyal, the publisher of Seagull Books, Naveen Kishore, become general dogsbody, and me, all pulling together to 'make the book ready for the Calcutta Book Fair!' This afterword will be necessarily brief.

'I had but that one arrow,' says Chotti at the end of the novel. What is the magic of Dhani Munda's magic arrow? Nothing but practice, repeats Chotti, attention to detail, focusing on the prey, caught in that ethical glance that undoes the distinction between love and its opposite. That focusing practice—*adhyan*—in Sanskritic Bengali—*is* magic. That is the trick of teaching as infinite relay, the very spine of historical change. I have no doubt that related words will be found in the world's languages. Here I note the uncanny resemblance with the Sioux ghost dance.[1]

The ghost is not the abstraction of the spirit, it has a ghostly body. And magic in *Chotti* is not the mere irrationality of the epiphenomenal; it carries the sweat of target practice. Through the ghost dance as through arrow practice, the ancestors are touched and asked for a way to cope with a future that seems to overwhelm the present. That last scene of the book, fixed in the freeze frame of a dance: 'Chotti on one side, S.D.O. on the other, and in between a thousand bows upraised in space. And a warning announced in many upraised hands,' is where Chotti finds the open end of the redemptive solution by memorating Dhani Munda: 'Chotti gives an innocent smile and says, I'll show ya.

Then says fast in the language of the Mundas, Dhani Munda! I'm raisin' yer name an' shootin' yer arrer today. To stay true, meself to meself.' The novel's suspended conclusion looks forward to the possibility of the magic coming alive again.

Chotti Munda repeatedly dramatizes subaltern solidarity: Munda, Oraon and the Hindu outcastes must work together. Today such a solidarity has a name: dalit. The seduction of an identitarianism in the name of the dalit can learn a lesson here. With a degree of regret, Chotti accepts that cultural identity must be—to take an altogether inappropriate metaphor that is easy for the reader to understand—museumized:

> Chotti returns home but the clouds don't lift from his mind. The day is coming. Mundas will not be able to live with their identity. In all national development work they will have to be one with those who, like Chhagan, are the oppressed of the land, and work as field hands, as sweated workers for contractor or trader. Then there'll be a shirt on his body, perhaps shoes on his feet. Then the 'Munda' identity will live only at festivals—in social exchange.

Between the performative of ritual transformed into performance and the power of a haunting magic anchored in practice the text charts the remote possibility of a resistant subalternity.

When in the conversation at the head of this book Mahasweta proposes subaltern solidarity as resistance to globalization, I am not ready to situate the remark as benevolent Luddism. World trade and the trade-related measures of 'development' are altogether dependent upon detail, and much of this detail is still located in large aboriginal, subaltern and sub-proletarian areas. More than the visible disruption of large-scale international meetings, as in Seattle (30 November–3 December, 1999), Naples (March 15–17, 2001), Genoa (20–21 July 2001) or indeed the material destruction of the temple of World Trade (September 11, 2001), subaltern disruption in detail can throw the global machinery of world trade out of joint. I am not suggesting that *Chotti Munda* is predicting this in 1980. I am suggesting that the novel can prefigure this for the canny activist reader.

In 2000, mourning the passing of old Harlem, I had written: 'how does one figure the cutting edge of the vanishing present?' I said nothing when Mahasweta spoke as follows during our conversation: 'I had such a great *asthirata* in me, such a restless-ness; an *udbeg*, this anxiety: I have to write, somehow I have to document this period which I have experienced because it is going away, it is vanishing.' I said nothing, but I was filled with elation to think that, already at the end of the seventies, Mahasweta had been driven by a kindred urge. Such resonances dictate the impulse to translate.

The last word, woman. If Chotti memorates Dhani at the end of the novel, at his own end Dhani memorates Sali, Birsa Munda's companion, and Pariwa, her son, adopted by him as his own. I want Mahasweta to unpack that proper name, Sali, which holds the names of the women who came out with axe, sword and stick to fight in the Ulgulan:

> Gaya with a sword, Maki, his wife, with a long *lathi*, their little son with a *bulwa*, grandson Ramu, 14 years, with a bow and two arrows, the two daughters-in-law with a *dauli* and a *tangi* respectively and the three daughters, Thigi, Nagi and Lembu with a *lathi*, a sword and a *tangi* respec-tively . . . we [Gaya and I] rolled into a corner . . . I on top . . . I was hammered from behind by one of the ladies . . . I thought at the time it was with an axe . . . but Sub-Inspector Iltaf Hussain tells me it was Gaya's wife, the most ferocious harridan of the lot, with a *lathi*: it was probably this old dame who flung the axe at the Sub-Inspector . . . I may add that at least two of the women had small babies in their left arms while brandishing arms with their right.[2]

Mahasweta's answer is illuminating: 'I will write, about Laro'—her informant in the Gua shooting—'Laro is someone I know, I will write about her. And about women participating, those were again tribals brought from the Chhotanagpur plateau, settled in Sunderbans, who took part in Tebhaga.' I begin from what I know, says this soldier.

I have followed Mahasweta Devi for over twenty years. I have seen, again and again, how her fiction overflows her plans. I will

look forward to fighting women, whatever their names, and look
forward to translating their story.

Gayatri Chakravorty Spivak
Columbia University
New Delhi, 6 January, 2002

Notes

1 I learnt of this first from the unabridged edition of James Mooney, *The Ghost-Dance Religion and the Sioux Outbreak of 1890* (Glorieta, N.M.: Rio Grande Press, 1973). For the animation of the ghost dance in 1970s activism, the text is, of course, Dee Alexander Brown, *Bury My Heart At Wounded Knee: An Indian History of the American West* (New York: Holt, Rinehart & Winston, 1971), a book Mahasweta came to love long after she wrote *Chotti Munda*.
2 Report of Deputy Commissioner Streatfield, cited in K. S. Singh, *Birsa Munda*, pp. 107-108.

adivasi: (lit. 'first inhabitant'). Indigenous person. Tribal. 8% of India's population.

Adivasi Samachar: Lit. 'Tribal News'. Newspaper.

Arjun . . . Brihannala: In the epic Mahabharata, the five Pandava princes spend their last year of exile in disguise. Of them, Arjun passes his time as a eunuch, Brihannala, cultivating only the 'womanly' arts.

August Movement: Also known as the Quit India movement of 1942. On 9 August 1942 the Congress Party and Mahatma Gandhi called the nation to participate in protests against colonial rule. The movement spread to many parts of India and thousands of people participated. It took a violent turn in many areas. Coming as it did in the middle of the Second World War, it caused considerable worry to the British Government and repressive measures were used to suppress it. Thousands of people were imprisoned and many killed. The Communists did not participate in the movement because they felt, with Germany's attack on the Soviet Union, that Britain was an ally in the anti-fascist struggle.

Birsa: Birsa Munda (1874–1901). Legendary leader of the Munda tribals of Chhotanagpur region in Bihar, who spearheaded a revitalization and armed resistance movement of the tribals, culminating in the Ulgulan, or armed uprising, 1899–1900. *Bir* means forest in the Mundari language. Munda is the name of the proto-australoid Munda tribe. It also designates the temporal head of the village.

Birsaite: Follower of Birsa Munda.

Bonded Labour: Compulsory labour which a person is forced or obliged to give free or at rates much below the market rate to a specific landowner from whom s/he may have borrowed paltry sums of money or foodgrains. The bondage may continue for generations. The original term for this through the text is *bet begari*, which includes all sorts of chores and labour which the landlord can require those indebted to him to perform, free of remuneration. When the traditional tribal land system was being replaced, under the British, by an alien land system, the Diku zamindars, the new masters, imposed on the tribals and others the concept of forced labour. Every year, for a given number of days, a person who was cultivating certain types of land belonging to the landlord was forced to give 15–16 days free labour, or even more.

Bonded Labour Act: Law enacted in 1976 abolishing bonded labour and providing a 'compensation package' for 'freed' bonded labourers.

ceiling: Part of land reform measures in independent India fixing the upward limit of the amount of land a person could own.

Chamar: Leather and hide worker, amongst the lowest in the caste hierarchy.

Congress: Indian National Congress—major political party since 1885. Under the leadership of Indira Gandhi in the context of the book.

Daroga: Officer in charge of police station.

Diku: Word used by the tribals of the area. Intruder. Alien. Exploiter (of the tribe), landlord, moneylender, trader, shopkeeper. In the narrow sense, 'Hindu'.

Dusad: Low in the caste hierarchy.

Emergency: Period starting in June 1975 for two years during Prime Ministership of Indira Gandhi, when the government empowered itself with extraordinary authority. Period infamous for authoritarianism, draconian laws and their abuse.

Ganju: Low caste.

Hoffmann's dictionary: Rev. John Hoffmann, S. J., was an expert on the language and culture of the Mundas. His definitive fifteen-volume *Encyclopaedia Mundarica* began to appear in 1930; the final volume was published by 1979.

Hul: Rebellion, movement, agitation, revolt. Synonymous with the great Santal Rebellion of 1855. Santals, Mundas and Oraons are the three largest ethnic tribal groups in eastern and east-central India.

I. G.: Inspector General.

Jalianwalabagh: A walled park in the city of Amritsar in the Punjab, which people could enter or exit only through a narrow alley. In 1919, public agitations against certain repressive laws of the British were taking place in many parts of India, and Gandhi was emerging as an all-India leader. On 13 April, 1919, several thousand men and women had assembled in Jalianwalabagh for a peaceful meeting. Armed British forces started firing on the assembly, blocking the only escape route. Over a thousand men, women and children were killed and many more injured. There was an outcry against the massacre all over the country.

Janata Party: Coalition of parties opposed to Indira Gandhi. Defeated Indira Gandhi in elections in 1977 and was in power for a short period.

Karam: A tribal festival, held in the rainy season, in which women play a major role. Like all tribal festivals, it is based on the worship of nature. Foodgrain seeds, fruits and vegetables are placed in woven baskets. When the seeds sprout, the women carry them to the karam tree for a puja or worship ritual.

Kashipur-Baranagar killing: Kashipur and Baranagar are adjacent localities in the northern parts of Calcutta, located on the river Bhagirathi, a densely populated area largely inhabited by the middle and lower-middle classes. In 1971, when the radical Naxalite movement was raging in West Bengal, Kashipur-Baranagar turned into a symbol of state repression. On 12–13 August, the entire area was cordoned off by the police and handed over to armed underworld goons taking revenge for the murder of a local leader belonging to the Congress Party under Indira Gandhi. West Bengal's administration was under the effective charge of a trusted lieutenant of Indira Gandhi, Siddhartha Shankar Ray. Those believed to have any association with the Naxalites were dragged out of their homes and slaughtered. The bodies were piled onto small carts and dumped into the river nearby. The carnage continued for a full forty-eight hours and the major political parties opposed to the Naxalites collaborated with the police in sealing off the escape routes. Over 200 people, mostly young men, are on record to have been killed in this single incident.

Khasi: A matrilineal tribe of the Assam and Meghalaya hills in northeast India, known for a high rate of education amongst women.

Kherwar: A movement named after the ancient tribal word for the Santals, a proto-australoid tribal group. The Santal rebellion of 1855–56 was the 'political expression of the idea seeking restoration of the primeval world'—K. S. Singh, *Birsa Munda*, p. 28. This was followed by a revivalist movement under Bhagirath Manjhi in the 1870s. Its roots were agrarian, the means socio-religious or devotional. The dream was for a Kherwar millennium, with the enemies of the race wiped out. Bhagirath was arrested and later released in 1877. Subsequently, the movement lost momentum.

Khuntkatti: Tenure of the members of the lineage (*khunt*) who reclaimed lands (*katti*). An ancient tribal land settlement pattern: when a particular village or settlement became overcrowded, heads of society would seek out another uninhabited place, and assess its suitability in terms of soil, water and wind currents. If deemed favourable, they would drive a pole (*khunt*) into the ground, the surrounding virgin forest would be cleared (*katti*), and a village would be set up. Each family would clear an area which would become their dwelling place. These original clearer-settlers were known as *khuntkattidar* or first inhabitants. Later, people not of the lineage of the first settlers were allowed to settle in these areas: servicemen of inferior status, relatives by marriage, etc.

Kurmi: Low caste, landless poor; tribals who were Hinduized.

Lala: Trader

Maintenance of Internal Security Act (MISA): Closely associated with the regime of Indira Gandhi. Introduced in 1972. Under the MISA, constitutional rights of an individual could be severely curtailed and thousands of people were actually arrested and put behind bars without regular trial for years. After the defeat of Indira Gandhi in 1977, the Act lapsed because the new regime did not renew it.

Marwari: Trading community from Rajasthan.

Mauritius: A reference to the recruitment of indentured labour for the sugar-cane plantations in Mauritius.

Mission: (Christian) missionary centres.

Mulkui: 1858 movement, also known as Sardari Larai. A legal and peaceful struggle led for forty years by the Munda Sardars, or chiefs, in protest against intrusions into their age-old agrarian system, particularly by the Church, which claimed tribal lands on the basis that many tribals had converted to Christianity. The tribals felt let down by the Church, particularly when it failed to help them against the Dikus who had gained control of their land. They sent several petitions and appeals to the government. They also sought help from some lawyers of Haora who fleeced them for years while pretending to put up their case before the Viceroy and Queen. These betrayals are a major cause for the tribal disillusionment with and distrust of the legal system, administration and Church. From 1890 the movement turned against all Europeans, who, the tribals felt, were complicit with the zamindars (q. v.).

Naxal: Political activists of the extreme left believing in armed revolution and working under various Marxist-Leninist-Maoist organizations. Name originates from Naxalbari, a rural area in north Bengal where the struggle of local peasants in 1967 led to the polarization of leftist political forces in the country. A new political party, Communist Party of India (Marxist-Leninist), was launched in 1969. Later many breakaway groups from the party set up their own organizations.The movement resulted in radical political activities, political violence and ruthless state repression on an unprecedented scale in certain parts of India, particularly West Bengal, Bihar and Andhra Pradesh. Various Naxalite groups are still active in many rural areas of Andhra Pradesh, Bihar and Madhya Pradesh and some parts of West Bengal. There is a support base for the radicals among the tribals and poor people of these regions, particularly in the area which is the locale of the book.

non-violent fighters: A reference to the participants in the Civil Disobedience movement spearheaded by Gandhi and the Indian National Congress, part of the ongoing independence movement in India.

Oraon: A tribal group of dravidian origin.

S.D.O.: Sub Divisional Officer. Administrative head of a subdivision. There are several in a district.

Sidhu-Kanhu: Two brothers, who were regarded as the 'chosen ones'—apostles appointed by their God (Thakur) in a revelation. Legendary heroes of the Santal Rebellion of 1855, that engulfed large tracts of Bihar (now Jharkhand). The brothers were killed by hanging by the British in Pakur, now in Jharkhand.

Sohrai: Three-day cattle festival that coincides with the 'new harvest' when new paddy is brought home in the months of October and November. Basically a thanksgiving to the cattle for having helped in cultivation. The cattle are bathed, fed, anointed with turmeric and worshipped.

Tebhaga: Agrarian movement (1946–47) before the partition of India, in the then undivided province of Bengal in British India (now the Indian state of West Bengal and the separate nation-state Bangladesh). The movement was based on the demand of the sharecroppers for two-thirds of the produce as opposed to the half share they were traditionally entitled to, even though they bore all the costs of cultivation. (The effective share was invariably much less than half, due to various illegal exactions imposed by the landlord.) The movement lasted for some months, and spread to several districts of Bengal, being particularly intensive in the north Bengal districts where sharecropping was widespread. Over seventy peasants died in clashes with the police and landlords. The movement was withdrawn when the government promised legislation on the subject. It took years after independence for the necessary laws to be enacted.

Telengana-Girijan: Region in Andhra Pradesh covering several districts, a strong base of support for the Communists in the forties and still a stronghold of the left radicals. Starting before India's independence (1947), and continuing till 1951, this vast region became the locale of a major agrarian movement under the leadership of the Communist Party of India. At one stage the struggle for land turned into a struggle for political power. After independence, the Indian Army was used to suppress the movement. Between 4000-6000 Communist activists were estimated to have been killed by the forces of the state and landlords and over 10,000 arrested. Considered a landmark in the history of armed struggle in the country. Girijans (lit., hill people) are the hill tribals of eastern Andhra Pradesh. This too is a traditional base of radical movements.

Ulgulan: 'The Great Tumult'. Armed uprising led by Birsa Munda from December 1899–January 1900 in the Ranchi and northern Singhbhum districts of Bihar. The uprising was suppressed, ending in the surrender of the insurgents, followed by the capture and death in captivity of Birsa Munda.

wax-house of epic fame: A reference to an incident in the Mahabharata in which the exiled Pandava princes are lured into a mansion constructed entirely of flammable materials, in an attempt to finish them off while they sleep, by setting the edifice on fire.

Youth League: The allusion is to the Youth Congress, a wing of the Congress Party under Indira Gandhi. The Youth Congress, under the effective control of Indira Gandhi's younger son, Sanjay Gandhi, came to be associated with many acts of tyranny and violence during the Emergency years.

zamindar: Landlord. Ranks expanded in the British Permanent Settlement of 1793.

The Selected Works of Mahasweta Devi

M ahasweta Devi (b. 1926) is one of our foremost literary personalities, a prolific and best-selling author in Bengali of short fiction and novels; a deeply political social activist who has been working with and for tribals and marginalized communities like the landless labourers of eastern India for years; the editor of a quarterly, *Bortika*, in which the tribals and marginalized peoples themselves document grassroot level issues and trends; and a socio-political commentator whose articles have appeared regularly in the *Economic and Political Weekly, Frontier* and other journals.

Mahasweta Devi has made important contributions to literary and cultural studies in this country. Her empirical research into oral history as it lives in the cultures and memories of tribal communities was a first of its kind. Her powerful, haunting tales of exploitation and struggle have been seen as rich sites of feminist discourse by leading scholars. Her innovative use of language has expanded the conventional borders of Bengali literary expression. Standing as she does at the intersection of vital contemporary questions of politics, gender and class, she is a significant figure in the field of socially committed literature.

Recognizing this, we have conceived a publishing programme which encompasses a representational look at the complete Mahasweta: her novels, her short fiction, her children's stories, her plays, her activist prose writings. The series is an attempt to introduce her impressive body of work to a readership beyond Bengal; it is also an overdue recognition of the importance of her contribution to the literary and cultural history of our country.

Mother of 1084
A novel. Translated and introduced by Samik Bandyopadhyay.

Breast Stories: Draupadi, Breast-Giver, Behind The Bodice
Translated with introductory essays by Gayatri Chakravorty Spivak.

Five Plays: Mother of 1084, Aajir, Urvashi and Johnny, Bayen, Water
Adapted from her fiction by the author.
Translated and introduced by Samik Bandyopadhyay.

Rudali: From Fiction to Performance
This volume consists of the story by Mahasweta Devi and the play by
Usha Ganguli. Translated and introduced by Anjum Katyal.

Dust on the Road: The Activist Writings of Mahasweta Devi
A collection of prose pieces. Introduced and translated by
Maitreya Ghatak.

Bitter Soil
Palamau stories by Mahasweta Devi.
Translated by Ipsita Chanda. Introduced by the author.

Our Non-Veg Cow and Other Stories
Translated by Paramita Banerjee. Introduced by Nabaneeta Dev Sen.

The Armenian Champa Tree
A novella. Translated by Nirmal Kanti Bhattacharjee.

Old Women
Two stories. Translated by Gayatri Chakravorty Spivak.

Titu Mir
Translated by Rimi B. Chatterjee.

The Queen of Jhansi
Translated by Mandira and Sagaree Sengupta.

Till Death Do Us Part
Five stories. Translated by Vikram Iyengar.

Outcast: Four Stories
Translated by Sarmistha Dutta Gupta

The Book of the Hunter
A novel. Translated by Mandira and Sagaree Sengupta.